D1293446

BRAVO ... FIRST CLASS TUTORIAL

"Once in a while you need to be reminded of the basics of effective marketing management in creating sustainable brands. We tend to ignore these proven principles thinking we already know them. In this book you get a first class tutorial on those basics that are essential to the success of your brand but augmented by a big dose of reality in the examples and analysis. Bravo!"

Sergio Zyman, Former Chief Marketing Officer,
The Coca-Cola Company, and Founder of the Zyman Group

FOR ANY BUSINESS PERSON WHO WANTS TO WIN

"Winning in business has always been about tireless, competent focus on the basics. COMPETITIVE POSITIONING is all about the "basic" that counts the most - your brand's position in the consumer's mind. For any business person who wants to win in this competitive marketplace this is a must read!"

Don Knauss, Chairman,
Clorox Corporation

STAND OUT FROM THE PACK

"COMPETITIVE POSITIONING replaces Richard and Mike's earlier work, Creating Brand Loyalty, as the new guide for developing brands that stand out from the pack. It provides a thoughtful explanation of the ideas that lead to great positioning, but it is also a manual that leads you from thought to action. The wisdom and insight, born from real world experience will change the way you think about building sustained leadership. If you want to get ahead in marketing, read COMPETITIVE POSITIONING, and put its principles to practice."

Stuart Raetzman, Vice President Global Marketing,
Alcon Laboratories, Inc.

A PATH TO THE HOLY GRAIL OF BUILDING BRAND EQUITY

"Insightful, pragmatic and a must read for any Marketer. Richard and Mike know their stuff and outline a path to the holy grail of building brand equity through COMPETITIVE POSITIONING."

Scott Epskamp, President & Co-Founder of
Leapfrog Online

BREAK THE BARRIERS OF CONFORMITY

"Richard and Mike constantly break the barriers of conformity to engage and reinvent. Their writing speaks to my own desire to achieve marketing excellence and propels me to work harder and dare to try new approaches. In COMPETITIVE POSITIONING they've done it again, writing with a style and passion that captivate from the first and deliver through to the last pages of the book. COMPETITIVE POSITIONING goes deep into theory without feeling heavy, and delivers practical solutions through tangible, clear and instructive examples. I would recommend this and their previous book, Creating Brand Loyalty, to anyone with a passion or simply a curiosity about marketing."

Gilberto Dalesio, Area Vice President,
Alcon Laboratories, Inc.

WILL HELP YOU RAISE THE BAR …
TO ACHIEVE MARKETING EXCELLENCE

"COMPETITIVE POSITIONING identifies best practices for creating brand loyalty. The work, while profound, is written in a conversational tone and presented in such a way that make the learnings "stick" and become embedded in the marketer's DNA. This book, through the practices, tools and processes Richard and Mike share, will help you raise the bar in your personal and organization's journey to achieve marketing excellence."

Charlotte E. Sibley, Senior Vice President Business Management,
Shire Pharmaceuticals

A MUST HAVE (AND DO!)

"Czerniawski and Maloney have created a pragmatic, no-nonsense approach for achieving excellence in brand positioning. Brought to life with a treasure trove of real-world examples, COMPETITIVE POSITIONING is simply a "must have" (and do!) for all marketers aspiring to create world class brands."

Thomas H. Chetrick, Vice President,
Advertising & Marketing Services,
Bristol-Myers Squibb

GIVE YOUR CAREER THE COMPETITIVE DIFFERENCE

"In a world of 'sameness' it's not just products but also marketers who are perceived as being undifferentiated. Any marketing 'professional' who is looking to distinguish herself needs to be able to achieve success in building enduring brands. She would, therefore, do well to dive into this book since Richard and Mike provide a wealth of tools, key principles, and resources to gain an advantage in developing a competitive brand positioning strategy, the blueprint for the brand. Even using one or two of the ideas in this book may very well give your career the competitive difference that years of hard work might never achieve."

Hank Provost, Vice President of Organizational Development
and Talent Management,
WhiteWave Foods Company

THE REAL DEAL … IT WORKS!

"COMPETITIVE POSITIONING is the real deal when it comes to developing leadership brands. It contributes best principles, practices, processes and tools. Working with Richard and Mike we have incorporated these into our European and Middle East operations. It has changed how we think and how we go to market to make us more competitive. It works regardless of category or country. It works!"

Dominique Boulet, Director Strategy & Business Development EMEA
Johnson & Johnson MDD

TWO OF THE WISEST SAGES …

"Richard Czerniawski and Mike Maloney have done it again. They have built upon the success and value of their previous book, CREATING BRAND LOYALTY and taken it to a whole new level with COMPETITIVE POSITIONING. Richard and Mike are two of the wisest marketing sages I have ever worked with and we are all fortunate to be on the receiving end of their collective wisdom.

Matt Seiden, President and CEO,
The Seiden Group, Advertising

SIMPLE, YET SO POWERFUL!

"The evolving media landscape and competitive marketplace has led many marketers to divert their focus to emerging media, integrated communications and new product introductions, leading us astray from job number one - creating a competitive positioning, the foundation of brand marketing. This book serves to refocus us all in the basic framework of and key principles in developing a competitive brand positioning. It is easy to read and understand. Simple, yet so powerful! I definitely recommend it to my marketing team and all who want to achieve an enduring competitive advantage."

June Bu, Executive Marketing Director,
Johnson & Johnson Consumer Products, China

DIRECTION ... FOR
MORE COMPETITIVE BRAND POSITIONING

"Creating brand value has to start with positioning. The complexity of doing business on a global basis requires quality time and effort in creating the right positioning. Richard and Mike are masters in this field and provide the direction and discipline for more competitive brand positioning."

Chuck Inman, Global Marketing Director, Marketing Training,
Alcon Laboratories

THE CORNERSTONE FOR
SETTING UP YOUR BRAND FOR SUCCESS

"In an ever increasing crowded market place, the ability to effectively position a brand is the cornerstone of setting up your brand for success. The many practical tools and real world examples within "COMPETITIVE POSTIONING" provide critical insights into understanding the best way to approach positioning and enable every marketer to achieve "marketing excellence."

Lori Kaplan, Executive Director – Global Commercialization,
Bristol-Myers Squibb Company

TEXTBOOK (AND BIBLE)

"Creating Brand Loyalty" has been my textbook (and bible) for eight years. Now, with "COMPETITIVE POSITIONING," Richard and Mike have identified ways to operationalize everything. This new work brings concepts to life through loads of examples, analogies, and stories. Not just enlightening, but fun to read."

Bill Weintraub, Professor at University of Colorado, Former CMO Kellogg, Tropicana, and Coors Brewing Company

INSPIRED A METAMORPHOSIS FOR OUR ORGANIZATION

"The principles we learned from COMPETITIVE POSITIONING inspired a metamorphosis for our organization. It changed not only what we communicate to customers, but also how we design new products and services going forward. It's no longer about how many features can be included in a product, but what brand positioning strategy will drive relevant, meaningful differentiation in the market to build a sustaining, leadership brand."

Laura Gustavson, Skeletal Health Business Leader, GE Healthcare Lunar

BE A MORE POWERFUL COMPETITOR

"Be a more powerful competitor by reading COMPETITIVE POSITIONING! Being competitive starts with brand strategy and a single powerful competitive positioning - something Richard Czerniawski and Mike Maloney know and share from success on the battlefields of the most fierce marketing wars waged across the globe."

Ron Hirasawa, Professor, Lake Forest Graduate School of Management

DON'T READ THIS AT YOUR OWN PERIL!

"To all marketers I say, "Don't read this at your own peril! This book cuts to the heart of brand positioning strategy and how to make it work to develop leadership brands. Sometimes marketers and their organizations see positioning as something to be draped over the product—like a wardrobe that reflects an identity. That's branding, at best. COMPETITIVE POSITIONING is about much, much more. It defines and utilizes brand positioning as the strategic backbone and cerebral cortex that provides brand stature and direction. Thanks Richard and Mike for putting brand positioning in its proper context and sharing best practices on how to make it more competitive in today's market."

Sal Uglietta, President,
Med Partners Consulting

BECOME BETTER

"This can really inspire all the marketers to become better in their discipline and strengthen their brands."

Jan Bles, Managing Director,
FrieslandCampina, Vietnam

INVALUABLE ... TO BUILDING
A WINNING BRAND STRATEGY

"An invaluable text offering a practical guide to building a winning brand strategy. The real world examples and cases allow for the brand team to directly apply the best practices to their brand. The text's focus on what and how to build a solid positioning for the brand is a must read for anyone touching the brand."

Altaf Shamji, Executive Marketing Director,
Bristol-Myers Squibb

COMPETITIVE POSITIONING

Best Practices for Creating Brand Loyalty

Richard D. Czerniawski
Michael W. Maloney

HUDSON HOUSE

To purchase contact:

Brand Development Network *International*, Inc.
368 North Country Club Road
Chanute, Kansas 66720
Tel.: 800-255-9831 / 620-431-0780
Fax: 800-489-8907 / 620-431-0771

Library of Congress Control Number: 2010934532

Czerniawski, Richard D.
        Competitive Positioning: best practices for creating brand loyalty/
    Richard D. Czerniawski, Michael W. Maloney.
        p.   cm.
Includes index.

ISBN: 978-1-58776-914-6

HUDSON HOUSE

675 Dutchess Turnpike, Poughkeepsie, NY 12603
www.hudsonhousepub.com   (800) 724-1100

Knowledge is more than information.
Knowledge is being able to apply what we've learned,
to be able to do it.
If we haven't done or can't do it, then we don't really
know it.
We need to get beyond information and acquire
knowledge.
We need to be able to do it!

COMPETITIVE POSITIONING is dedicated to all those
marketers committed to developing leadership brands and
making marketing matter.

Foreword - How to Use This Book

At the university level, one merely needs to correctly answer the professor's questions to enjoy his favor and gain a favorable grade: Identify the five essential elements of a Brand Positioning Strategy Statement and you get an "A" for your work. But the workplace and the marketplace are not the university. They represent the "real world." And in the real world you need to do more than correctly identify the five essential elements of a brand positioning strategy. You need to be able to develop an ownable, competitive, and enduring brand positioning strategy to create brand loyalty. This takes skill. In fact, it takes a considerable level of skill to accomplish successfully—a level few marketers will master.

Reading this book will, no doubt, provide you with valuable information. It introduces a number of new concepts, such as the Perceptual Competitive Framework, the "5 Cs" Add-Valuation Method, and *Pro*sitioning. It also contains tools, such as the Benefit Ladder, to enhance your productivity. These tools will not tell you "what" to think but, instead, will encourage "how" you think. "What" you think is the Creator's gift to you. It encompasses your unique talents and is born of your experiences. "How," on the other hand, transcends corporate, country, cultural, and even category boundaries to leverage "what" you think. It represents a critical strategic ingredient for helping make your brand to be more competitive in the marketplace.

But these alone will not transform you as a marketing manager unless you approach this book with *"beginner's mind*," are an active reader (one who considers ways to apply what you read), and put your learning into action.

"Beginner's mind" is a Buddhist term to connote a mind that is like that of a child. It is a mind free from bias, stereotypes, and preconceived notions. It is fully awake to each moment, in the moment. As a famous Zen monk stated, "To the expert there is only one solution. To one with beginner's mind there are many solutions." Challenge your assumptions. Don't assume that you know (or, for that matter, we know) everything about marketing. Grow to know by examining everything you currently believe, and everything we write, to separate fact from fancy, reality from fantasy, and principles from dogma.

Be an active reader. We provide you with many, real brand stories and examples drawn from a wide variety of categories. Use these to help make the principles and practices we share come alive for you. Put these stories and examples into context with your brand, and its situation. Use them to stimulate your imagination and, yes, creativity as to what you might do to create brand loyalty.

Finally, put the learning into action. Stop to engage in the exercises we share and the productivity tools we provide by applying them to your specific brand, in your specific category, and in your geographic market. Don't just read through the exercises and tools. Use them. They are available not only in this book but also online; you can download them from our website, ***www.competitivepositioning.info.*** They are made available for you to use in developing your competitive brand positioning, building your brand, and winning in the marketplace.

We wish you a productive journey as you use this book and employ your talent in creating brand loyalty through the development of a competitive positioning to transform your product into a brand.

Contents

Authors' Notes

You may perceive what you believe are inconsistencies regarding how we have handled trademarks and certain words. At times we capitalize a word and at other times we use a lower case letter for the same word. Handling this was a real challenge for us. We worked hard to make it easier for everyone to understand and be on the same page, and to avoid needless redundancy.

Specifically, we have attempted to capture brand trademarks using upper and lower case letters as represented in each brand's communications. Additionally, we have noted a trademark registration or copyright (again, as per the brand communications) immediately following the first usage of the brand name. Thereafter we have dropped their registration or copyright symbol.

As per the use of upper and lower case letters for words, we have chosen to use upper case as the first letter for:

1. Words and terms that we have created such as Marketect, Power Positioning and *Pro*sitioning, among others;

2. Names of all our tools, which we also created, such as the Brand Positioning Strategy Statement format featured in this book, Brand Positioning Add-Valuator, etc;

3. All lead elements of the Brand Positioning Strategy Statement when we refer to them as part of that document, namely Target Customer, Perceptual and Literal Competitive Framework, Benefit, Reasons-Why, and Brand Character. If they are not capitalized then we are talking either about the resultant impact on the customer, a constituent part of the positioning statement or making a general reference.

As per the use of brand logos on the book cover please note: Citation of these trademarks implies no endorsement or approval of any kind, as the marks are here duplicated for display without the consent of the owners. The marks depicted in this presentation are the property of their respective companies.

One final note, DISPATCHES – Insights from the Marketing Front, are articles we write and distribute electronically. They contain a section titled "Boats & Helicopters." This refers to application of the learning from the article, via specific action steps, to help make your marketing more productive.

We hope you find this helpful in clearing matters. We also hope it provides you with an informative and enjoyable reading experience.

Introduction

It's been 10 years since AMACOM, the publishing arm of the American Management Association, published our first marketing book, *Creating Brand Loyalty—The Management of Power Positioning and Really Great Advertising.* Since then, the book has experienced widespread readership, with more than 10,000 copies sold around the globe. Additionally, we have gone on to write more than 400 *DISPATCHES*™ articles dealing with marketing management. We have also trained more than 10,000 marketing managers through our various programs—the Brand Positioning and Communications College, the High Impact Advertising College, the Discovering Customer Insights College, and the Marketing Analysis and Planning College programs, among others. Additionally we have empowered, and assisted, scores of marketers in creating strategically appropriate and more competitive brand positioning strategies, creative briefs, and marketing plans.

We can truly say that we have continued to learn during these intervening years between when we first wrote *Creating Brand Loyalty* and today. We have learned from our consulting practice working with top-notch managers from some of the world's most admired and successful companies, the thoughtful act of writing to share our learning, interaction with our student marketing practitioners, and a business life that marries reflection with action. We have learned how to build leadership brands that break the shackles of, what we have identified as, this "age of sameness," where products and organizations are basically the same or, at least, perceived to be so. (And, "perceptions" are "reality.") This learning is essential to create relevant, meaningfully differentiated brands in an age of sameness, particularly as customers are becoming more demanding and discriminating. For, if we do not have the knowledge or, more importantly, the skills to deal with this, we allow our products to be reduced to commodities.

This new book, *COMPETITIVE POSITIONING—Best Practices for Creating Brand Loyalty*, builds upon our earlier work and continued learning regarding brand positioning and, all things, brand marketing. It is devoted to sharing best practices, tools, principles, and processes for creating a competitive, enduring, and ownable brand positioning strategy that transforms mere products, consisting of features and attributes, into brands that enjoy a special relationship with customers based upon shared values, and reinforced by positive experiences. It is a skill required of all marketers and their organizations if they are to survive, no less thrive, today.

This book addresses how to create brand loyalty through the development of a competitive brand positioning strategy, articulated in the Brand Positioning Strategy Statement, and the practices of *Pro*sitioning, and Power Positioning. We made a conscious decision not to extend this work into (advertising) communications (as we did in our previous book) but, instead, to focus on brand positioning strategy. This focus is born of the universal need for a brand positioning strategy to serve as the blueprint for creating a successful brand. Not all marketers are involved in developing advertising. But everyone should be, and needs to be, involved with developing, or executing, the brand positioning strategy, in order to market brands as opposed to merely sell products.

COMPETITIVE POSITIONING deals with "how," not "what," the marketer should think to leverage his or her unique talents in creating a brand positioning strategy that will contribute to the development of a healthy, competitive brand. It provides the discipline and allows the marketer to provide the art, in creating a winning combination to compete more effectively in today's marketplace of product proliferation, sameness in product and organizational performance, increased marketplace pressure to discount pricing, absence of low-hanging fruit (such as the ability to grow through increased distribution and price increases) and more circumspect customers, and in the face of the conundrum posed by the organization's demand for more growth even as it slashes resources for marketing support.

This book is built upon our many years of client experiences in successful brand building through the development of strategically appropriate and competitive brand positioning at leading companies such as Procter & Gamble,

Johnson & Johnson, Frito-Lay, and Coca-Cola, among many others. It captures what we have learned in our work beyond the shores of the United States, in places such as Beijing, Singapore, Shanghai, Sydney, Bangkok, Ho Chi Minh City, Istanbul, Paris, Rome, Dusseldorf, Barcelona, Madrid, Warsaw, Prague, San Paolo, Mexico City, Buenos Aires, Santiago, Caracas, Toronto, Montreal, and scores of other world cities. It has been proven effective in industries and categories that span health care (pharmaceutical and medical devices), fast-moving consumer goods, and services, as well as others.

The marketer who reads this book and puts into practice the proven principles, practical tools, and quality processes it lays out can expect to learn how to go about *creating brand loyalty* by:

- Developing a competitive brand positioning strategy, using the Brand Positioning Strategy Statement, to elevate your product, or service, from a commodity driven by price promotion into a vibrant brand;
- Providing relevant differentiation for your brand offering against your competition to drive customer preference;
- Establishing your brand's positioning in the minds of your customers by employing each of the brand's marketing activities to drive customer preference;
- Evolving your positioning in real time to grow your competitive edge; and
- Building successful and healthy brands to withstand the vagaries of the economy and the marketplace.

COMPETITIVE POSITIONING does not offer a bromide that with one reading will remedy the many, significant marketplace challenges and ensure success. Quite the contrary, it will require a lot of work from you. For the earnest and dedicated marketing professional, this book will mean much more than gathering information. It may serve to challenge the conventional wisdom of your organization, industry, and country and, perhaps, even your personal comfort zone. It will empower you by seeding the requisite skills to win in the marketplace. It will assist, if you are successful, in restoring the marketing function in your organization to a leadership role in driving the top line and in transforming your marketing from good to great. We hope you will find that it arms you with best practices that will lead to superior strategic thinking that, in turn, will develop the brand building leadership essential to creating brand loyalty.

Thank you for giving us this opportunity to share our learning regarding best practices for creating brand loyalty through the development of a competitive positioning strategy. We wish you great success in making your marketing matter in both the marketplace and your organization.

CHAPTER ONE

"It's job number one!"

"The best way to predict the future is to create it."

—*Peter Drucker*

Chapter 1

Positioning—The
Foundation for Brand Marketing

Unlike many other books on the subject of brand building, *COMPETITIVE POSITIONING* takes the client's (i.e., the brand marketing manager's) perspective. A client's perspective is rooted in *sound strategic marketing management* that is focused on the customer, and the competitive marketplace. That's our professional background. That's our passion. We are not ad agency people, nor are we academics. We have been and continue to be real-world marketing practitioners who have held virtually every position in brand marketing, from brand assistant to chief marketing officer to general manager. Sound strategic "brand" marketing management begins and ends with a *competitive positioning* strategy, which is articulated in the Brand Positioning Strategy Statement.

So, What's Positioning?

The answer to this question is rather interesting. Managers will state that positioning is your target audience, or your benefit, or, perhaps, what you want customers to think about you (such as the image), or what you say in your advertising . . . and so forth.

True, we all have a passing knowledge of positioning. After all, we've been positioning ourselves and others virtually all of our lives. We get a poor grade on a test at school and we begin to think of ways in which we might serve up (i.e., position) this unpleasant piece of news to that critical and demanding species of beings we refer to as our parents:

The way we serve up this unfortunate occurrence is limited only by our imagination (whose creativity is typically in direct proportion to the perceived penalties), applied in context to our parents' hot buttons. (If only we could harness that imagination in our work to create a competitive "brand" positioning strategy!)

We are "positioning" all the time. How are you going to explain to your spouse why you were two hours late to celebrate your anniversary with a romantic dinner at that exclusive restaurant that you had to reserve six months in advance? Or, how will you serve up an assistant for promotion—particularly one of whom your boss is not particularly fond? Or, how will you deal with potential objections you anticipate from a penny-pinching customer to a price hike that you are about to take? Positioning is a full-time job. It's also "job number one" when it comes to employing sound strategic marketing in building a competitive brand that drives customer preference and establishes an enduring relationship with those customers.

When we think about positioning, we are really getting at how we want an intended group of prospective customers (be it one or many) to perceive our *brand*. More precisely, we define brand positioning *as the way we want customers to perceive, think and feel about our "brand" versus competition.* It's the specific piece of turf we want to occupy in potential customers' minds and hearts as they view the market landscape before them. Positioning can be captured simply in the following statement:

To _____,
                    (Target Group and Need)

_____ is the brand of _____
        (Brand)   *(Competitive Framework)*

that _____
                          (Benefit)

The reason is _____
                          (Reason-Why)

The brand character _____
                          (Brand Character)

This positioning strategy framework has been around for decades and has guided the thinking behind the development of many of the leadership brands we know, and choose, today.

Positioning comprises five elements (which are treated in detail in subsequent chapters devoted to each one). These are:

- Target Customer Group (including Need);
- Competitive Framework;
- Benefit;
- Reasons-Why; and
- Brand Character (which was added back in the 1970s).

While most managers have some understanding of positioning, few have a real appreciation for the basic concept of *brand positioning*. They are distant admirers, as opposed to committed practitioners. This is evidenced by the fact that few brands even have a brand positioning statement. Unfortunately, many marketers are just too busy in their "right-sized" environments to do anything but react to e-mails and execute their projects. And they find precious little time to even execute. Moreover, those marketers that do "position" limit it to advertising messaging, rather than establishing the brand entity.

But, if you don't have a brand positioning statement for your product, you could be shortchanging its potential. You are merely selling a product with features and attributes that are basically the same as those of its competitors. Worse yet, you could be rudderless, leaving your product to float wherever the changing currents (the next new product features, or latest fad) take it.

By the way, if you do not have a written Brand Positioning Strategy Statement, does that mean you do not have a positioning? Hardly. The *positioning* is how customers perceive your offering relative to its competitors. They do or will have a perception of your offering, but it is unlikely to be the one you would want or need to *create brand loyalty*. Instead, it is probably a perception insinuated by your competitors about your product. In this highly competitive world, we should not surrender our duty to position our offering to our competitors. If we do, we, and our offerings, are going to be the losers in the marketplace.

Brand Versus Product

Brand positioning asserts the reason-for-being for the "brand" against competitive products, or services, among select customers. The Brand Positioning Strategy Statement *serves to provide the organization with a blueprint for the development and franchise building of the brand.* The word "brand" is distinct from "product." A product encompasses mere physical attributes and features. As Walter Landor, founder of the design firm Landor and Associates, stated, "Products are made in the factory, but brands are created in the mind." A brand represents a constellation of values and experiences that forge a special relationship with customers. For instance, let's consider baby powder—Johnson's versus generic retail versions. Do you know the ingredients in Johnson® Baby Powder?   There are just two: talc and fragrance. Guess what's in the generic store product. You got it! The same two ingredients: talc and fragrance. But Johnson's Baby Powder carries a significant premium. A recent store audit showed it to have a 60% price premium over the chain drug store product (read "generic").   Why would consumers pay 60% more for Johnson's Baby Powder than for a generic competitor? It's the "Johnson's" brand. It is a special promise of quality, trust and, as one marketer put it, "love." Imagine "love" in a canister. (We've got to get ourselves some of that!) This is the power of a brand versus a product.

Since the brand positioning (articulated in the Brand Positioning Strategy Statement) is the blueprint for the brand, it must *precede* the development of all sub-strategies, such as pricing, distribution, packaging, and advertising, to name just a few of the many marketing-mix elements we employ in promoting our brand. It is the only way we can reliably establish our brand in the marketplace. Recently, we were facilitating a Brand Positioning Strategy Workshop for a worldwide brand. At lunchtime during the first day's session, the client stopped to review proposed packaging. Can you imagine? That's a real no-no! They should know better. Brand positioning comes first. Packaging and everything else dealing with "branding" should follow the brand positioning.

When we first establish a clear, single-minded brand positioning strategy, everything we do serves to communicate it and, at the same time, reinforce it so it sticks in the marketplace. The brand positioning strategy serves to inform, and grow, from our marketing activities.

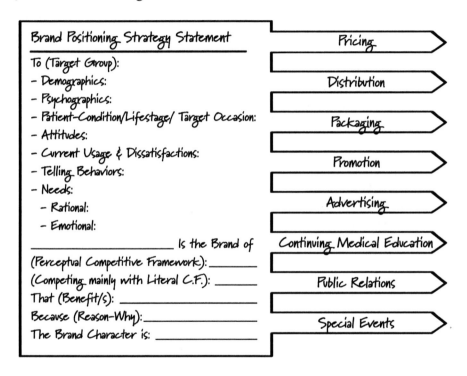

Brand positioning that sticks in the marketplace and firmly takes hold with customers becomes its "equity." It creates value for the brand that goes beyond the mere physical properties of the product, sales, and/or market share position.

Those companies without a clearly articulated Brand Positioning Strategy Statement will, more often than not, chase their tails squandering precious support dollars to introduce new marketing, promotion, and public relations and advertising campaigns on an annual basis that go nowhere with customers. What's more, the brand will lack the integrity needed in its marketing-mix elements to "stand for something." It will fail to establish a meaningful basis for positively influencing customer preference, ultimately confusing customers and diluting the marketer's efforts. Without a competitive brand positioning strategy, marketers limit themselves to selling products and/or merely servicing sales, not building brands. Without a competitive brand positioning strategy the organization is reduced to making sales one transaction at a time, rather than forging enduring relationships and building brand equity.

Products are commodities. Brands have value. As John Stuart, former CEO of Quaker Oats Company, stated, "If this business were split up, I would give you the land and bricks and mortar, and I would take the brands and trademarks, and I would fare better than you."

Still Water Runs Deep

An iceberg makes for an interesting metaphor for the importance and role of brand positioning. Unlike what was shown in the blockbuster movie *Titanic*, those unfortunate ships (and their crews and passengers) that meet their demise by a collision with an iceberg are struck by what they cannot see. No, this isn't about the impenetrable fog that obscured the vision of the crew of the *Titanic*. Nor was it the darkness of night that blinded the crew and passengers to the danger that lay before them. Ships are more likely to collide with that part of the iceberg that lies below the sea. The largest mass, about 85 to 90%, of an iceberg lies below the sea, where the human eye cannot see. Similarly, the largest and most important driver in creating a brand is its competitive brand positioning strategy. It is that which the customer does not see. The numerous marketing-mix elements we use and, in particular, the marketing tactics we execute at the various customer touch-points, are what, ultimately, make the positioning real and come to life. But without a competitive brand positioning, one does not have an iceberg. One merely has floating surface ice, as in ice cubes (albeit large ones). These supersized ice cubes might put a dent in a ship, but they are not likely to sink it. We marketers are in the business of sinking ships—that is, competitive products. So we need the substance afforded by the brand positioning strategy.

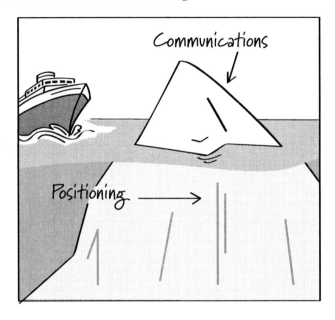

The Brand Positioning Strategy Statement establishes, in *strategic language*, the *competitive reason* for customers' selection of your *brand* rather than that of your competition, and the unique relationship you hope to enjoy.

- **Strategic language.** One of the areas we have found to be most vexing to marketers is the specificity required in wording one's positioning. Marketers, and rightfully so, scrutinize the words they use to pen (nowadays, "word process") their brand positioning strategies. However, most often the effort goes wrong in attempting to arrive at the customer language for the basic brand proposition. Customer language is the province of resource providers such as your advertising agency, not the marketing team. The agency can do it better, much better than you can! (If not, you are either on the wrong side of the business or you had better get yourself a new creative team.) Instead, exacting efforts should go into the strategic thinking and its articulation. It's about what you want to stand for, not how you communicate it to your customers. How you communicate it comes later in the marketing process, much later. So, get clear on the strategic concept and leave its translation to customers for your creative resource people and teams.

- ***Competitive reason.*** The marketer needs to go beyond mere product benefits that are generic to a given category or class of products and identify a meaningful way to differentiate the nascent brand against its competition (more on this subject when we get the "benefit," in chapter 7).

Positioning Example

Tide provides an instructive example regarding brand positioning and, for that matter, the use of the Brand Positioning Statement we shared with you earlier in this chapter. Here's an example of an inferred brand positioning for Tide® Laundry Detergent:

Inferred Tide Brand Positioning Strategy

TO (Target Group & Needs) Moms with active children and husbands, who need (1) consistent outstanding cleaning and (2) total care for their families' clothes (as in keeping them looking new, etc.).

TIDE IS THE BRAND OF (Competitive Framework) Laundry Care Detergent

THAT (Benefits) is the best choice for consistent, outstanding cleaning and total care for the family's clothes.

BECAUSE (Reasons-Why): 1. Heavy-duty cleaners & stain removers (Powerful Enzyme Technology); 2. Special fabric protectors ("Protective Fiber Complex"); 3. Value-Added Branded Ingredients (Dawn, Febreze, Downy); 4. Only fabric care product to receive a Good Housekeeping VIP award.

THE BRAND CHARACTER IS A perfectionist (with traditional family values) whom you can count on to always do the job right, and go beyond what's expected to do even more for you.

For years, Tide Laundry Detergent has stood for being the "heavy-duty cleaning detergent." Tide has been positioned as the detergent that gets out the dirt that families get into. Yet Tide has extended its line of products. It has evolved its positioning from a heavy-duty cleaning detergent to the brand of total laundry care. Tide now gets clothes clean and cares for them in myriad ways, such as keeping colors from fading and fabrics from fraying. Tide plays out its brand positioning in all its marketing-mix elements to make it stick in the marketplace. It's no wonder that this 60-plus year brand dominates the laundry detergent category in North America.

Going beyond the "Age of Sameness"

We live in an "age of sameness." And, if we happen to enjoy product advantages (or think we do), we should expect that these are temporary. Determined and creative competitors (which is what we all face in our highly competitive categories and markets) will neutralize whatever product advantages we currently enjoy. Think about it; when you compare one product to another in the same category, you see a basic sameness. Think for a moment about your brand, your company. Chances are your product's physical attributes are not dissimilar from its competitors'. Pricing, distribution, terms, and other important elements are also on par with those of other brands and companies. Not even knowledge is sacrosanct from this encroachment of sameness. Look at your marketing colleagues, or even yourself. Chances are high that the marketing managers in your company have experience working with other companies prior to joining your current organization. So, too, your product research and development, sales, and purchasing managers have a knowledge and experience base that was imported from some other company or companies. Just about everything is the same; if there is a difference, it is one of degree that is typically difficult for prospective customers to distinguish or not very meaningful.

In this age of sameness, marketing spells the difference between life and death or, at the very least, between great and poor performance. In this age of sameness, "how you think" can be the critical difference in gaining a sustainable, competitive advantage. We must think differently, and different (as in distinguishing our offering from competitive entities). We must think brands. We must think competitive positioning to create leadership brands. How the marketer thinks represents the company's and the product's strategic weapon for not just surviving but thriving through creating brand loyalty.

But, first, there is a myth that needs to be dispelled. The myth is that creativity is for people in certain functions. Creativity is for the agency people and, more specifically, agency creative personnel. Moreover, the myth extends to confining creativity to select uses. For example, it's okay to be creative when transforming strategic language into customer language. It is not only acceptable but also highly desirable to be creative in developing language that will appeal to, and resonate with, customers. For other people, or at other times, we give lip service to creativity but do not put our money where our mouths are. Imagine the reaction if the company's chief financial officer were labeled as "creative." (Did he contribute to the financial crisis that has rocked our world?)

Or, how about this one: "Interesting idea, but has any one in the category done this? Well, we don't want to be the first."

If we are to break out of this age of sameness, we need to be extraordinarily creative in the way we think (and, certainly, act). Creative strategic thinking is a requisite for every marketing manager, every organization. It is absolutely essential in the development of a competitive brand positioning. We need to be creative strategists who can envision a future and a game plan to get us there. And, as Peter Drucker said, "The best way to predict the future is to create it." Each of the five essential elements of the Brand Positioning Strategy Statement provides us with an opportunity to ply our creative strategic thinking. Each provides us with an opportunity to develop a competitive positioning strategy for a brand and, in that manner, set our offering, whether it is product or service, regardless of the industry, category, or country, apart from the competition in a way that is meaningful to our, and prospective, customers. Anyone can easily fill in the Brand Positioning Strategy Statement template. But, it is the creative strategist who will create a positioning to build a brand and enable a competitive advantage to be gained and sustained in the marketplace. Strategic discipline must be married to creative strategic thinking (which, come to think of it, is the "art") for the ultimate success.

The Marketect

Unfortunately, many marketers do not do a very good job in differentiating their offering from those of their competitors. They contribute to reinforcing this "age of sameness." They pore over the marketing research, studying the landscape for opportunities, and settle upon the spot with the largest sales volume and pool for customers irrespective of what or who is currently occupying that space. They then commit their companies to spending vast resources against trying to gain that space. They don't consider who (as in what brand) is already there, what that brand will do to defend its turf, and what relationship it has with its customers. As a consequence, these marketers cost their companies significant losses in terms of real and/or opportunities costs. We refer to these marketers as "small m marketers."

Then there is the smarter marketer. He sees the same landscape but looks for a place that he may occupy. This is a place where it would be difficult for competition to follow (either because it is not large enough or because to do so would dilute an already solid position in the market). We call these marketers "niche" players. But, to the leadership of many companies, "niches" are not desirable. They are considered, well, too small. Yet, we know that niche marketing can prove to be highly profitable and, in many cases, while corporate leaders may not call their efforts niche marketing, it is really what their line extensions are in reality.

But the smartest marketer is the "Marketect." We coined this term by combining the words "marketer" and "architect." Like the architect, the Marketect has two duties:

1. Develop the blueprint for the brand, its brand positioning strategy (articulating it in the Brand Positioning Strategy Statement); and

2. Provide the stewardship to make sure that the brand is built to the specifications of the positioning blueprint.

But the Marketect does more. She uses creativity to break the shackles of sameness as perceived by customers to drive preference and create brand loyalty. The Marketect realizes that she cannot win within the parameters of the current marketplace landscape (as defined by conventional marketing research). So she changes how customers perceive the landscape in a way that will lead to customer preference for the Marketect's offering.

Sound pretty incredible? Well, it is! If you stop to think about it, there are a number of prominent examples of Marketect thinking. The iPod comes to mind as a shining example. It changed how we all think about receiving, sharing, and playing music and knocked the CD music industry on its ear. Then there's Nokia. It changed how we think about cell phones. It went beyond technology to make these devices fashion statements. The iPhone took the development, and wow factor, of smart phones even further. Sure, you say, technology is sexy, but my product is rather pedestrian. Well, what's more pedestrian than water? Perrier began to change how those in the United States perceive water back in the mid-1970s. Today, children in the U.S. are drinking bottled water rather than tap water (which contains fluoride), such that cavities are on the rise. That's Marketect thinking. No, the cavities are not the thinking of a Marketect—it is, instead, the ability to create a new market from products that are basically the same.

Let's borrow a page from Apple Corporation's playbook when we go about undertaking the development of our competitive positioning and creating the Brand Positioning Strategy Statement: Let's "think different," and while we're at it, "think differently."

KEY POINTS, PRINCIPLES & PRACTICES
Summary

✓ Positioning is "job number one" when it comes to sound strategic marketing and building a brand.

✓ We define brand positioning as *the way we want customers to perceive, think and feel about our "brand" versus competition.*

✓ A brand is more than a product. A product comprises mere physical attributes and features. A brand represents a constellation of values that forge a special relationship with customers.

✓ Brand positioning (articulated in the Brand Positioning Strategy Statement) should serve to provide a blueprint for the development and franchise building of the "brand." Therefore, brand positioning should precede the development of all sub-strategies such as pricing, distribution, and packaging, to name just a few of the many marketing-mix elements.

✓ Products are commodities. Brands have value.

✓ The Brand Positioning Strategy Statement establishes, in strategic language, the competitive reason for customers' selection of your brand rather than that of your competition, and the unique relationship you hope to enjoy.

✓ Brand positioning comprises the following five elements: Target Customer Group and Need; Competitive Framework; Benefit; Reasons-Why; and Brand Character.

✓ We live in an "age of sameness" where products and services are virtually indistinguishable.

✓ In this age of sameness, "how you think" can be the critical difference in gaining a sustainable competitive advantage. It represents your company and product's strategic weapon in creating brand loyalty.

✓ If we are to break out of this age of sameness, we need to be creative strategists who can envision a future and a game plan to get us there. Each of the five essential elements of brand positioning provides us with an opportunity to ply our creative strategic thinking.

✓ Think like a Marketect. Work to change how customers perceive the marketplace landscape in a way that will favor your brand offering.

✓ Like an architect, capture your competitive vision for the brand in the Brand Positioning Strategy Statement. And, like the architect, conduct the stewardship to ensure the brand is built according to this blueprint.

✓ Strategic discipline must be married to creative strategic thinking for the ultimate success.

✓ Think different, and think differently.

THE CONCEPT OF BRAND VERSUS PRODUCT POSITIONING

This issue of *DISPATCHES*™ explores the difference between "brand" versus "product" positioning statements.

So What's a Brand?

Let's start at the beginning with a definition of a brand. *The brand is a constellation of values that goes beyond the mere physical attributes of the product to include intangibles in establishing a bond with customers based upon meaningful experience.* A brand creates enduring equity (i.e., the worth that customers bestow upon it). It's more than product. It's more than a trademark. Products, and their trademarks, come and go, but brands live on. Products may be replicated, but brands have a unique identity and place in the competitive marketplace and minds of their customers.

Brand Positioning

Efforts at creating a "Brand" Positioning Strategy Statement usually fall short, producing a "product positioning strategy." The product positioning, while it may have elements of brand positioning, gets at what the product does at a physical level. It's about today's offering, the here and now. It is short term and shortsighted, as contrasted to the more precious asset of the brand. It ignores the deeper emotional connection and meaning that brands have with their customers. Take a mere product out of the marketplace and what do you miss? In the vast majority of categories, you have one less meaningless choice in the confusing array of products that characterize this "age of sameness."

But a true Brand Positioning Strategy Statement gets at the whole offering. It gets to a higher order benefit. It defines the meaning between the brand and customer. It clarifies the unique and competitive *reason for being* for the brand. Unlike a product positioning, the brand positioning:

1. ***Reflects its customers.*** Customers identify with the brand. It is a source of identity for them. It may not be an exaggeration to say that in some cases the brand even helps complete the customer. Marlboro is more than a cigarette to its loyalists. It extends its identity of rugged individualism and the free-ranging spirit of the American West to all who affiliate with the brand.

2. ***Reveals a distinctive personality.*** Apple computer is countercultural and, at the same time, approachable. Microsoft (read PC) is traditional and remote. It seems to many people that Microsoft and other makers of PCs care more about serving the needs of big companies than about serving individuals. Pepsi-Cola is somewhat countercultural to Coca-Cola®'s clean-cut, all-American persona. Perhaps consumers choose Pepsi-Cola not on its taste but on the badge inherent in the choice of a "new" generation.

3. ***Shares its culture.*** Perrier and Evian are, well, French. Mercedes-Benz is German throughout. Coca-Cola and McDonald's share a taste of (North) America with the remainder of the world. But culture goes beyond geographical boundaries to get at the heart of the organization. The Body Shop® and Patagonia® have eco-minded cultures that span the world.

4. ***Builds a relationship with its customers.*** Starbucks pours more than a cup of coffee. It serves up community. Starbucks is more than a place. It's a portal to what's new and hip in our society. It's also their clients' "third place" (first place is home; second place is work or school, depending on one's lifestage). And Starbucks is not just an employer. It makes its baristas shareholders so that they have a stake in serving its customers well.

The brand communicates, through everything the marketer does, how the customer should interpret the whole offering. In turn, the specific offering reinforces the brand positioning strategy.

Paths to Building Brands

Brands come into existence through two major paths. The first is through the vision of its creators. It's a conscious effort. These come from people who dare to dream and work to make their dreams a reality. The dream is their version of the brand positioning. We're familiar with this path. It is the path blazed by Richard Branson of Virgin, Howard Shultz of Starbucks, Anita Roderick of the The Body Shop®, and Jeff Bezos of Amazon.com, Inc., among others.

The second path is the more common. The brand starts as a unique product offering. Over time, it develops into a brand due to the thoughtful planning and stewardship of its manager(s) or, as in so many cases, through unconscious (i.e., unplanned) efforts. It develops through the myriad activities initiated over years to support it in establishing a relationship with customers. While Amazon.com, Inc. may have started with a vision, it is evolving into more than the "World's Largest Bookstore" through iterative experiences selling other merchandise coupled with a large dose of ambition and need to succeed. And, while Gatorade may have started as an isotonic beverage mix to replenish lost fluids of collegiate athletes, today it is essential equipment for any athlete (regardless of competitive level) who desires a competitive edge. The brands most of us manage were born of this second path.

Getting to Brands

The key to constructing a brand rather than a product positioning statement is to perceive the brand as a vision of the future. We need to crystallize and articulate that vision. We need to go beyond stating product benefits to define what meaning the brand holds for its customers. We need to rethink how we use its Competitive Framework. We cannot look upon it as merely a classification of the competitive segment but must see how we want it to be perceived by customers (e.g., as a totally new segment). We also need to create a brand personality that emanates from the soul of the brand, the brand bundle, its culture and relationship with customers.

The Brand Positioning Strategy Statement is all about providing meaning, purpose, and value to the whole product in establishing a brand relationship with customers. It can serve to immunize our offering from competitive inroads. It can generate enduring equity. It can provide a platform for line extensions. What is more, it can give everyone who works on the brand a sense of value (e.g., Apple revolutionizing the world).

BOATS & HELICOPTERS

1. Using the Brand Positioning Strategy Statement, define the brand's positioning as currently perceived by customers for the category in the marketplace. Is it defined by the relationship, experience, and/or higher order benefits? Or, is its positioning defined by product features, attributes, and/or benefits? Do you have a brand or product positioning?

2. Create a vision of the "meaning" you want to establish for the brand with customers. Make sure that you go beyond articulating mere product benefits. Remember, product benefits can be replicated by the myriad like products that abound in this age of sameness.

3. Use the Competitive Framework section as a way to state the identity you want the brand to have with its customers. Step out of using the "standard of identity" or category definition to define your brand identify. Failing to do so will serve only to commoditize your offering. Try to define what you want customers to perceive your offering as being (e.g., a new category or segment).

4. Create a brand personality (i.e., Brand Character) that emanates from the soul of the brand, the brand bundle, its culture and relationship with customers.

5. Subject the new Brand Positioning Strategy Statement to the following question:

> *"If the offering reflected by the positioning strategy statement were to be taken out of the marketplace, would the customer miss anything?"*

If the answer is "no," it's unlikely that you have a Brand Positioning Strategy Statement. You probably have a product positioning strategy. At best it's a poor "brand" positioning strategy. So get back to work.

6. Develop a plan to eliminate the gap between the currently perceived positioning and your vision for the brand in creating a competitive positioning and articulating it in the Brand Positioning Strategy Statement.

CHAPTER TWO

"We're chasing our tails for 18- to 49-year-old idiots when 10,000 people are turning 50 every day."

— *Howard Stringer, Former CBS president on the folly of network TV ignoring older viewers. (Chicago Tribune, April 17, 1996)*

Chapter 2

Selecting and Serving the Right "Bull's-Eye" Target Customer

*T*hink about it. That's the heading for the column in which the quote that opens this chapter appeared more than a decade ago. Think about it. Mr. Stringer makes a rather provocative comment. And, he's someone to whom we should listen when he speaks. He is not only the former president of the CBS television network, which is quite a prestigious and influential position in the world of media, but he currently serves as Chairman, CEO and President of Sony. In fact, he is the first Westerner to be named chairman of this Japanese company, a role in which he has served for more than 10-years. Queen Elizabeth II knighted him at Buckingham Palace in 2000, so he's really Sir Howard Stringer. He has our attention, and we hope he has yours, too. The quote from Sir Howard suggests a number of issues worth surfacing with regard to selecting the right target customer.

- It identifies the practice of marketers and their companies to define their target audience solely, or largely, by demographics (i.e., age, gender, income, education, or position, such as "purchaser," or, in the case of the health care industry, the type of practice, such as "internist" or "orthopedic surgeon"). In this instance, the target is 18- to 49-year-olds. Unfortunately, this doesn't help us marketers much when it comes to discovering customer insights, developing brand positioning and marketing-mix strategies, and corresponding tactics, or creating effective messaging, since it ignores critically important factors such as psychographics, behaviors, attitudes, and needs. And, these factors may vary significantly *within* a given demographic segment.

- Moreover, it should make us aware of the common practice of defining our target in the same manner as we have always done—or the way our competitors define it. This practice of running around in circles after 18- to 49-year-olds has probably been in place for many years, decades even, without question. Although the quote is more than a dozen years old, the practice is still going on. Also, it represents the demography (age) shared by all the major network competitors, undermining marketers' ability to be competitive with the other major networks (through differentiation of the target sought) and, even, opening the door for cable and other mediums to attract older viewers and to grow into a more potent competitive force.

- Mr. Stringer's statement also evidences the mindless way many companies compete. Specifically, here is a significant trend in demography, the aging of America (and, for that matter, much of the rest of the world. Every seven seconds someone turns 50-years of age somewhere in this world. And, since the dawn of humankind, of all the people who have lived to be 50-years of age or older, more than half of them are living today.). Yet, it is clear from Mr. Stringer's statement that the TV networks are ignoring the over 50-years of age population. It is ignored in programming. It is ignored in casting.

One of our colleagues, Richard Cook, former executive director of the Johnson & Johnson Marketing and Advertising College, tells us that on one fine morning he was awakened by the sound of something akin to a sonic boom. He ran from his bed to the window to look up into the sky, expecting to see a low-flying jet breaking the sound barrier. He looked in all directions, but the sky was clear. There was no aircraft of any kind to be seen. It then dawned on him that he had turned 50-years young on that day and that the sound he had heard was caused, not by a jet but, by him as he fell out of every marketer's demographic target. *BOOM!*

This large and growing demographic segment is likely to remain largely ignored by marketers until that time when it has either grown much larger and powerful (how much larger and wealthier must we grow?) and/or some competitor demonstrates it is able to successfully and profitably serve it.

Then, others will follow, perhaps, even, to the point of ignoring their current franchise base. This is likely to put into play a pendulum effect, with marketers swinging mindlessly back and forth from one target group to another. Or, it can lead to the development of multiple target groups, as in "primary" and "secondary," which most marketers cannot serve adequately, no less competitively. (So don't even try.)

By the way, a study reported by Michael Schneider of *Vanity Fair,* that appeared in the Chicago *Tribune,* shows that the audiences of the so-called Big 3 networks has grown older than ever. The median age for CBS has turned 55, that for ABC has turned 51, and that for NBC has reached 49. The report suggests that this is a function in a change in programming from comedy (which attracts younger viewers) to procedural dramas such as *Law & Order,* which appeal to older viewers. But, this graying of the networks may be attributed to one or more of these factors: a conscious decision to pursue older viewers (however, we doubt that it is this one); a failure to execute against the 18- to 49-year-old targets with their programming choices; an exodus of younger viewers from television to other mediums; and/or the inexorable aging of the population.

- So, given the quest for the same demography, we may confidently infer the absence of meaningful segmentation among the major television networks and, if we want to get real, within the categories in which many marketers compete. There are undoubtedly a wide variety of segments of viewers that may be more precisely classified and defined contributing to a brand positioning that differentiates one television network from another (such as the Hallmark Channel, the Disney Channel, the Food Network, Bravo and, men, let's not forget Spike – all found on cable TV). Also, the identification of more precisely defined segments should encourage the development of programming that better serves and fulfills the specific needs of a given target segment. Instead, we are fed the same type of programming from each of the Big 3 major networks. (Please spare us from another so-called reality show of teens and/or 20-somethings sharing their insipid, vacuous lives of sex, profanity, infidelity, alcohol and other mind-numbing drugs, and just plain nonsense.) No wonder these three networks continue to lose market share.

- By the way, the term "idiots" brings into focus two other important factors in defining the target group: current habits and mindset. In the case of the term "idiots," one gets the impression that the target is certainly not very intelligent (to say the least) and that the group's viewing habits may be well served by the mindless drivel served up by these networks. Perhaps this explains the reason for the boom in reality shows.

The customer is the most important asset of the brand and company. Nothing is more important. It's what gives the brand its legitimacy and value. As former Procter & Gamble chairman Edwin Artzt said: "Brand value is very much like an onion. It has layers and a core. The core is the user who will stick with you until the very end." Marketing is all about *satisfying customers better than your competitors* to create brand loyalty. But it doesn't appear that we marketers have an adequate understanding or respect for customers beyond exacting a transaction (i.e., a sale) that benefits us.

How we go about choosing and defining, and ultimately serving, the target group has significant implications in the development of competitive positioning and establishment of a brand. We need to wake up to the importance of the customer and find a better way to choose and define the Target Customer group (in the Brand Positioning Strategy Statement) other than demographics (the media target), past practices (the way it was), or competitive behavior (the herd effect).

Choosing the Target Segment

A segment is *a grouping of potential customers*. It is about making choices. The fact of the matter is that we cannot be all things to all people. So it is imperative that we make choices regarding which customers we will pursue in our quest to create a relationship, and which ones we will not pursue. It is about making sacrifices for the greater good of the brand. As Kim Mullarkey, former vice president of marketing for LifeScan, the maker of the OneTouch® BSL (blood sugar level) monitor, is fond of saying, "Marketers need to practice the discipline of sacrifice."

We need to identify and then find a strategically appropriate match between different target segments and our ability to *create meaning* with them. Consider testing two positioning concepts for the same product—concepts "A" and "B." We share concept "A" with 2,000 potential customers. It receives a mean purchase rating of a "3" on a 5-point scale where "5" means the customer claims she will *definitely purchase*, "4" means *probably purchase*, "3" means *maybe/maybe not purchase*, "2" means *probably not purchase*, and "1" means *will definitely not purchase*. It so happens that all 2,000 respondents claim a purchase interest of "3." Positioning concept "B" receives a mean purchase rating of "3" also. However, 1,000 potential customers rate it a "5," while the remaining 1,000 rate it a "1."   Which positioning concept do you believe represents the best potential?

		Purchase Interest				
	Mean Rating	#'s of Customers Rating				
		5	4	3	2	1
Concept "A"	3.0	–	–	2,000	–	–
Concept "B"	3.0	1,000	–	–	–	1,000

If you are like nearly everyone to whom we pose this question, you have selected concept "B." The reason is obvious. Concept "B" has a segment of potential customers to whom the positioning is meaningful. They claim they will definitely purchase the product as positioned in concept "B." That's a really good thing!

But what typically happens in this kind of situation? Management, or the demands for additional volume, pushes marketers to revise the positioning of concept "B" in a futile attempt to move the purchase interest of those respondents who rated it a "1," *definitely will not purchase*, to a more favorable purchase intent. Now, what happens when we change the positioning of concept "B"? You know it! The purchase intent of those who rated it a "5," *definitely will purchase*, declines. And, they're the only customers that matter when it really comes down to making good on their claimed purchase interest. So when one of them reduces his purchase interest you lose volume. When one of those respondents whose claimed purchase interest is a "1" moves up to a "2" or a "3," you will not realize incremental volume. And that's a fact!

It just goes to show you cannot be all things to all people. Nor can you be some one thing and have meaning (as in driving preference) to all people. Sorry, but you have to carefully select a segment with which you can establish a compelling meaning to drive a preference win over the competition. And, even if you could be all things to all people, like Coca-Cola, for example, your offering would be vulnerable to a competitor who segments the market, like Pepsi-Cola. You may recall that Pepsi-Cola pursued the "new" generation. We're not just talking about chronologically young consumers. Instead, the new generation includes consumers who have a young mindset. Guess what? Many of us in the over-50 demographic believe we are part of that generation. Now, that's a pretty large segment, don't you think?

As soon as a market is created, competitors rush in to slice-up the pie and to lay claim to a segment (a slice of it!). The market for anti-depression medicines is a sterling example. There are some 20 different brands, several from the very same class of drug (SSRIs), each vying for a different segment of the category. Effexor XR is positioned as solving the unresolved symptoms of depression and preventing relapse; Zoloft provides relief from the broadest spectrum of mood disorders; Wellbutrin SR® promises relief without the unwanted side effects of other antidepressant medications, such as sexual dysfunction and weight gain; Cymbalta is positioned as relieving the physical and emotional pain of depression. That's segmentation. That's about standing for something with someone very specific.

Anti-Depressants

We are not going to deal with how to identify the market segments in this book. That's a job for your marketing research managers. They'd be more than happy to assist you in identifying the various segments, their defining characteristics, and even their size. Instead, we want you to know that you must choose before you can define your target. The segment you choose will represent the *most likely prospects, those who have a similar set of values, attitudes, and/or needs, that our brand (whether it be a product or service) can satisfy better than the competition.* In this way, we focus against all potential users of the brand in a manner that will be relevant to them. We urge marketers to go beyond defining the target segment by demographic profiles, past practices, or the way the competition is doing it.

1. *Most likely prospects.* The focus on *most likely prospects* is made up of two major issues. First, we must decide what is the most important constituency, the one in which we most need, and are most likely to be able to instill brand loyalty. Second, we must identify who is most likely to purchase, use, or recommend our intended brand within a given constituency.

- ***Most important constituency.*** Is it the purchaser or gatekeeper? Is it the ultimate user? Is it the key influencer or one who recommends the brand? Is it the surgeon or the physician? Is it the purchasers at the hospital? Or is it the payer constituency? For example, in the toothbrush category, three major constituencies present themselves. One is the dental professional, who represents a key influencer in the purchase behavior of a distinct segment of consumers and whose influence explains the success of Oral-B (a premium-price product). A second is the retail trade, which is responsible for pushing the product out to and upon those consumers who are, quite frankly, less involved with oral hygiene and getting it to price-conscious shoppers via distribution (i.e., making it available), merchandising, and pricing. A brand such as Tek owes its existence to the retail trade activity through which they promote, with aggressive promotion pricing, to push the product through to the consumer. The third constituency is the consumer. Reach® Toothbrush was the first successful toothbrush brand positioned to the consumer constituency. However, today, toothbrush brands such as Oral-B and Crest have also been aggressively pursuing this consistency, with Oral-B capitalizing on its hard-earned professional heritage. Each constituency has different implications for positioning and, ultimately, the marketing of the brand.

- ***Who within the constituency?*** Within each of these major constituencies, one needs to choose further. For example, if we choose to go with dental professionals (i.e., key influencers), we have further choices to make. Do we target dentists? Or dental hygienists, who order product and dispense it to patients? If we go with dentists, should we select a specific specialty such as orthodontists? Or periodontists?

  In our case of marketing to the consumer constituency, one has to choose between toothbrush purchasers, gatekeepers, and users. There is overlap. A purchaser can also be the gatekeeper (for a household) and a user. In fact, Reach® Toothbrush chose moms, whose role in the household of the mid-1970s put them in the position of purchaser, gatekeeper, and user of toothbrushes. Mom chose and bought for the family. When she did buy, she purchased something like 2.7 toothbrushes per purchase occasion. What mom purchased determined what dad, the children, and she used to practice good oral hygiene. But not all moms qualify as being part of target prospects.

2. *Similar set of needs and concerns.* In order to identify the *most likely prospects*, it is essential to also understand and capture their *values, attitudes, and needs*. This enables us to go beyond mere demographics to capture the true Target Customer segment and, thereby, all potential users of the brand, not just the product. These values, attitudes, and needs serve to unite, and attract, prospects of a similar ilk, our Target Customer market segment, for our brand.

The Reach® Toothbrush, like today's Sonicare brand, carried a substantial premium (albeit not so significant in the absolute) when compared to toothbrushes marketed through the retail trade. With a premium-price brand, one has to identify who within the constituency would be willing to pay a premium price. After all, not all moms share the same attitudes, values, and needs when it comes to oral health care. In peeling back the onion within the broad target of moms, one will identify a segment of mothers who attempt to do their absolute best to protect their family's teeth against cavities and to avoid costly, painful dental visits. These moms are likely to ensure that their children receive regular checkups at the dentist's office, purchase and use an advanced toothpaste formulation such as Colgate Total® or Crest Complete®, and even have and encourage the use of dental floss.

Another interesting example is found in the carbonated soft drink category—diet Coke. (The lower case "d" is not a misprint. Diet Coke was introduced with a lower-case "d," since it was a great-tasting cola that just happened to be low in calories.) Prior to its introduction, women (particularly dieters) constituted the low-cal soft drink segment almost entirely. During our time as marketers at Coca-Cola USA, we believed the market was ripe for expansion and that it could be expanded with a better-tasting low-calorie cola entry. Instead of going solely after women we set out to attract males also, and not just dieters either, but anyone who appreciates great taste in a cola without the unwanted calories. The key copy words behind the campaign idea, "Just for the taste of it," coupled with the lower-case "d" in the trademark diet Coke (which has since been changed to a capital "D"), evidenced a broader target defined by attitudes, values, and needs and not by mere demographics such as gender.

3. *Our brand can satisfy.* Obviously, we need to be able to satisfy the needs and concerns of the target group. Had Reach® Toothbrush not demonstrated its superior cleaning efficacy (particularly for those hard-to-reach back teeth) through its product design features and attributes, clinical studies, and better checkups, it would have ultimately failed with consumers. Had diet Coke not had a unique, full-bodied great cola taste, it would not have been able to grow the low-calorie segment, increase the composition of male consumers, or achieved the leadership position in this same market segment. The product and brand bundle has to deliver on your promise to, and fulfill the expectations of, the target, or you will fail miserably! In other words, the perception you seek to create must be capable of becoming a reality to your Target Customer segment.

Let's fast forward to the modern past and examine the Coca-Cola Company's introduction of C2. Perhaps you may recall it. Coca-Cola C2 was a mid-carbohydrate (carb) soft drink introduced to capitalize on the low-carb craze. ("Craze" is probably an inappropriate word, since we tend to consume far too many carbs in our diets, which is leading to the rapid growth of obesity and Type 2 diabetes.) It failed miserably. Those consumers concerned about carbs didn't need Coca-Cola C2. They could choose to consume Diet Coke or Coca-Cola Zero, which has no carbs! Consumers perceive carbs (actually calories) as an essential characteristic contributing to taste. Moreover, they believe that if you remove even one calorie, then taste is going to be compromised. And, if the consumer is not going to get all the taste she truly craves, then she will opt for the lowest calorie (carb) soft drink. Which brings us (and consumers!) back to Diet Coke and Coca-Cola Zero. By the way, Coca-Cola Zero is segmenting on two planes. One is gender (male); the other is taste (like my Coca-Cola—The Real Thing).

Bull's-Eye Target Customer of One

Once we have chosen our customer segment, we need to clearly define the prospective customer within it so that we may create a competitive positioning and own it. The Target Customer group is typically poorly defined in positioning strategies through the identification of shared demographics, socioeconomic levels, medical condition, or generic category needs, among others. But, as mentioned, this way of segmenting and, in turn, defining the Target Customer is not very meaningful. It lacks the level of specificity needed to enable us to really understand customers so that we can connect with them. We need to understand our target so well that we can accurately predict how the target will react to a specific piece of stimulus. Package design, promotional events, public relations, and so on, are all stimuli. And, we should feed our target only stimuli that will motivate him to behave in a predetermined manner that benefits our brand (i.e., achieves the Marketing Objective, the brand's overarching behavior objective essential to realizing the sales forecast). The segment, when approached from the top down, and rather vaguely at that, becomes a mere abstraction that is only somewhat more meaningful than pursuing everyone in developing the Brand Positioning Strategy Statement, single-minded proposition, or any of the brand's marketing initiatives.

So, how might we define the Target Customer? We need to move beyond mere abstraction and deal with something that is concrete, something that is real. That's our *target customer of one*—the bull's-eye. Who is the bull's-eye Target Customer of one for your brand and what it represents? Find that one person, a real living and breathing human being. Once you can see her clearly in your mind, you define her, using the seven essential components we teach in our Brand Positioning and Communication College program. These are demographics; psychographics; patient-condition/lifestage/targeted occasion (choose one depending upon the category or your unique situation); attitudes about her situation as it relates to the category of products; current brand/product usage and dissatisfactions; other relevant, telling behaviors; and, finally, needs, both rational and emotional (that the brand can win on!). In this way, we identify the Target Customer segment. This will result in a more relevant and actionable target segment composed of matching psychographic profiles, and having similar feelings and attitudes about the category and/or specific situation, and shared needs.

Often, when we refer to the "bull's-eye Target Customer of one" in our seminars, someone will counter that he doesn't want to limit his target for fear of limiting sales potential. While experience shows that a sure way to fail is to try to be everything to everyone, this concept shouldn't limit sales potential but enhance it. Specifically, it enables the marketer to really understand the bull's-eye mindset and to establish a positioning and a story to allow him to capitalize on more sales opportunities with the most "right prospects." Also, it establishes the bridge for the marketer regarding those factors, which meaningfully differentiate the brand from competition and pave the road to the story, which gets at the heart of the matter for customers.

We need to fix this relevant target clearly in our mind. Many a legendary copywriter fixed a photo of a potential bull's-eye customer on her desk and wrote copy to that specific individual. It helped her to relate to a real live human being, not an abstraction. The resultant messaging made for a productive stimulus in winning customers and growing healthy brands. We can achieve a similar end by locating and defining a Target Customer of one, the bull's-eye.

The Target Customer Profile

The first step is to identify someone we know who falls at the epicenter of our segment for our brand—the bull's-eye. One does not need to even know the segment in which he falls. It is fine to merely know someone for whom our brand is a perfect match, as if we were making a marriage (and we are, in some way). This person represents the segment, although without marketing research we will not know how large it is. This person is our bull's-eye Target Customer of one, our customer.

Once we have the bull's-eye customer clearly in our mind, we answer a host of questions about him that provides us with the info we need to define the Target Customer (which is the fist element we need to address in the Brand Positioning Strategy Statement) clearly and completely. The questions are similar to what one would find in an Attitude, Awareness, and Usage (AA&U) marketing research study. These studies cover three basic areas: personal, category, and brand-specific information. The answers are specific responses about what you know of this real, bull's-eye Target Customer.

We've provided two examples of questions, one with inferred responses. The first is for Curves Health Clubs and Fitness Centers for Women. We've inferred the responses. The second is a series of questions relating to a prescription analgesic (although it could be for any class of pharmaceutical products) to illustrate how you can modify the specific questions for another constituency, in this case health care professionals, and your information needs. These are examples, not absolutes! Modify the questions according to your needs and the unique characteristics of your category and/or country.

Target Customer Profile
Inferred Curves - Example
(Personal)

Name: *Jena Davis*

Gender: *I'm a "real" woman, obviously.*

Age: *36*

Marital Status (Married to/How Long): *Charles, for 12 years*

Children (Ages): *Charlie, 8, and Amy, 5*

Occupation: *Primary School Teacher*

Education: *B.S. in Education*

Personal Auto: *Ford Escort*

Currently Working On: *Me (stated emphatically)! I want to be less hard on myself and more forgiving.*

Favorite Leisure Activity: *I don't have much time for leisure activities with preparing lesson plans, grading papers, and caring for my family. But when I do get time, I like to walk in the country.*

I Stay Home to Watch (on TV): *Dancing with the Stars*

Last Good Book I Read: *The Secret*

Newspapers/Magazines I Usually Read Include: *"O, The Oprah Magazine" and "Real Simple", plus the daily newspaper*

My Favorite Music/Performer Is: *Natalie Cole. My husband, Charles, sang "Unforgettable" to me shortly after we began dating, and it was our wedding song. I guess I'm sentimental and go for romantic music.*

The Last Vacation I Took Was: *We rented a cabin in Yellowstone Park.*

I Love to Shop For: *I shop for my children. I used to like buying clothes for myself. But I felt I never really looked good in anything. I would buy fashions that flattered me, you know, as in "hid my fat." But I'd outgrow them. I also like to buy purses. Now if only I had money to put into them (laughs). I do feel more comfortable about buying clothing for myself now.*

My Favorite Shopping Place: *Target. I like that they give you what they say, "Expect More. Pay Less." Their stuff is not so pricey. Yet it doesn't look cheap. It has style.*

What My Friends Say about Me (When I'm Not in Their Presence): *Oh, my, how she is changing. She looks so much younger now.*

Current Weight: *You are a naughty boy, aren't you? First you ask my age, then my weight. You know you shouldn't be asking a woman that (with mock admonishment). Let's just say I'm not where I want to be, but I'm getting there.*

Ideal Weight: *Well, I've lost about 50 pounds already. I just have a few more to go. I don't expect to look like a model. I don't have that kind of body. Quite frankly, I don't know anybody who does. But I would like to be able to fit into a size 12 dress.*

If I Could Change One Thing about Myself, It Would Be: *To have more self-confidence; to not be afraid to try new things; to feel less self-conscious in my skin. Oh, that's three things. But I think they are all related.*

My Personal Hero in Life/Why: *Oprah Winfrey. She has overcome a difficult childhood and being a black woman in a white, male-controlled world. She is a champion of women. She works so hard to empower other women,* *regardless of color. And, while she is super-successful, she has her struggles, too. She has had to deal with weight issues. She's real. She's not a phony.*

(Category)

Attitudes/Beliefs about Weight: *Being overweight is definitely not a good thing. I don't think anyone would intentionally try to make herself overweight. Overweight people are terribly discriminated against. And, of course, it's not healthy. It stresses your joints, your heart, your life. You simply don't have the energy, whether it be physical or mental, to engage in life beyond work and caring for your family. And even that is compromised. You feel self-conscious and just want to hide out at home.*

Potential Ways to Manage Weight: *There's the diet thing. I can't tell you how many of those I've tried. There's exercise, if that doesn't kill you. Then there's surgery, and, believe me, at one time, when I really felt desperate, I considered it.*

Attitudes Regarding These Practices: *If it's too demanding, it is not going to work, whether we are talking exercise or dieting. All these systems tout how easy it is to "shed" pounds and develop a beach body in only minutes a day. If it were so easy, we'd all have beach bodies. They are downright demoralizing.*

What Practices Do You Do: *I exercise and diet sensibly.*

How Come to Try/Use These Practices: *I was always a chubby kid. I put on more weight in my freshman year at college, and it just seemed to creep up. Then I started work, and the pounds accumulated. I don't think the food they serve in our school cafeteria is all that healthful. And when I was pregnant with Charlie, my weight really soared. After I gave birth, I found I just couldn't shed the pounds. So I became desperate and tried them all, with the exception of the surgery. But I went so far as investigating it with my husband. Then I settled on a sensible exercise and nutrition program through Curves.*

Why Do You Engage in More Than One Practice: *Because it's not one thing. Exercise and nutrition go hand in hand. You have to have a balance. You can't exercise and then go pig out. And you can't just diet without getting your body into gear if you want to lose and keep your weight off and have some level of fitness for life.*

What's Worked for You/Why: *Curves (Health Clubs and Fitness Centers), that's what has worked for me. They cater to women like me. They understand women.*

What Hasn't Worked/Why: *Anything hardcore. They're over the top. I don't have time to devote my life to exercise and dieting. It's too extreme.*

When Something Isn't Working, How Does It Make You Feel: *Well, it makes me feel very depressed. I feel like I'm a complete failure, not just with this but then I question my role as a mother, wife, and teacher.*

What Do You Do When It's Failing: *You mean what I did as in past tense because Curves has worked and is working for me. With the others I tended to blame myself. It probably resulted in my doing more of the wrong things, like eating the wrong foods, and too much of them, to comfort myself.*

What Do You Expect a Practice to Do for You: *To work without killing me.*

What Is the Role of Gyms/Health Clubs in Your Management: *Well they're not for me. They cater to the young hardbods, of which I am not one. They are over the top.*

What's Most Important to You in Choosing a Health Club: *That they are not hardcore. That the people who use it are real people like me.*

(Brand Specific)

What Do You Know about Curves: *Oh, it's really great. I mean, you have to do the work, but they know what it takes to be successful, and they are so encouraging. They know women. It's founded by a husband-and-wife team, Gary and Diane Heavin.*

How Did You Come to Learn about Curves: *I was at a teacher's workshop and saw a college friend of mine who also struggled with her weight. She had lost so much weight I almost didn't recognize her. She told me about Curves and encouraged me to give it a try. At that point, I felt I had nothing to lose, since my next step was going to be surgery.*

What Is the Role of Curves in Your Weight Management: *It's a Godsend. It has made all the difference. I make time in my day for Curves. It takes about a half-hour, and it's worth it. My husband, Charles, is worth it. My children are worth it. Come to think of it, I'm worth it, too. Now I'm sounding like a commercial, aren't I?*

What Do You Feel Are the Advantages of Curves: *They understand women like me. The other women there are like me, too. The Curves center isn't populated by the "Barbie" dolls of the world or macho men that make you feel self-conscious and out of place because your body isn't perfect like theirs. And everyone is so encouraging at Curves, not just the staff, either, but the other girls like me. We encourage and help each other to be successful*

What, If Any, Are the Disadvantages: *Well, you do have to do the work. And you can't binge on Haagen-Dazs, which I'll tell you from experience does "not" work.*

Who Is A Good Candidate for Curves/Why: *I'd say, real women like me. Women who have had a weight issue and have tried just about everything else. Women that can't put up with the scene at the hardbod gyms where the women there strut about all made up donning their bright and shiny spandex.*

Who Is Not a Good Candidate for Curves/Why: *As I've said, the hardbod glamour queens. And men are definitely not permitted.*

What Would You Tell Other Women about Curves: *It works. It really does. It worked for me, and it can work for you. It will make a difference in your life, how you look and how you feel. I'd also say, join us. We'll help you do what we've done and are doing.*

Here are sample questions for the health care practitioner (HCP) constituency. The subject is pain management. Take note that there is an additional consideration when addressing the HCP, her patient and the condition for which he is being treated. The patient is addressed in this questionnaire when we get to the "Brand X" section.

Target Customer Profile
Health Care Practitioners
(Personal)

- Name:
- Age:
- Marital Status (Married to/# of years):

- Children (Ages):
- Medical Practice:
- # Years Practicing:
- What Doing When Not Practicing:
- Reason Became a Physician:
- What Enjoy Most about Their Practice:
- What Enjoy Least about Their Practice:
- What They Want Their Patients to Think of Them:
- What They Want to Be Known for beyond Being a Physician:
- Most Memorable Medical Success:
- Personal Hero (e.g. Lance Armstrong) Because:

(Analgesia Category)

- Attitudes/Beliefs Regarding Treating Pain:
- Rising Trends in Your Field Regarding Treatment Therapy/Modalities:
- Fading Trends in Your Field Regarding Treatment Therapy:
- Goal in Treatment Therapy:
- Key Challenges in Treating Pain:
- What Treatments Using:
- What Is Key Decision Factor in Treating:
- How/Why Using Different Treatments:
- How Come to Use These Treatments:
- Most Effective Treatment:
- What Do When Patient Is Failing Treatment:
- How Feel When Patient Failing Treatment:
- Current Unmet Needs in the Treatment of Pain:
- Most Promising Treatment(s) on the Horizon:
- What Is the Promise of These New Treatments:

(Brand X)

- What Do You Know about X:
- How Come to Learn about It:
- Who Is Your Ideal Patient for X:

  - Name:
  - Age:
  - Condition (including concomitant conditions/concerns):
  - Currently Treating With:
  - Reason for Switching to X:
  - Anticipated Outcome:
- What Expect Patient Will Think about X:
- Perceived Advantages of X versus Other Competitive Options
  (be specific):
- Perceived Disadvantages of X Versus Other Competitive Options
  (be specific):
- What Patients Are Not Good Candidates for X:
- Why:

Yet another practice to take note of is that we should identify those customers for whom our brand is not a good match, as in *"What customers or patients are not good candidates for your brand?"* We should make it clear whom we will not pursue, whom we do not wish to serve. And be clear regarding "why" these people are not good candidates for your brand and its limited resources.

Target Customer Profile—Practical Tips

Now it's your turn to complete the Target Customer Profile for the bull's-eye target for your brand.

1. Go to our website, ***www.competitivepositioning.info***, to download the Target Customer Profile tool.
2. Eliminate, add, and modify questions to meet your specific needs (as in category or country).
3. Then think of that someone you know well and who you feel is the perfect match for your brand. You are now ready to put the tool to its full use.

Here are some practical tips for pulling together a sound Target Customer Profile. Check your work for each of the following:

- *Be as specific as possible.* You know this person. When we know someone, we can be specific. The more specific we are, the easier it is to address the questions needed to clearly and completely define the Target Customer group. A clear and complete definition of the Target Customer aids in the development of all marketing-mix elements and decisions. Leaving out sections suggests we don't know our customer. If we don't, it is time to find out more.

- *Look for brand name connections to shed further insights into the target.* In the Curves example, we learn that Jena Davis drives a Ford Escort, watches *Dancing with the Stars*, and reads *O, The Oprah Magazine*. These connections help us identify habits and understand attitudes. They allow us to be in resonance with our customer.

- *Reflect the customer's attitudes and habits, not yours or your agency's!* We are profiling the customer, not ourselves. We tend to be more upscale and urbane (particularly if you are an agency creative living in a condominium off Central Park South in Manhattan) than the bull's-eye customer. At a meeting with a marketing director for a canned meat product we pulled together a Target Customer Profile. The marketing director stepped back and snickered that the bull's-eye target couldn't possibly be correct. He said that no one in his neighborhood fit the profile we had created. We pointed out that his neighborhood was filled with doctors, lawyers, and business moguls like him, who wouldn't be caught dead eating 79-cent canned meat (unless it was their mission in life to market it). He lived in a neighborhood where the mean price of a home is nearly two and one-half times the average home price in the United States—in an obscure part of this country, no less. His Target Customer lives in a home valued at a fraction of the cost of his home, is blue collar, is significantly older, and so on. Do we need to say more?

- *Give the customer's reason for selecting your brand, not the conventional wisdom of the manufacturer.* It is important to know why the customer selects your brand rather than competitive offerings. Sometimes we think we know the answer to why she chose our brand when we really don't know. Manufacturers' responses tend to be rational, and are rationalized to fit with their world perfectly. Customer responses tend to appear somewhat less rational and fit with their world—the real world!

- ***Check for consistency in attitudes and habits to ensure integrity of the profile.*** We ought to be able to get an accurate picture of the bull's-eye customer and predict her behavior based upon a resultant deeper understanding of the customer. If we find (unexplainable) inconsistencies, then we have not accurately defined the target, nor will we have the precision needed to provide proper direction and aid decision making as we develop our positioning and work to establish it with what we do in the marketplace.
- ***Confirm with (qualitative) research.*** Check it out! We like to use the Target Customer Profile tool at, and following, focus groups. We either fill these out for the alternate customers (i.e., ours and various competitors') as the groups progress, or we have the respondents fill out a profile on themselves before the focus group begins. Focus groups give you a better feel for the customer than the endless pages of statistics presented in quantitative research. Certainly, using both types of research increase our understanding. When our research work is complete, we pull together the many profiles and construct the one bull's-eye Target Customer on the basis of everything we learned. (This is not an amalgam of diversity but a crystallization of lifestyle, attitudes, habits, and needs of the bull's-eye target.)

When you are satisfied with the Target Customer Profile you've created, you are ready to capture and define the Target Customer using the Strategic Target Tool.

Strategic Targeting

As mentioned earlier we define the strategic Target Customer using the following elements: Demographics; Psychographics; Patient-condition/ lifestage/targeted occasion (depending upon your category or country situation); Attitudes about one's situation as it relates to the category of products; Current brand/product usage and dissatisfactions; Other relevant, telling behaviors; and, finally, Needs, both rational and emotional (that the brand can win on!).

We simply extract the information from the completed Target Customer Profile tool. The strategic elements and the source for each, captured within the Target Customer Profile, are listed here:

Defining the Strategic Target Customer

Strategic Element	Source*
• Demographics	Personal
• Psychographics	Personal
• Patient-Condition	Brand Specifics
• Lifestage	Personal
• Occasion-State	Personal/Brand Specific
• Attitudes	Category/Brand Specific
• Current Usage/Dissatisfactions	Category
• Telling Behaviors	Category
• Needs	Brand Specific/Category

* Target Customer Profile Tool

Building upon our Curves example, here's what the definition of a strategic Target Customer would be in the Brand Positioning Strategy Statement if we were to use Jena Davis as the Target Customer of one:

Inferred Curves Strategic Target Customer Example

Demographics: *Women 35+ from C&D Households*

Psychographics: *Perceive themselves as "Yo-Yo failures," have low self-esteem*

Condition: *Believe they have always been overweight, currently obese, may suffer health problems brought on by being overweight, such as high blood pressure and diabetes, may even suffer from depression.*

Attitudes Regarding Condition: *Dislike themselves. Strongly feel their weight situation is a turn-off to others and limits their ability to enjoy success, happiness, and even the simple things in life.*

Current Usage and Dissatisfactions: *Tried all kinds of diets but found they don't work for them (either don't lose the weight or it comes back* *quickly—"Yo-Yo"). Tried traditional fitness gyms but fail them because they are self-conscious among the "hardbods" and, therefore, inconsistent in working out.*

Telling Behaviors: *Binge eating, wearing oversize clothing to hide their weight, making excuses for not appearing in public, refraining from engaging in physical social activities.*

Need(s):
- **Rational:** *A proven program that can really help them lose weight.*
- **Emotional:** *Confidence to be successful.*

Here's yet another example, this one directed at health care practitioners (i.e., Medical Doctors). It is implied for Lipitor, a cholesterol-reducing drug, and is based upon Lipitor's promotional materials.

Inferred Lipitor Strategic Target Customer Example

Demographics: *GPs, Internists, Cardiologists, Endocrinologists, and Lipidemiologists*

Psychographics: *"Goal-Oriented" Disease Combaters*

Treating Patient-Condition: *Treating adults, typically 35+ with hyperlipidemia and multiple risk factors (some combination of family history, high blood pressure, age, high BSL, low HDL, smoking, and so on) for CAD and ACS (heart attacks and stroke).*

Attitudes Regarding Treating Condition: *These physicians are concerned that, left untreated or not properly treated, the condition could lead to serious complications and premature death. They believe the key to successful outcomes is to get key lipid numbers to healthy goals for these patients and thereby to avoid CAD and ACS.*

Current Usage and Dissatisfactions: *They currently prescribe diet and exercise as first-line treatment, followed by statins when the former fails. They are frustrated that, no matter how much better the lipid profile becomes, they still can't reach the desired levels for their patients with both diet and exercise and/or with other statins.*

Telling Behaviors of HCP: *Refer patient to dietician. Provide counseling to change lifestyle.*

Need(s):
- **Rational:** *Achieve heart-healthy lipid goals for more of their patients; and*
- **Emotional:** *Self-assurance that they are doing their best to reduce their patients' risk for CAD and ACS.*

Beyond Demographics

Okay, so now we can see that there's more, lots more, to defining the strategic Target Customer than just demographics. Demographics are inadequate as the *sole element* in defining your Target Customer. Demographics represent, at best, a media target. They assist us in identifying specific mediums, vehicles, and programming through which to reach our target. But, by themselves, demographics typically do not help us identify most likely prospects for our brands or to develop target appropriate tactics.

If we were to specify our target as males 25–34 years of age, we expose ourselves to a wide range of socioeconomic backgrounds and mindsets. There is a vast difference in need mindsets between a 25-year-old and a 34-year-old, particularly if they occupy different lifestages (e.g., single versus married; married without children versus married with children). This need mindset difference is compounded by race, education, occupation, values, and other factors.

Imagine for a moment that we are marketing men's clothing. The typical target definition might be males 25 years of age and older with incomes greater than $35,000 who have completed some college. Now consider two males, both 34 years of age. Both have incomes of $55,000 per annum. Both have college experience. One is a sanitation engineer (what some consider to be a "garbage collector") in Valley Stream, Long Island. The other is a high school French teacher in Winnetka, Illinois. It is very likely these two will be miles apart, not just in geography but in interests, needs, values, taste, and so on. A simple demographic description is insufficient for defining the target when positioning our clothing line. We need to know more.

Psychographics—Values

Psychographics is about mapping the mind. It gets at the deep seated values and mind-sets of people. It is determining what they hold to be true and dear. Roping customers by their psychographics, in addition to attitudes and needs, not only transcends demographics but assists us in creating a brand that is relevant to the strategic target group we have selected to serve. It helps us be more effective. In being effective, we put our companies in a position to be truly efficient on the basis it matters most—conversion of customers to our brand, creating brand loyalty, and realizing premium margins and profitability.

A number of successful brands reflect a target group that is based upon a mindset that relates to needs rather than demographics. Here are a few examples:

Target Customer Psychographics & Needs - Examples

Crest Toothpaste	"Family Protecting" moms concerned about their families' oral health care, particularly the avoidance of cavities for their children
Pepsi-Cola	People who think young!
American Express	"Prestige-conscious" frequent travelers who crave recognition, attention, and special service
Michelin Tires	"Highly anxious, safety-conscious" parents of young children
Microsoft®	Computer-using "standard seekers" who want to avoid mistakes and be covered with the standard in technology
Apple	"Creative explorers" who dare to be different and want a computer that will leverage their talents by catering to their creative passions

You can probably think of many more examples. In fact, it is probably a good idea to do so. Take a few minutes to leaf through one of your favorite magazines and look for three examples of brands that reflect a strategic Target Customer group with a psychographic profile.

Brand	Psychographic
•	
•	
•	

Microsoft is an interesting example. Microsoft has outdone IBM in setting the standard for computer operations and dethroned that blue chip company many, many years ago in achieving the preeminent position in the computer industry (software, of course). In its heyday, IBM practiced FUD, which stands for **F**ear, **U**ncertainty and **D**oubt. Whenever a competitor was about to introduce a new, advanced computer technology, IBM would announce its intention to introduce an IBM solution in the very near future. Customers, perceiving IBM as the industry leader and standard, would forgo the competitive offering because of their fear, uncertainty, and doubt that it would perform up to the level of whatever it was that IBM would introduce. But, Microsoft leap-frogged over IBM. It then became the "standard," catering to those "standard seekers."

Similarly, Intel has been playing this same game on the basis of its leadership role in the computer microchip market. The reason Microsoft and Intel have been able to achieve this desired effect is that they prey on a customer mindset that holds these companies as the "standard." These customers do not want to make a wrong decision (i.e., Fear, Uncertainty, and Doubt). As you know, Microsoft has since flubbed some recent introductions (can you say "Vista"?), and Intel has followed, rather than led, more innovative (and lower-priced) competitors in a few instances.

Think different. Think Apple and Mac. The psychographic profile of Apple's target customer is quite different from that for users of personal computers (read "Microsoft"). Whereas the PC is the industry standard for those who do not want to make a wrong purchasing decision (as in "It isn't compatible and doesn't play well with other computers"), Mac users perceive themselves as being different and thinking differently. They, like Francis Ford Coppola, the creative genius, brilliant director, entrepreneur, risk taker, and independent thinker who appeared in a classic ad campaign for Apple many years ago that suggested that Target Customers "Think Different," want to stretch their wings and create their masterpieces, whether it be a presentation, a film, or a graphic design. They might be dubbed "creative explorers."

Is it any wonder, then, that Macs are used by creative folks such as ad agency types, designers and architects? Is it any wonder that the PC is the commodity of the corporate world? Not really. Everything Apple does for Mac serves this specific psychographic target customer. Just think for a moment. Which would you expect to bundle the best spreadsheet software—PC or Mac? Which of the two do you believe would bundle the best film editing software—PC or Mac? Need we go any further?

Here's one target group to avoid: "early adopters." Marketers, particularly for new products, identify the psychographic target as "early adopters." This is nonsense. We do not build a brand from early adopters. Think about it. Early adopters gravitate to whatever is new. You don't have to give meaning to them beyond the news of "new." They will seek out your new product and find it. And what happens to these early adopters when the next new thing comes along? You got it! They go from being early adopters of your offering to "early exiters." They are onto someone else. At best, you enjoy a fling with them, not an enduring relationship. Here are other clichés to avoid:

Clichés to Avoid

- "Active Adults"
- "_____ Concerned" (e.g., "health concerned")
- "Seeking more control over _____"
- "Lead Adopters"
- "Category - Involved"

Patient-Condition/Lifestage/Targeted Occasion

The choice among patient-condition, lifestage and targeted occasion is specific to your brand category and situation. If you are working with pharmaceutical or medical device brands, you have the additional requirement to identify the bull's-eye patient and the patient-condition for your product. By condition, you must go beyond the generic condition. If you tackle pain, you need to specify whether your product addresses acute and/or chronic pain sufferers. You may even want to address the type or source of pain. You also need to take into consideration concurrent conditions the patient may have, which could impact the efficacy or safety of the compound and play a role in the physician's decision to choose one drug compound instead of another. Certainly you need to consider the severity of the condition and whether the patient has been previously treated and, if so, with what pharmaceuticals. These are some of the many considerations you need to address regarding patient-condition, along with the patient's demographics, psychographics and, perhaps, vital statistics and attitudes regarding the condition.

In our Lipitor example, the patient-condition is defined as *"adult, typically 35+ with hyperlipidemia and multiple risk factors (e.g., some combination of family history, high blood pressure, age, high BSL, low HDL, smoking) for CAD and ACS (heart attacks and stroke)."*

Our pharmaceutical product is not going to be for all patients with a given condition. Physicians typically do not prescribe that way. They prescribe different compounds in a given category to different patients on the basis of what they believe are the needs of that patient. Also, many of our clients have more than one brand to treat a given condition; examples are HIV antiviral and oncology drugs. Each of their products is expected to treat a different patient type and/or a different stage (another consideration) of the disease.

Lifestage is utilized most frequently in positioning consumer products and brands, particularly financial products. It addresses a particular point in the consumer's life, such as "student," "single professional," "married with children," "dual income, no children" (DINKS), "empty nester," and so on. Lifestage plays a big role in defining a consumer's needs, and consumers' needs at any given lifestage tend to be very similar.

Targeted occasion can be used for positioning food and beverage products. It includes factors related to who, where and how the product is used (e.g., target, time of day, at home or away from home, alone or with others).

We need to determine which, patient-condition, lifestage, or targeted occasion, is most appropriate to address in defining the Target Customer for our category and, importantly, our product and brand.

Attitudes

Attitudes address the target customer's feelings about his situation as it relates to your category, his condition, treatment options, and so on. In the Curves example, the strategic Target Customers' attitudes are that they *"dislike themselves. Strongly feel their (over) weight situation is a turn-off to others and limits their ability to enjoy success, happiness, and even simple things in life."*

The attitudes for the "Goal-Oriented" Disease Combaters in the Lipitor example are: *"These physicians are concerned that, left untreated or not properly treated, the condition could lead to serious complications and premature death. They believe the key to successful outcomes is to get key lipid numbers to healthy goals for these patients and thereby to avoid CAD and ACS."*

These attitudes are specific to the psychographic profile of the target. They, along with "current usage and dissatisfactions," help guide us to their needs.

Current Usage and Dissatisfaction

It is important for us to identify what our prospective target is using and his dissatisfactions. Don't be afraid to name "names"! In the analgesic category, brands such as Advil, Aleve, and Excedrin® have been comparing themselves to Tylenol® for years. Obviously, their competitive target is Tylenol, since that brand has enjoyed category leadership and has been the standard of care for many years. Each claims superiority to a Tylenol product (and here we wish for you to note the distinction we make between the words "product" and "brand"), undermining consumer confidence in not only the Tylenol product, but the brand. This is not to suggest that you need to be comparative in your communications. No, we are not saying that! Instead, we need to think comparatively in order to identify any dissatisfaction that your product or brand might exploit.

In the Curves example, the target group is clearly dissatisfied with its current options. In fact, current options have failed these women. Their current usage and dissatisfactions are: *"Tried all kinds of diets, but they don't work for them (either don't lose the weight or it comes back quickly—"Yo-Yo"). Tried traditional fitness gyms but found they don't work for them because they are self-conscious among the 'hardbods' and therefore inconsistent in working out."*

But, perhaps, the Target Customer you are seeking does not consciously feel any dissatisfaction with current products. Ah, the real question is whether you can lead him to feel dissatisfied. Often, unless there is a product problem, we don't realize we are dissatisfied until something better comes along. Or we are willing to tolerate what we have because we believe it is the best technology has to offer. We tolerated the bitter taste of the artificial sweetener saccharine (since it was the best artificial sweetener available) until aspartame, in the form of NutraSweet®, came along. We tolerated NutraSweet until Splenda® came along and enabled us to cook with an artificial sweetener. And, we tolerated Splenda until Stevia came to our attention.

Similarly, the cholesterol-reducing brands Pravachol and Zocor set the standards for performance until Lipitor came along. Lipitor proved superior in reducing cholesterol. Physicians appreciated that there was something more that they could now accomplish with their patients who used Lipitor. In other words, the availability of the superior cholesterol-reducing power of Lipitor led these physicians to realize their dissatisfaction with what they had been prescribing for their patients, a dissatisfaction that they had not been previously aware that they had. Now Crestor is leading physicians to be dissatisfied with using Lipitor to treat a select population of their patients who suffer from arthrosclerosis.

Sometimes, we can add an additional "need," which our brand can satisfy. For example, gaining an additional indication can lead customers to be dissatisfied with their current choice. This may have been evidenced when Tide Laundry Detergent for cleaning clothes introduced its formula "Wear Care," which keeps fabrics from fading and fraying and keeps them looking new longer. Other examples occurred when Ortho Tri-Cyclen birth control brand gained an indication for clearing mild to moderate acne, and when Bayer®

Aspirin brand was able to claim that it helps heart health. Bayer has been discovering and proving its ability to satisfy needs incremental to the target's need for an effective analgesic. These additional capabilities, which serve to satisfy additional needs, undermine the target group's satisfaction with what it currently uses.

If the dissatisfaction isn't evident on the surface, our job is to dig deep and discover what our brand can do to make target customers realize they are less than fully satisfied or to exploit our brand's capabilities to satisfy additional, incremental needs.

Telling Behaviors

This factor, "telling behaviors," adds valuable texture to the strategic Target Customer definition. It thereby provides us with a deeper understanding of our prospective customers. It consists of, and results from, direct observation of *what else they do* consistent with treating the condition, their lifestage, or occasion relative to the category. In the Curves example, the Target Customer engages in *"binge eating, wearing oversize clothing to hide her weight, makes excuses for not appearing in public, and refrains from engaging in physical social activities."* This is quite telling and is one of the factors contributing to the design of Curves facilities, where there are no mirrors. The absence of mirrors, and of male membership (men are not allowed to join), helps these women feel less self-conscious about their bodies and about being judged (even if it is they who are judging themselves).

The "Goal Oriented" Disease Combater goes to great lengths to help her patient fix his cholesterol problem before it leads to potentially catastrophic consequences. The actions *"Refer patient to dietician; provide counseling to change lifestyle"* reveal a depth of commitment and dedication to her patients.

Needs

These are the *sine qua non* of the strategic target definition. There are rational (i.e., physical and functional) and emotional needs. We need to address both types of needs. Starbucks presents a good example. Starbucks satisfies the need for a more flavorful coffee as well as the need for a comfortable place to hang out. These are physical/functional needs. But Starbucks also satisfies an important emotional need of the consumer to be put into a *self-rewarding frame of mind.* This linking of rational and emotional can be very powerful. (In fact, when we complete editing this chapter we're heading out to Starbucks to reward ourselves.)

We tend to have a good handle on the needs of customers in our particular category. However, our knowledge is typically confined to *generic needs,* namely those that are common to the category. We need, excuse the pun, to go beyond generic needs and find those needs that our product or brand (if the physical product is not up to it) can satisfy better than the competition. Winning needs (i.e., those needs that we can win with) lead to winning benefits because needs and benefits are two sides of the same coin. If we have a need that we can win with, then we automatically have a benefit that we can win with, as long as the need is relevant to our Target Customer.

Need — Benefit Connection

Two Sides of the Same Coin

We could devote a whole chapter to needs. In fact, we do. Read on to the next chapter. But, before you do, it is a good idea to take a shot of capturing the strategic Target Customer definition from the Customer Target Profile in the following Strategic Targeting Tool.

Strategic Targeting Tool

Use the Curves and Lipitor examples found earlier in this chapter to guide you in defining your Target Customer for the Brand Positioning Strategy Statement.

Strategic Target Customer Tool

- Demographics: _____
- Psychographics:_____
- Patient-Condition/Lifestage/Occasion: _____
- Attitudes: _____
- Current Usage and Dissatisfactions: _____
- Telling Behaviors: _____
- Needs:
  - Rational: _____
  - Emotional: _____

Be Precise

Peter Drucker said something to the effect that the 30-second commercial is the most crafted message in language. Think about it. Thousands of hours go into the development of one spot. There are the hours needed for the development of the positioning, customer research, the agency briefing, creative development, pre-production, production, editing, and on and on and on. In order to be effective, the television spot (or, for that matter, print ad) must communicate a relevant benefit in a clear, provocative manner.

We expect the advertising to be clear. But, marketers often communicate in a less than clear fashion to their agencies and customers. They tend to be imprecise in their word choice and direction. Chalk it up to time pressure, intellectual laziness, poor training, indecision, or something else; it still has the same ill effect. Clear positioning starts with a clear definition of the Target Customer. Choose each word carefully.

Guiding and Checking Your Work

Here's a way to check your strategic Target Customer to ensure that it is technically correct and competitive, The Brand Positioning Add-Valuator checklist tool (which appears on the next page). Assess each of the following nine points by noting whether you "Don't Agree," "Agree Somewhat," or "Strongly Agree." Tally each box and step back to take stock of where you are with defining your Target Customer for the Brand Positioning Strategy Statement. Importantly, identify the indicated actions you must take to achieve a "Strongly Agree" rating and then take those actions.

Brand Positioning Add-Valuator

Strategic Targeting	Don't Agree (0)	Agree Somewhat (3)	Strongly Agree (5)	Indicated Actions
1. Speaks to a clear, well-defined target segment				
2. Contains a demographic				
3. Captures and labels a psychographic, noting it in quotes				
4. Identifies a specific condition, occasion, etc.				
5. Expresses the target's attitudes about the situation				
6. Identifies what products the target is currently using (name products) and dissatisfactions				
7. Expresses "telling" behaviors				
8. Identifies both rational and emotional needs				
9. Ensure that these are needs the brand can win with				
Total Score				

Integrity

If you think about your favorite television series, one that has lasted for years, you'll probably note the integrity of the main characters. When we speak of integrity, we are referring to predictability of behavior in any given situation. You know how Sam Waterston will respond as Jack McCoy in the long-running, but recently cancelled (after more than 20-years), series *Law & Order*, when confronted with certain types of characters or situations. That is character integrity.

This doesn't happen by accident. The screenwriter has probably put together a biographical sketch of the character, taking him from cradle to grave. Both the screenwriter and the actor have immersed themselves in the character. They become Jack McCoy. Unless they are schizophrenic, the integrity of the character will be present in all situations, across time.

Similarly, we need to know and understand our Target Customer group equally as well and define it so that it tells an integrated story where all the parts fit perfectly. Check for linkage of both behaviors and attitudes. Everything, absolutely everything, must link together.

Choose to Serve

Now that you are satisfied with your strategic Target Customer definition, you have made a choice, a most important choice, regarding whom your brand will serve. It is not the customer who serves the brand but the brand that serves the customer. The objective is not just to serve but to serve this customer better than your competition. The objective is to serve your customer in such a way that you delight him so much that it creates a bond that, in turn, inspires unswerving loyalty to your brand. Continue on with the development of your Brand Positioning Strategy to identify how you will go about serving your Target Customer.

Considerations for Better Serving Customers

A review of a broad spectrum of marketing practices from alternate sectors, categories, companies, and countries leads us to the adoption of a few additional considerations in better serving our chosen customer segment. Among those worthy of note are:

- Look to new technologies within your company, outside research organizations, and even other categories for their potential application to your brand. These technologies should lead to satisfying new customer needs or to meeting current needs in a better way.

- Brainstorm ideas for new marketing initiatives aimed at better satisfying your Target Customer on a regular basis. Reserve funds in your budget to test (in limited geographic markets) several of these new initiatives every year. Read the results for your target. It's the one you have chosen to serve. Successful business building initiatives should then be used to build an arsenal of proven marketplace initiatives, which can be launched on a broad basis to stimulate predictable behaviors from your target.

- Get out of the ivory tower to meet your consumers and customers. Go where they go. Do what they do. Go out not to sell them but to learn what and how they think, and what they do, and why they do it.

- Think about ways to add value to the brand from the point of view of your Target Customer, going beyond the physical attributes of your product. What can you do in the areas of selling terms, packaging, distribution, information, customer experiences, and so on to enhance customer perception of your brand? Creating brand loyalty is about adding value.

- Work to delight your customers. Go beyond satisfying "needs" to fulfilling "wants." Give your customers what they don't expect and what your competitors haven't considered or wouldn't consider providing them. Anticipate and lead.

- Be where your customers go and serve them when and how they want to be served.

- Advocate on behalf of your customer. Drive the Target Customers' needs, wants, and values through the organization. To paraphrase the late President

John F. Kennedy, "Ask not what your Target Customer can do for you (your brand, company) but what you (collectively) can do for your Target Customer." Don't settle with being a "voice of the customer." It's too passive. Advocate (isn't that what champions do?) on behalf of your Target Customer. Push the organization beyond what is convenient for it or what is merely acceptable to customers, and urge it to do those things that will win the hearts and minds of your Target Customers in creating brand loyalty.

Talk to your customer in a manner that will strike a responsive chord. We see so many (poor) examples of ads that attempt to talk to customers in a manner that is stilted, expected, overbearing, pretentious, and patronizing. Remember that we are engaging with human beings through our advertising. An ad aimed at health care professionals does not need to be in some prescribed format (boring). Use language, layout, ideas, and visuals that capture the Target Customer's attention and win her over to your way of thinking.

KEY POINTS, PRINCIPLES & PRACTICES
Summary

✓ The Target Customer group is composed of most likely prospects that have a similar set of needs and concerns that our brand can satisfy.

✓ It is important to identify the customer constituency and the key target within that grouping when selecting a target.

✓ Don't attempt to be all things to all people. It's a sure way to fail, particularly in an era of (very) limited resources for marketing.

✓ Demographics are inadequate as the sole element in defining the Target Customer group. Demographics represent, at best, a media target, not a creative or decision making target.

✓ Therefore, the definition of the Target Customer group needs to go beyond demographics. A good definition is made up of the following components: Demographics; Psychographics; Patient-Condition/Lifestage/Targeted occasion; Attitudes; Current (brand or product) usage and dissatisfactions; Telling behaviors; and Needs (both rational and emotional).

✓ Not all elements are equally important in selecting and/or marketing to the Target Customer.

✓ Defining the Target Customer group represents a balancing act. We are balancing the size of the group with our ability to deliver a meaningful message. We are also balancing efficiency and effectiveness.

✓ The best way to get efficiency is to first be effective. In being effective, we put our brand in a position to be truly efficient on the basis it matters most— conversion of customers to our brand, strengthening brand loyalty, and realizing premium margins and profitability.

✓ Make your target prospect real. Move beyond an abstraction, and identify someone you know who is the heart of your target segment. This is your bull's-eye customer.

✓ The bull's-eye customer is the ideal for your product. S/he reflects the values, practices, attitudes, and need mindset that makes your product and the benefits it delivers a perfect match.

✓ Remember, trying to be all things to all people is a sure way to failure.

✓ Use the Target Customer Profile tool to develop a better understanding for the brand's bull's-eye customer. Reflect the customer's attitudes and habits, not yours or your agency's attitudes and habits.

✓ Confirm the bull's-eye customer with (qualitative) research. Check it out!

✓ Alternate target constituencies require separate Customer Target Profiles and, most likely, brand positionings.

✓ Define your target using the Strategic Targeting Tool.

✓ Be precise in defining your Target Customer.

✓ Identify those customers whom you choose not to serve by compromising the brand's meaning and diluting its limited resources.

✓ Serve your chosen customer. Strive to serve them better than your competition in everything you do.

✓ Talk to your customers through all your marketing-mix elements, including your advertising, in a manner that will strike a responsive chord.

✓ Advocate on behalf of your Target Customer. Push the organization beyond what is convenient for it or what is merely acceptable to customers, and urge it to do those things that will win the hearts and minds of your Target Customers in creating brand loyalty.

Insights On Brand Development From The Marketing Front

BECOME A CHAMPION OF CUSTOMERS

"We are the champions—my friends
And we'll keep on fighting
Till the end
We are the champions
We are the champions
No time for losers
'Cause we are the champions of the World"
Queen

During the debrief for a Customer Driven Marketing program we conducted for a medical device company, one of the participants posed this question to the senior manager who hosted this learning event: "What one thing should we do following this program?" Obviously, this participant felt she needed further direction. While we were somewhat taken back that she did not know what to do, we did feel her question demonstrated candor within an organization that is attempting to transition from small-"m" marketing, which is service-to-sales oriented, to customer-driven marketing, which is brand marketing.

Not being asked the question directly, we had the opportunity to reflect upon rather than just react to it. We suggested to our host the following answer to the question, which is the essence of customer-driven marketing:

"Be a champion of customers
to deliver relevant, meaningful differentiation
that creates brand loyalty."

There's a lot of advice in these 14 words. Let's take this advice apart piece by piece, starting at the end and finishing at the beginning, to ensure that we capture its complete meaning.

- ***Create brand loyalty.*** The word "create" means to bring a customer into existence. "Brand" is not about artistic branding devices such as your logotype, icon or colors. It's something more, much more. It's all about a special relationship with the customer that goes beyond not just the branding elements but also the physical attributes of the product. It's a bond. Keep in mind that "loyalty" is a two-way street. It is not just something, albeit a big something, that goes from customer to marketer. It also goes from marketer to customer. Loyalty is marked by unswerving devotion to the other.

- ***Deliver relevant, meaningful differentiation.*** When we use the term "relevant," we mean providing something that is perceived to be important to, and by, our present and prospective customers. But it is not enough to be merely relevant. Our competition may also be relevant. And, the relevance may be generic. Our relevance must be "meaningfully differentiated" from the competitions' if we are to drive preference and create brand loyalty. We should always be on the lookout for ways to be uniquely relevant to our customers.

- ***Champion of Customers.*** With the word "champion," we are defining a requisite role in customer-driven marketing. To be a champion is to exemplify excellence in promoting and supporting customers' needs to the organization such that all resources are focused against meeting those needs. As champions, our first obligation is to our customers, not to our sales force or even to our organization. Our objective is to serve (the right) customers and to serve them better than our competition. "Customers" are our focus. Instead of looking inward to the organization and what it believes, that focus requires that we turn out attention outward to the world of our customers. We become *customer-centric*, not product-centric. We interact with our customers to serve them. Sound like heresy? Sound *eccentric* (please excuse the pun)? Well, if we serve our customers well, we are also serving our organization and sales force well, too!

- ***Become —.*** Are you there yet? Are you a champion of customers? Only you can answer that question. But even if you answer in the affirmative, there's always more you can do to develop further into one who serves customers. It's a transformation from being "inner" directed, selling what we have, to being "other" directed, advocating for our customers. It's also about becoming better as marketers. It's about striving for true marketing excellence.

BOATS & HELICOPTERS

How do we transform ourselves to become champions of customers? Here are some thoughts for your consideration:

1. *Choose.* Our brands cannot be all things to all people. So we have to make choices. The first choice deals with people. What customers will we devote ourselves and our organization, to serving? This requires thoughtful segmentation of the customer population. Once that is completed, we must choose the specific segment we plan to target from among the diverse customer segments. Then, we commit ourselves to creating a mutually beneficial and enduring brand relationship. This will enable us to focus and marshal the organization's resources to create impact, relevant impact.

With the target selected, we go on to create the Brand Positioning Strategy Statement. Consider the statement "our brands cannot be all things. . . ." We must choose what the brand will represent, the meaning we wish to establish with our target that will serve as the basis for our brand relationship. If we fail to choose here, our brand meaning becomes diluted and may even blend with that of the competition. The consequences of failing to choose the brand's meaning can result in a weak relationship with customers, one that is dependent upon the customer's relationship with the sales force (rather than the brand or the organization) and/or price incentives.

2. *Advocate.* Get to know, really know, your customer. You don't get to really know the customer by reading research reports. You have to get out of the office and be with customers. Observe what they do. Importantly, learn why they do what they do. But don't stop here. Do what's needed to ensure everyone on the brand team (both internal and external to the organization) really knows the Target Customer. We should know the target so well that we can anticipate his needs. We should know the target so well that we can predict how he will respond to our initiatives. Whatever initiative you undertake, ask yourself whether this reflects the values of your Target Customers and serves their needs.

Drive the Target Customers' needs, wants, and values through the organization. To paraphrase the late President John F. Kennedy, "Ask not what your Target Customer can do for you (your brand, company) but what you (collectively) can do for your Target Customer." Don't settle with being a "voice of the customer." It's too passive. Advocate (isn't that what champions do?) on behalf of the Target Customer. Push the organization beyond what is convenient for it or what is merely acceptable to customers, and urge it to do those things that will win the hearts and minds of your Target Customers in creating brand loyalty.

3. *Act.* Act in a manner consistent with that of one who serves. Serve your customer in a way that borrows from and builds upon the Brand Positioning Strategy. Don't just talk a good game (as in merely telling through advertising or sales presentations to customers); play a good game. Reflect the brand positioning in absolutely every initiative, everything you do! Practice "Power Positioning."

4. *Respond.* Former New York City mayor Ed Koch was often quoted as asking New Yorkers, "How am I doing?" or, as he would say it, "How'm I doin'?" He was interested in knowing how well he was serving his constituents, on getting their, not his, assessment. He was attempting to be responsive to the needs of his neighbors, the city dwellers. Inherent in his question was a larger question, "What else might I do for you?" Or, "How might I better serve you?" Let's not stop with the execution of each initiative. Get in there and find out how it was received by your customers. We're not talking about "pass" or "fail" marketing research, either. What we mean is finding out what happened (did the initiative generate the behaviors we targeted?), why it happened (how did customers feel about the initiative and why they responded this way?), and what we could do in the future to make our initiatives more productive.

What we learn enhances our understanding of our Target Customer and of our brand relationship with her, provides important feedback for future actions, leads to the discovery of "legitimate" and "productive" insights, inspires appropriate advocacy on the Target Customer's behalf, and directs how the entire organization should act in serving our customer in a way that is relevant and meaningfully differentiated from our competition's efforts. It is about being responsive (how we should adapt to achieve behavior objectives), not reactive (blindly rushing from one initiative to another with knowledge of neither performance or underlying causal factors). It's about creating a learning organization.

Become a champion of customers. Become a champion of the world.

CHAPTER THREE

"Here's the sure-fire way to distill a lot of potential (including 'categoric') Brand Positioning needs down to the winning ones:

1. *From the research-based list of, say, ten rational and emotional needs, identify those that are significantly more important than the others;*
2. *From those five or six, identify the ones that are currently unmet or not completely well met;*
3. *From those three or four, choose the one or two that our brand can meet better than our competition—either on a real or perceived basis;*
4. *These become the "winning"—and only—needs in our Brand Positioning."*

—Dave Roche, Brand Development Network International

Chapter 3

Completing the Strategic Target with Winning Customer Needs

The first and biggest challenge any brand-building team faces in assembling a competitive Brand Positioning Strategy Statement is that of *choosing* the right needs, the needs that the brand can satisfy—in fact or in perception—better than other brands in the same category or class. So challenging is this choosing that, more often than not, marketers default to "categoric" needs (ones that all brands must satisfy at some basic level to compete in the category—like preventing cavities for toothpastes or reducing cholesterol for statins). Or, even worse, they default to too many of them, making it virtually impossible for the customer to know what one or two things the brand truly stands for.

As we noted in the previous chapter, however, when constructing the strategic target for the brand's positioning, it is absolutely essential to make choices—choices in the market segments the brand will target and choices in the precise needs that will best satisfy those segments. So, the "sure-fire" process that our colleague Dave Roche consistently advocates in our training programs is an excellent one to put into practice whenever the team is building a positioning for a new brand or proactively positioning that of an established brand. Why are choices so important? Because the brand is aiming for a *strategic* Target Customer in its positioning. Many marketers have an idea of the *size* of the target they seek, but not so many have a good idea of the *type* of target they seek. They have a *volumetric* sense of the target they desire (normally, the bigger the better) but lack a *strategic* sense of that target. What makes a target strategic, of course, is the same thing that makes any business approach or method strategic: *It is consciously chosen to secure a competitive advantage.* And the needs selected for the positioning Target Customer must be ones that, when satisfied as Benefits, give the brand a real or perceived competitive advantage.

Implementing a Needs "Discovery Mechanism" Process

While our four-step process for distilling down to the right, winning needs is a good one, it's only as good as the marketplace and customer research that informs it. Truth be told, most marketers find their interaction with real customer needs to be pretty limited. If they are working on an established brand (especially a very large one), they may review only the known category needs when an every-five-year Usage and Attitude or Market Segmentation Study comes in. And, more than likely, they pretty much take for granted that there is an inherent "needs structure" to the category that has been well established over time and rarely changes.

But, in fact, much like the tectonic earth plates under our feet, a category's needs structure is shifting, evolving, and emerging in some fashion all the time, whether we perceive it or not. Marketers who spend even a little time working in new product development know this to be the case. (They are, probably, the closest to being customer needs "experts" in the organization—or at least they should be!) And, if you talk with new products marketers about customer needs, you learn a number of key operating principles for selecting the right brand positioning needs:

1. *It's not sufficient to stay current with shifting and emerging needs; you have to get out ahead of needs trends—with a Discovery Mechanism Process.* Such a process, as the name implies, aims to establish ongoing research mechanisms—from formal studies to informal observations and chats—so the brand team can regularly review findings and "discover" need shifts, on an almost real-time basis. To be more specific, this process involves a series of consciously triangulating from among a number of customer data points (including, but not limited to, the following):

- Talking to customers on a regular basis, not merely in scheduled qualitative events like focus groups and in-depth interviews but also while they are shopping and while they are using category products;

- Chatting with and listening to customers across a wide range of social media; soliciting their feedback on category satisfactions and dissatisfactions. as well;

- Fielding creative ethnographic methods—ways to observe and interact with customers during actual category usage;

- Fielding occasional quantitative studies, particularly ones that enable attitudinal and behavioral trend-tracking;

- Observing and borrowing from methodologies that uncover need shifts in other, related categories—for example, adapting what some beer marketers do when they quietly "buy out" a local bar for an evening and "plant" brand team members throughout the bar to engage customers in casual conversation;

- Using intuition, based upon past experiences as a category customer, to guesstimate underlying need shifts and swings.

Again, it's most important to conduct a good number of these formal and informal methods as part of an ongoing effort and to set regular times, say once quarterly, for the brand team to review the latest findings and generate hypotheses about the marketplace need structure.

Having a Discovery Mechanism Process—with both traditional and nontraditional methods at work—to keep ahead of needs changes can really give a brand an advantage. Shown on the next page are just a few examples from relatively recent times of brands that have used some nontraditional methods to discover advantageous emerging needs:

"Need" Discovery Mechanism - Examples

Brand	Discovery Mechanism	Need Discovered
▪ Starbucks	Live channel observations in Milan (Italy) cafes	Coffee-drinking as a self-rewarding experience (Emotional Need)
▪ Bayer 81mg Aspirin	Borrow findings from a competitor-sponsored clinical study (Bufferin)	Low-dose aspirin regimen as a healthy-heart provider (Rational Need)
▪ Knox® NutraJoint Gelatin	Taking part in live chat rooms—with arthritis-suffering customer	Eating gelatin (with glucosamine) daily to maintain flexible joints (Rational Need)

2. *To build the most compelling, competitive brand positioning, you usually must link up both functional and emotional needs.* While there are exceptions to this principle, most brand builders operating in today's "age of sameness" agree that it takes both functional and emotional benefits for a brand to gain a real or perceived advantage. And the key to successfully gaining this advantage lies in the careful linking of the functional to the emotional. This all makes good common sense, especially when backed up by that age-old theory called Maslow's Hierarchy of Needs. If you recall, Maslow's hierarchy stipulated a couple of things: (a) People require, first and foremost, satisfaction of their basic functional needs—food, clothing, shelter; (b) people also seek satisfaction of higher-order, emotional needs—like self-actualization—but these can be satisfied only after the functional ones are satisfied. In other words, one links with and leads to the other. (More about Maslow in chapter 5.)

There are any number of brands that have effectively implemented a brand positioning with well-linked, meaningful functional and emotional needs. One brand we have particularly admired in recent years has been the Imagin Artificial Knee from Johnson & Johnson's DePuy Orthopedics Division. For a while, the Imagin Knee was the only one available in the market that both bent and rotated, satisfying the functional need of many knee replacement patients to regain full motion of their knee joint. But the brand-team was not content to go to market communicating this functional need advantage. They added (linked!) to that functional need a relevant, compelling emotional need: feeling the "joy" of being mobile again. It was a winning need-state combination that came across in patient marketing materials this way: "Imagin: Restoring the Joy of Motion."

   3. *When assessing which needs to go with in the brand positioning, you want to know both the relative order of importance (within the target segment, not the entire market!) and how well your brand and competition deliver against those more important needs.* Knowing these things with any certainty obviously requires some compelling data, typically from a quantitative study. But, when working with any quantitative study, the idea is *not* simply to look for performance gaps (between important needs and customer satisfaction levels); rather, the idea is to go "prospecting" within the implied need-state structure to find hidden veins that might pay off—as the following client did:

Case History

A client in the sanitary protection business recognized that achieving a parity performance on the top two functional needs of the category was all its core competencies would allow. So, how to find a way to win on some other meaningful customer need? This client elected to move further down the *emotional* needs hierarchy and focused against an emerging *mindset* best described as "Feeling more like your natural self." This represented a need that their brand positioning strategy could incorporate; it also was a need ranked lower on the general category list—but considerably higher on a highly opportunistic target segment within the category's list. Prospecting, in this case, led to a perceived emotional advantage.

4. ***More than anything else, innovation is what makes the relative order of importance rankings change within a given slate of customer needs.*** For many years, consumers were reasonably satisfied with their toothpaste brand, since nearly all could virtually eliminate cavities (one functional need), prevent plaque and tartar build-up (another functional need), and fight bad breath (yet another functional need). In the U.S. market, being able to effectively meet all of these needs kept the Crest brand number one for decades. But then came the Colgate Total® innovation—a "strategic ingredient" (that is, patented) that could provide a full 12 hours of germ protection (a new functional need). You could argue that most consumers never knew they had such a need; once they learned about the need, however, it became an important one—important enough to catapult Colgate Total® to the number one position in the U.S. market.

Sometimes the innovation leads to a suddenly, much more important emotional need. When Nokia innovated mobile phone design by making the very first (and, at the time, only) cell phones that were minimalist in size and "sexy cool" in look, they effectively made the need to "feel more contemporary and cool in expressing myself" important to mobile users—especially to younger users. This "fashion innovation" not only enabled Nokia to leap from number three worldwide in market share to number one; it also led all key competitors to satisfy the emotional need and then to try to satisfy it even better than Nokia (e.g., as Samsung has done with design innovation).

Portraying the Need-State Landscape

In addition to providing customer needs operating principles such as these, new product development marketers are also typically adept at providing some insightful models for displaying or portraying a category's need-state structure or "landscape." Honestly, it's hard to imagine any brand—not just new brands under development—aiming to craft a brand positioning without first constructing and studying a map of the existing category need-state landscape.

A good example of the effectiveness of such mapping can be seen in some classic work done by Mexico's major cookie and cracker manufacturer (shown on page 77). Using progressive qualitative research (one-on-one interviews and focus groups) in markets across the country, the manufacturer derived a reasonably reliable picture of the need-state landscape. More specifically, as shown in the bubble map, they found that cookie and cracker consumers evoked 11 important need-states that fell into six need-state "camps." These need-state camps then formed the foundation for the manufacturer's first *portfolio positioning matrix*. And, with inputs from heavy users of both cookies and crackers, they were able to link up distinct product traits—like "layers of ingredients" and "food value ingredients"—with each of the six need-state camps—which, in turn, became the bedrock for their individual cookie and cracker brand positionings.

Cookie Need-States and "Camps"—Mexican Market

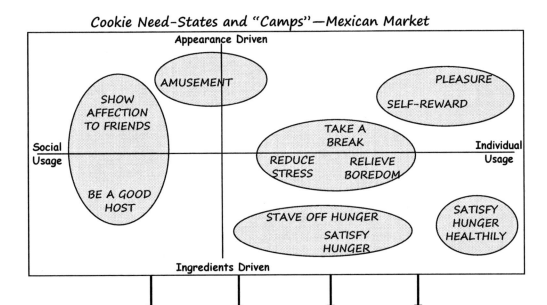

Cookie Product Trait and Need-State "Camp" Linkage—Mexican

MORE EMOTIONAL ————————————————————— MORE RATIONAL

| NEED-STATES | INDULGE MYSELF | CHANGE MY MOOD | | SHARE GOOD TIMES W/ FRIENDS | FEED ME | |
		AMUSE ME	COMFORT ME		SATISFY MY HUNGER	GOOD FOR ME
PRODUCT TRAITS	1. Very sweet 2. Chocolate 3. Layers of ingredients 4. You can taste the fat	1. Colorful 2. Shapes 3. Play-value sizing and portions	1. Lighter – Texture – Portion 2. Mild sweetness; good with beverages	1. Good pieces – Sized for handing around 2. Fillings and special flavors	1. Heavier texture 2. More bulk density/ grams per piece	1. Food-value ingredients – Wheat – Grains 2. Less sugar 3. Plain looking (dough-like)

What is especially telling about this qualitative work with Mexican consumers is that the consumers themselves—not the brand marketers—linked certain visible, tangible product traits they had long been familiar with to needs they typically had met by consuming brands having those traits. In other words, if the manufacturer really wanted to meet the "Indulge Myself" need-state, it would need to offer a brand with extra sweetness, layers of ingredients, some chocolate, and a rich, "full-fat" taste—which, of course, it did. With a consumer-constructed need-state map such as this, the process of selecting which needs to include in a brand's positioning becomes a whole lot easier!

But, wait, you may say. What about the volumetrics of these need-states? This Mexican map doesn't help the marketer understand which ones are likely to provide the biggest volume opportunity for the brand. Well, with a willingness to invest in more marketplace data-gathering, there is yet another map-model that can not only size up need-states relative to one another but also provide volume indications for the various target segments in the market. You might call this a "Targeted Occasion-State" model.

A few years ago, one of the major U.S. beverage manufacturers, determined to get a much more "granular" look at the various target segments and their beverage needs as they changed throughout the day, set about to build such a model. Such a look added two new dimensions to the conventional view of marketplace need-states: target segments (instead of everyone in the market) and day-part or occasion. The company purchased actual consumption data that could be broken out by beverage type by target segments over the course of a day. Using another consumer-generated need-state study—in which consumers identified (much as those in the Mexican cookie market did) which beverage types typically fulfilled which need-states—the company was able to group these beverage types into a need-state "volume base." What resulted was 11 volumetric "targeted occasion-state" charts like the one presented on the next page (one for each of the 11 beverage need-states elicited from consumers):

Targeted Occasion-State: *"Pick Me Up"*
(Volume includes: All coffee and coffee drinks; all caffeine carbonated soft drinks; hot tea)

Target/Psycho & Age Day-Part % Volume	Generation "No" (13-19)	Generation Apart (20-29)	Boomers (30-49)	Power Generation (50+)
Breakfast	4.8%			
Between Breakfast and Lunch	7.7%			
Lunch	16.7%			
Between Lunch and Dinner	23.2%			
Dinner	26.7%			
After Dinner	20.9%			
TOTAL	100%	100%	100%	100%

From this partially reconstructed chart you can see the percentage of total coffee and coffee drinks, caffeine carbonated soft drinks, and hot tea volume consumed by the Generation "No" target segment at various times of the day. But, since these beverages make up the total "Pick Me Up" need-state, you can also see when this need-state is most important to this segment and decide if you have the right beverages to best satisfy the need-state at those times. If you had all 11 of these targeted occasion-states, you would ultimately have direction-setting for both new product development (to fill gaps in the company's total brand portfolio) and for choosing which need-occasions to satisfy with which brands.

A final word: Obviously, neither of these need-state maps is a perfect portrayal of its respective market. As we saw, the Mexican map is based upon only qualitative research; the U.S. model, while based upon quantitative research, involves the cross-hatching of two distinct studies. But what should be inspiring about these two approaches is that the brand builders sought out their target consumers for help in linking up the right brands with the right needs.

Three Big Questions—About Needs

Even when we have the help of market research, it seems there is no end to our quest for understanding customer needs better. In our work with clients—during consulting assignments or training sessions—we are often asked about this most fundamental of brand positioning (and strategic targeting!) elements. But some questions get asked a lot more than others. Here are three, can we say, "classic" questions that marketers everywhere keep asking again and again, along with our best shots at answering them:

Q1. *Do we actually create needs from time to time, or do we merely discover ones that have always been around but are unexpressed by customers?*

A. Our first inclination is always to answer this question with another question: "Does it really matter if we create them or merely help customers finally express them?" But that rarely satisfies anyone. So a better response might be to look at developments in the marketplace over, say, the past 25 years or so. For example, 25 years ago, did some people have a need for reducing their cholesterol? For sure, many had the need to prevent heart disease and heart attacks. But who knew, then, that there was a more basic, underlying need called reducing cholesterol in the arteries? We could not say that the Mevacor and Lipitor and Zocor brands *created* this need, but we sure could say that these brands—with their enlightening new clinical studies—helped to express the underlying need in a way that many customers could appreciate.

Or take another example: Did Apple and its iPod create the need for more conveniently carrying our music around with us? Or was this need created by Sony when it launched its original Walkman? Or, is it more likely that there was always a low-level *desire* among some people to easily take more of their music with them and these brands—through their product innovations—found ways to expand that need to a much larger target?

The more examples you consider, the more you come to the conclusion that it is very, very rare for either a small entrepreneur or a large company to actually *create* a totally, never-thought-of-before need. That's why the Discovery Mechanism Process we outlined earlier in this chapter is so important to implement—to give marketers better odds of unearthing those unexpressed needs and turning them in to winning needs for their brands in the marketplace.

Q2. *Can a brand really win with a "categoric" or "class-effect" need?*

A. Not usually or easily, is the best, first answer. Category or class-effect needs tend to be, by definition, those that each brand in category or class can satisfy. In fact, pharmaceutical brands do not typically receive FDA approval to enter a market unless they can demonstrate some base level of satisfaction against the class needs—such as efficacy, safety, and tolerability. Of course, some brands can demonstrate they satisfy a category or class-effect need better than others. As we saw earlier, Colgate Total® was able to demonstrate longer-lasting efficacy against bacteria than other leading toothpaste brands; for a long time Lipitor was able to demonstrate better efficacy at reducing total cholesterol, LDL, and triglycerides than other leading statins.

But there are other ways that clever marketers position their brands as better solutions to categoric needs. Take Snickers®. Has any other confection brand ever matched its perceived better satisfaction of the category need "hunger satisfaction" (between meals)? You could argue that Snickers won this perception through nothing more than sheer persistence—never missing an opportunity in its positioning implementation—packaging, merchandising, advertising, Internet—to link hunger satisfaction to the brand (as in, "Hungry? Grab a Snickers." or, "Don't Let Hunger Happen to You. Snickers." or, currently, "You're not you when you're hungry. Snickers Satisfies."). Or, how about what the drug brand Nexium did so masterfully in its positioning to doctors and patients in the United States? It coupled a parity performance against the class-effect need (relief of GERD, or gastrointestinal reflux disease) with a winning performance against a related, unmet need—esophageal healing.

So, yes, there are ways to win with or even take perceived "ownership" of a category need. Finding them usually takes out-lasting or out-thinking the competition.

Q3. *Finding a way to differentiate the brand against a functional need is one thing, but how do you differentiate the brand against an emotional need?*

A. One of our favorite questions! Not because the answer is easy, but because answering it demands thinking about emotional needs with a "counter-to-the-herd" mentality. It demands that marketers resist the usual and refuse to insert tired, overused, and often meaningless emotional needs such as *confidence*, *control*, and *empowerment* into their strategic targets. Do you have any sense of how many brands in how many categories have claimed to satisfy emotional needs like these? No, the way to find an emotional need that your brand can satisfy and others cannot is to (1) find a target segment or two that other brands in the category are not squarely positioning their brands against, and (2) through persistent, deep-digging research with those segments, find a need that is virtually opposite to that of the competition. It's sometimes called a strategy to "go where the competition isn't."

And the classic example of this very strategy is what MasterCard began in the late 1990s with its repositioning of the brand against the satisfaction of an important emotional need among a large and growing consumer segment, "Credit Card Pragmatists—people who appreciate those simple moments that really matter in life." Neither Visa nor American Express could have pulled off this same repositioning, for the simple reason that both of those brands had invested too many years and too much money in the "opposite" emotional need—feeling like you are important, with enviable status. Going with a meaningful emotional need that the competition cannot easily (or comfortably) copy is the absolute best way to incorporate a winning emotional need in the brand positioning.

Guiding and Checking Your Work

Here's a way to check your brand positioning needs to ensure they are technically correct and competitive. Assess each of the following six points (which appears on the next page) by noting whether you "Don't Agree," "Agree Somewhat," or "Strongly Agree." Tally each box and step back to take stock of where you are with your needs choices. Importantly, identify the indicated actions you must take to achieve a "Strongly Agree" rating and then take those actions.

Brand Positioning Add-Valuator

Customer Needs	Don't Agree (0)	Agree Somewhat (3)	Strongly Agree (5)	Indicated Actions
1. The Needs are derived from actual customer research—qualitative and or quantitative.				
2. The Needs are also "cross-checked" via informal research methods—from an ongoing Discovery Mechanism Process.				
3. Needs selected relate to the specific Target Segment(s) chosen for the Positioning Target.				
4. The Needs are ones the brand can "win" with against the competition—on a real or perceived basis.				
5. There are both Functional and Emotional Needs the brand can win with.				
6. The Needs are not merely "categoric" or "class-effect."				
Total Score				

KEY POINTS, PRINCIPLES & PRACTICES
Summary

✓ Customer Needs are perhaps the most important of the seven essential elements within the Brand Positioning Target. They are also what the brand will "pay off" in the Benefit part of the Brand Positioning Strategy Statement. As such, they should be Needs the brand can "win" on versus competition—on either a real or a perceived basis.

✓ The need-structure of any category keeps shifting and evolving, with today's less important ones becoming tomorrow's more important ones. It's critical, then, to implement an ongoing Discovery Mechanism Process (comprising both traditional and nontraditional research techniques) to stay ahead of the shifting and evolving structure.

✓ New product development marketers usually represent an excellent resource for established brand marketers who wish to keep up with innovations that may be shifting the market's need-structure and to keep abreast of the latest research techniques for use with customers.

✓ Most brands in today's "age of sameness" require both functional and emotional needs in their brand positioning, and these needs should be well linked (in keeping with Maslow's famous "hierarchy of needs" theory).

✓ Any brand positioning development work should start with a reliable "map" of the current category's needs landscape. There are a couple of "map models" that can help in generating such a landscape. In one of these, consumers/customers link familiar product traits with the needs they typically have satisfied by those traits; another model adds a volume component to each need-state ("Targeted Occasion-State" model).

✓ Marketers rarely create new needs. Rather, the real art and science of working with needs occurs when the marketer—through innovative and ongoing customer interaction—finds a meaningful, emerging need before the competition does—and leverages it for a winning difference in the brand's positioning.

✓ It *is* possible to win versus competition with a "categoric" or "class-effect" need, but doing so usually requires more persistence than the competition puts forth in taking ownership of that need. It may also require a more clever way of linking that categoric need to another important need that is *not* categoric—one with which the brand can meaningfully differentiate its positioning.

✓ The most powerful differentiating emotional needs are the ones that take the brand "where the other brands are not," needs that other brands cannot easily or comfortably duplicate.

✓ Finally, as stated in chapter 2, for the strongest brand positioning, aim to go beyond satisfying needs to fulfilling wants.

WHEN EMOTIONAL NEEDS WORK...
AND WHEN THEY DON'T

Ask any group of marketers what it takes to build a winning brand these days and you will get one answer over and over again--it takes making an emotional connection with the Target Customer. Most of these marketers will make the answer even more specific; they'll say it takes adding an emotional need (and corresponding benefit) to the brand's positioning. The thinking goes something like this: so many branded categories comprise products that perform at parity; brands cannot "win," therefore, with product or functional needs; rather, they can only win by going to a "higher order need"…an emotional one.

At first glance this line of thinking makes sense. But upon closer consideration, you can see at once a glaring flaw in the thinking. And that flaw is simply that adding an emotional need to a Brand Positioning Strategy Statement is something any brand can try. So, Brand Q adds an emotional need to its established, parity functional need, say, something along the lines of "lowers your blood sugar (the functional one) so you can be free to live your life (the emotional add)." Next thing you know, Brand R—in the same category—copies this…and then Brand S, and so on. The category now has three brands with both parity functional and parity emotional needs, and no one has a "win."

How does this happen so readily? We think there are two principal reasons:

1. Probably the bigger reason of the two is that most marketers either don't know how to get at meaningful emotional needs/benefits in their categories, or they continue to rely on out-moded, ineffective research methods in their attempts. What we see clients doing time and again—across all kinds of

categories—is generating a lame list of potential emotional needs to explore with consumers. You know the kind of list we mean when we say "lame"—one that includes all the overused, trite, usual suspects like: "puts you in control"; "gives you freedom"; "provides peace of mind"; "gets you your life back"; "empowers you" (sound familiar?). These lists are typically pulled together internally, often with the help of the ad agency account team. You can see why they would be so predictably similar, regardless of category—clients and their agencies are simply regurgitating what they see and hear daily in ad after ad.

Then, to hinder the emotional need exploratory process even further, they take these lists to focus groups where moderators do what they've always done—try to get consumers to rank order the importance of the emotional needs on the list. Invariably, when the groups end, the client concludes that nothing is conclusive, so they select one of the emotional needs that was talked about the most.

2. The other main reason for so many brands having over-used, parity emotional needs in their positionings is that so many marketers don't seem to understand that what makes an emotional need work is its direct link to a *real or perceived functional need*. The reason Michelin has had such success with its "so much is riding on your tires" psychic-safety need-benefit is simply that Michelin tires were already perceived as being the safest, longest-lasting tires on the road. The reason Hallmark has maintained greeting card leadership for so long via its "when you care enough to send the very best" emotional need-benefit is simply that Hallmark has been recognized as the best at card design/verses forever. The reason that Gatorade has won so big in the sports beverage market with its added emotional need-benefit of "having it in you to be a winner" is that everyone knows the liquid itself is preferred by alpha athletes. And the reason that Tylenol (generally a parity-performing analgesic) is able to win with an ownable emotional need-benefit of trust/safety is that just about everyone knows Tylenol is recommended by more hospitals and doctors than other analgesics. In short, each of these additional emotional needs links directly to something *tangibly differentiated* about the product.

And therein lies the key principle behind emotional needs that work versus those that don't: just like winning functional needs, winning emotional needs need to be differentiated too. The best way we've found for this differentiation to happen is when the emotional follows directly from some differentiable product/functional benefit or reason-why. If you think about it, it makes perfect sense. Why do we trust <u>any</u> brand more than another? Why do we attribute more psychic satisfaction to any one brand over another? In almost every case it's because our experiences with that preferred brand tell us it works better, or at the very least, is more likely to work better. Our emotional attachment is grounded in something real.

BOATS & HELICOPTERS

1. If you are truly serious about discovering the right emotional need/benefit for your brand, start by taking the pledge to conduct the search differently. Hire a panel of psychologists. Send the brand team out to live with your loyal users for a week. Find some chat rooms to listen in on. Get customers to express their emotional needs in a new language (like sounds or colors)—anything but dead benefit terms. Contract with a non-traditional customer intelligence service. Hire a dramatic actress to be your interview moderator. Whatever methods you employ, make sure you keep digging deeper and deeper.

2. At the same time, take another hard look at your brand and at the product underneath that brand. What tangibles might each contain within them that would link up with emotional needs and benefits? And are these linkages truly differentiated in some way from other brands in your category (be honest!)?

3. Whatever happens, don't settle for a categoric emotional need—like the ones virtually all the direct-to-consumer Rx brands use in the U.S. They're like wallpaper in a meeting room: what nobody notices.

CHAPTER FOUR

Something to think about:

Q: *I desperately need a competitive edge, but I'm stuck with a parity-performing product that I can't change. What do I do?*

A: *Try changing your competition!*

Chapter 4

Setting the Competitive Framework
for a Competitive Edge

The answer posed to the question on the preceding page may, at first glance, appear rather clever but highly impractical. For, despite the desperate straits a brand faces, how can it literally change its competitive set? A detergent (like Tide or Surf) competes with other detergents and laundry cleaning aids; a prescription drug (like Lipitor or Crestor) competes with other similar drugs, broadly referred to as statins. These fast-moving consumer goods categories and drug classes are virtually set, often even legally so. No wonder most marketers typically accept them as givens.

But, upon further consideration, the marketing team behind Tide might well argue that the Tide brand is perceived by the consumer as being much more than simply another laundry detergent. With line innovations like Tide with Febreze and earlier formulation improvements like "Wear Care," the brand goes beyond ordinary detergent boundaries to something like "Clothes Cleaner and Preserver"—or maybe, better yet, "Clothes Care" (no wonder, in fact, that a leading line extension is now dubbed Tide Total Care). Likewise, thanks to Lipitor's clinically proven ability to prevent coronary heart disease, that blockbuster brand is perceived by American physicians and patients as much more than simply a cholesterol reducer. It is an "Event Preventer."

Whether you agree with these interpretations or not, one thing is clear: More and more brands—often with parity-performing products underneath them—are aiming to go beyond their obvious competitive set boundaries and create the perception of being something more. And, if you recall our definition of Brand Positioning in chapter 1, *"the way we want customers to perceive, think, and feel about our brand versus competitive entries,"* this creation of perception through the Competitive Framework makes a lot of sense. It is no longer sufficient for marketers to merely identify their brand's literal competitive set (that's the easy part anyway!). No, to be more competitive nowadays the brand marketer must creatively explore and develop a *Perceptual Competitive Framework.* In fact, as we'll see, the Brand Positioning Strategy Statement should include not one but two dimensions of the Competitive Framework: the literal (LCF) and the perceptual (PCF).

Of course, articulating the Perceptual Competitive Framework is only the first step. After that, it takes tangible initiatives—such as line extensions, product improvements, packaging architecture and design changes, product "designators," merchandising placement, and advertising—to ensure that the consumer or customer will readily perceive what the brand intends. In other words, getting to a competitive Competitive Framework takes an action plan.

We'll take a look at some examples of brands with compelling, sustained Competitive Framework action plans in the following pages. But before we do that, let's return to the question and answer exchange that opened this chapter. Is it really possible to change your competition (or at least add to your current competition)? Consider the classic example of a paper-product brand known worldwide:

Case History

First introduced in the United States in the 1920s, this brand was initially positioned as a "disposable cold-cream remover." In those days, women who wore makeup used cold cream each night before going to bed to remove their makeup; naturally, they required something to wipe off and hold the "goo" being removed from their face. The brand built a nice little business within a competitive set that probably included things like cotton balls, toilet tissue, and washcloths. But then some forward-thinking marketer on the team suggested that, without any major changes to the product (but some to the packaging architecture), the brand could be more advantageously positioned as a "disposable handkerchief." In that way, it would be competing with more and different products like cloth handkerchiefs and napkins, and it would be increasing its use occasions substantially—throughout the day (as opposed to one use in the evening for removing cold cream) and by both genders and all ages. Can you name the brand?

(The answer is on page 108.)

Identifying the Literal Competitive Framework

With examples like this, you can perhaps begin to see some advantages of thinking beyond the brand's obvious competitive set. But, of course, each brand needs to have some easily recognizable competitive set to "belong to"—if for no other reason than to ensure the intended positioning target readily remembers the brand when needs it can satisfy arise. As the authors of *Winning Brands* put it, every consumer or customer has a set of "mental drawers" in her head; these drawers open automatically when various needs arise. For example, if I awaken with a painful backache, my subconscious mental drawer labeled "back pain" opens and shows me the various options I have to take care of the problem: Analgesics, both oral and topical, are in the drawer for sure; maybe some pain patches like Therma-Care or Tiger Balm will be there, as well. There may even be some procedures to go along with these products—like taking a hot shower or calling for a massage or making an appointment with a chiropractor. The point is, if your brand is a substitute for one of these, it obviously needs to be in the drawer! We like to call these substitutable competitors the *Literal* Competitive Framework (LCF) because they are literally the brands and services that our brand interacts with and sources volume from.

Most well-established brands communicate their Literal Competitive Framework in the most basic of ways. Fast-moving consumer goods typically have a designator on their packaging—usually right under the brand logo—that identifies the category or set.   Sometimes these designators are referred to as "standard of identity" nomenclature.   So, under the Tylenol logo we see the words "Pain Reliever/ Fever Reducer"; under the Tide logo we see the words "Laundry Detergent"; and under the Gatorade logo we see the words "Thirst Quencher"—at least until very recently.   Even pharmaceutical brands normally follow this standard of identity classification.   For example, under the Lipitor logo we see the word "atorvastatin," which clarifies precisely what type of statin Lipitor is.

Another very basic way that packaged goods brands indicate their literal set is through their retail merchandising location.   Remember you grandmother's admonishment, "You will always be known by the company you keep"?   Well, brands are also at least partly known by the company they keep, by their retail "neighbors."   We expect brands like Neutrogena, NIVEA, and Olay to regularly be found in the Health and Beauty Aid section of the store, more specifically in the Skin Care aisle.   In a way, these consistent retail classifications inform and reflect our individual mental drawers.

But even with everyday helpers like standard of identity labeling and retail category sectioning, there are also times when brands choose to do more to ensure that their brand's Literal Competitive Framework is being communicated.   One common approach is using advertising to make it crystal clear.   What are some of those times when a brand marketer might want to go beyond packaging and in-store signals to identify very clearly for the target the literal framework?

Advertising the Literal Competitive Framework

Here are some of the more common reasons for spotlighting the brand's Literal Competitive Framework in advertising:

1. *When brand line extensions (or new indications for pharmaceutical and medical brands) open up new sources of volume.* If the marketplace already knows the brand and its longstanding competitive set well, it only makes sense to inform everyone when there is a change to that set.   For example, when Campbell's Soup launched its new Soup at Hand® packaging for virtually instantaneous, on-the-go soup, the brand seized upon an immediate opportunity to expand beyond its entrenched set of canned soups. The new single-serve, portable format enabled the brand to compete with virtually any "in-hand nutrition." In one of its first print ads, Campbell's simply showed a split page with an unnamed granola bar at the top and a Campbell's Soup at Hand at the bottom. The headline brought it all home: "Routine." (next to the granola bar) and "Rousing! Eat something good on the go." (next to the Soup at Hand). And at the very bottom of the ad are the simple words "Campbell's Instead." Through this simple communication, the between-meal nutrition-seeker now opens her "mental drawer" and sees not merely energy bars but also Campbell's!

   2. When a brand has the option of sourcing volume from a smaller, "sub"-competitive set or from the established "gold standard" (which typically dominates the established competitive set). Actually, in some categories, brands have wrestled with this option for years. Take sanitary protection. U.S. tampon brand marketers have gone back and forth in their advertising by sometimes positioning their product as a better alternative to *other tampons* (about 40% of the total market) and other times as a better alternative to *pads and liners* (about 60% of the total "san-pro" market). Of course, which competitive set to go up against is often an opportunistic choice: If the brand has a legitimate performance advantage over other leading tampons (say, with a new extension), then it only makes sense to exploit that news. But the brand may at other times perform no better than other tampons, yet show better absorbency or comfort than certain pads—so why not let san-pro users know that?

   One of our favorite recent examples of taking on the "gold standard" in advertising comes out of Argentina for the NutraSweet brand. Now that it is more than 25 years old, many consumers around the globe know NutraSweet as a leading artificial sweetener. They also know a few of the more prominent competitors that make up the artificial sweetener competitive set: Equal, Sweet'N Low, and, more recently, Splenda. In Argentina, NutraSweet chose to position itself outside this "artificial" set and directly against the sweetness standard, sugar. In one particularly clever television spot, a woman makes coffee for her husband at the breakfast table while he peruses the morning paper. He sees an article there that says that 90% of women "fake it" with their husbands, and he inquires if she has ever "faked it" with him. She catches herself quickly and responds, "No, you would be able to tell if I did." She then asks him (with her back to him, hiding her actions) whether he would prefer sugar or NutraSweet in his coffee. He replies, "Sugar." At this point, she empties one packet of NutraSweet into his coffee (still unseen by him) and hands him the cup, and he drinks with obvious satisfaction. The spot ends with these simple words on the screen: "NutraSweet: Tastes as good as sugar."

The positive implications of this kind of literal framing are twofold: (1) The sugar user (or dual sugar and artificial sweetener user) is incited to try NutraSweet and find out how indistinguishable its taste is from that of real sugar, and (2) the sugar user may infer that, among all those artificial sweetener choices out there, NutraSweet is the one that is better-tasting. One other thing this advertising approach illustrates is that you don't have to beat the "gold standard" to source volume from it!

3. ***When a brand needs to fend off unexpected competition—particularly that deriving from advances in technology.*** Take, for example, some of the skin care brands—especially their line extensions in the burgeoning anti-aging segment. Virtually all of these products, whether from Neutrogena, NIVEA, RoC®, or Olay, are essentially lotions in a bottle that are applied to the surface of the skin. They clearly compete with one another—until some advance like Botox injections or laser resurfacing comes along. And, while it is true that both injections and laser applications are more invasive procedures, in some instances they steal volume from the tried and true lotions.

At times like these, it may behoove the marketer to remind the anti-aging lotion user that her brand offers wonderful youth-enhancing efficacy *without* the potential risks associated with more invasive treatments. No wonder, then, that Neutrogena has run some print ads showing its Visibly Firm (with copper) cream alongside a hypodermic syringe with the simple headline: "Is it possible to have younger-looking skin without resorting to collagen injections?" And, along similar lines, Olay Regenerist has run print with a list of invasive procedures (Botox, laser resurfacing, chemical peel) that have all been crossed out; only the word "Regenerist" at the bottom of the list remains fully visible. Referencing a new, "more advanced" competitive set, as these ads do, may actually get some consumers to think twice before giving up their topical skin care for treatments; it may also suggest that these new treatments are not all that much more effective, anyway.

4. *When a brand has a provable (and meaningful) advantage over its key competition.*   We generally label advertising developed in this case as "comparative," and the risks-rewards associated with comparative advertising have long been debated among marketers. Most buy into the principle that leading brands should never condescend to acknowledge or give any free media exposure to their lower-ranking competitors; they also typically accept, therefore, that comparative advertising is reserved for the "upstarts" in the competitive set (numbers two, three, or four), which have less to lose. And, of course, outside the United States, comparative advertising is widely scorned as an American phenomenon—and, in most places, it is illegal, anyway.

Regardless of your personal philosophy on the advisability of running comparative advertising, there are case histories after case histories of brands that have gained significant business results via the clever (and timely!) use of ads that showcase their brand's "win" over its closest competitor or even the entire competitive set. Though it now happened well over 30 years ago, does the Pepsi Challenge ring a familiar bell?

But you don't have to go back in time to see its effects at work: On any given day, U.S. television ads for Advil or Aleve directly claim that their pain relief is stronger, faster, or better than that of Tylenol. And it is becoming more and more common to see direct-to-consumer magazine ads for prescription drugs that pit one brand against all the others in its class.

These, then, are some of the more common reasons for actually advertising the brand's Literal Competitive Framework to the customer or consumer. Still, it is relatively rare for marketers to use advertising to communicate the Competitive Framework. That's why it makes all that much more sense for most brands to create, to nurture over time, and eventually to own a Perceptual Competitive Framework. As mentioned at the start of this chapter, this dimension of the Brand Positioning comes across in virtually everything the brand does.

The Perceptual Competitive Framework: Getting Started

We've found that a really useful place to start the search for a differentiating perceptual framework is with diagramming, as in the longstanding, even classic, tree diagram for the *Jell-O* brand:

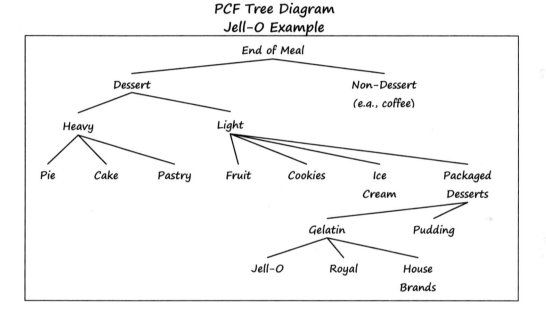

PCF Tree Diagram
Jell-O Example

A good way to draw a diagram like this for your brand may be somewhat counterintuitive: Start in the lower right-hand corner of a blank page, and work your way up and left-center as the possible segments or markets open up. In this fashion, *Jell-O's* most immediate Competitive Framework is all other gelatin brands, which is only one of the subsets underneath a broader framework called "Packaged Desserts," which is only one of the subsets underneath the even broader framework called "Light Desserts," and so on.

Over time, the *Jell-O* brand sees opportunity in competing for a broader set of substitute products—actually, opportunity to increase its source of volume (thereby expanding its Literal Competitive Framework) but also opportunity to be perceived as something more than just another gelatin or packaged dessert (thereby identifying options for expanding its Perceptual Competitive Framework as well). There is a catch, however, in both of these opportunities: *the Jell-O product line-up has to deliver on the key benefits associated with these expanded frameworks*. To be taken seriously as an alternative to more formal "heavy" desserts, Jell-O needs to offer something akin to those kinds of desserts. So they introduce the Jell-O *No Bake* line of desserts, comprised of things like *Chips Ahoy!* pie that uses Jell-O as a key ingredient. To be taken equally seriously as an anytime treat, Jell-O offers a new, single-serve packaging format that allows for on-the-go snacking with such items as Cheesecake Snack, Sundae Toppers, and Smoothie Snacks…effectively taking the brand beyond "End of Meal" to "Non-Meal Treat," an even higher level on the diagram.

Mainly through the introductions of flavor and form line extensions, the Jell-O brand has effectively expanded its literal source of volume; it has also dramatically changed the brand's perception in the minds of consumers—from that of an after-meal dessert to an anytime snack treat. Let's look at one other brand that has just as effectively expanded its perceptual framework, but by using even more marketing mix elements than line extension: Gatorade.

A few years back, one of the marketing leaders for Gatorade was quoted as saying that the company intended to have the brand perceived by consumers as much more than a leading sports beverage. They intended the brand to eventually be seen as *"ultimate liquid athletic equipment."* Upon first hearing, such a notion sounds almost absurd. But if you could actually pull it off and be perceived as essential athletic equipment—for all kinds of athletic endeavors and all levels of performance—well, imagine the advantage you would have over your competition. How did the Gatorade marketers come up with this "athletic equipment" notion? Well, we don't know for sure, but perhaps they employed the tree diagram as Jell-O did and found the following (which appears on the next page):

PCF Tree Diagram
Gatorade Example

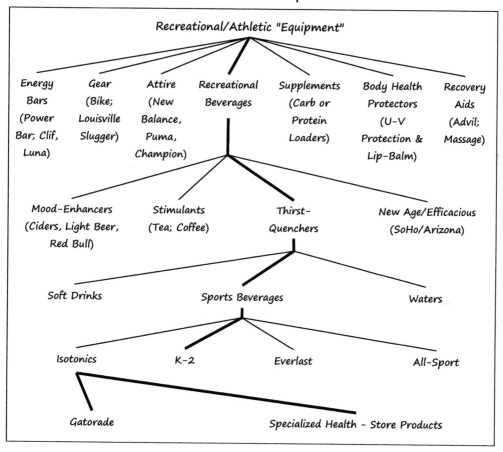

While we cannot be sure this is how Gatorade envisioned its sports beverage or thirst quencher as a subset of other recreational equipment, we *do* know that the brand has used the athletic equipment perceptual framework to guide all of its marketing efforts. For example:

- Gatorade pioneered the pop-up sports cap bottle, making the average bottle more equipment-like;
- Packaging for Gatorade powder is in the shape and color of its famous sideline coolers, also a type of equipment;
- Gatorade widened the mouth of its bottles to enable faster gulping, something athletes need;
- When it launched a water sub-brand, Gatorade named it Propel Fitness Water, not merely "water."

Articulating the Complete Competitive Framework in the Brand Positioning

So, by now we have examined the two dimensions—Literal and Perceptual--of the Competitive Framework that we urge every brand to include in its Brand Positioning Statement. And, to keep things real simple, we even like to use an easy format that links the two dimensions in a side-by-side fashion:

Competitive Framework Tool - Examples

Brand	Is The Brand Of_____ (Perceptual Frame)	Competing Mainly With____ (Literal Frame)
Gatorade	Ultimate Liquid Athletic Equipment	--Powerade, Lucozade --Water and enhanced waters --Fruit drinks
McDonald's	Family Fun and Food Destination	--Burger King, Wendy's --KFC, Subway --Mall arcades --Zoos, parks
Olay Regenerist	Revolutionary Cell Care	--L'Oreal --Neutrogena --RoC (and other leading anti-aging brands)
Virgin Atlantic Airlines	Travel Entertainment	--British Airways --United, American, Delta
Snickers	THE Between-Meal Hunger Satisfier	--Kit Kat, Hershey Bar, Reese's --Fritos --Power Bar
Kellogg's Special K	Shape and Weight Maintainer	--Corn Flakes, Rice Krispies --Adult cereals --Slim-Fast

Notice some key principles at work in each of these inferred examples of complete Competitive Framework articulation:

1. The perceptual frame is "anchored" by a telling noun: Equipment, Destination, Care, Entertainment, Satisfier, or Maintainer. Each of these should ring true to the target customer or consumer; ideally, over time each of these nouns should be more ownable by these brands than by others.

2. The literal frame starts by listing the closest-in, strongest volume-interacting competitors and then proceeds to identify (in most cases) some further-out but logical alternatives to the brand. These further-out competitors should link to the perceptual frame. For example, Fritos is probably the most satiating of the big-name Frito-Lay snacks (it is certainly one of the most densely made), so it would be the salty snack hunger satisfier—and there is always some interaction between salty snacks and confection.

3. As we saw with Gatorade, each of these brands owes it to its respective target group to communicate its perceptual frame in all that they do. McDonald's has certainly communicated its "family fun and food destination" well over the years, being the pioneers of playgrounds on restaurant property, the Happy Meal, and many Ronald McDonald appearances and events on-site. In some places (like India), McDonald's even designates their locations as "Family Restaurants."

4. Perhaps most important of all, the perceptual frame should lead to or *set up* the brand's Benefit(s). Based on these examples, we would expect to see in the Benefit section of the Brand Positioning Strategy Statement for Olay Regenerist that it promises even younger-looking skin; we would expect Kellogg's Special K® to promise women that a daily diet which includes Kellogg's Special K will help them keep their weight and shape better. You can think of the Perceptual Competitive Framework as similar to the assist in basketball—it sets up the basket or the "score."

Getting the Competitive Framework Done Right—Some Final Perspective

There's really no magic in out-thinking your competitors when it comes to setting the vision and pushing the boundaries for your brand's Competitive

Framework. But there are two things you can do that increase your odds of succeeding at these endeavors a great deal: (1) be sure to involve both creative and analytical thinkers in the process—people who work on your promotion or advertising agency creative teams usually speak a different language than most of us marketers…which can really help in finding those potential "telling nouns" that anchor the perceptual dimension of the framework; (2) encourage everyone who develops the Competitive Framework to maintain an open mind, along the lines of the following tale:

> Two monks from different holy orders were arguing heatedly over a rather practical matter: whether it would be proper to smoke while praying. One, a hard-line thinking monk, insisted that to do so would be offensive; the other, more open-minded monk saw no real harm in it. Because they could not agree, they decided to ask their superiors. When they had done this, they met again to compare answers. The hard-liner confidently asserted, "It's as I knew it would be— my superior said emphatically, 'One must never smoke while praying.'" "That's funny," the open-minded monk replied, "I asked if it would be all right to *pray while smoking*, and my superior readily responded that praying at any time is good thing."

Being able to see your brand and its potential competition with such flexible perspective as this can make all the difference.

Guiding and Checking Your Work

Here's a way to check your Brand Positioning Competitive Framework to ensure it is technically correct and competitive. Assess each of the following six points by noting whether you "Don't Agree," "Agree Somewhat" or "Strongly Agree." Tally each box and step back to take stock of where you are with your Competitive Framework choice. Importantly identify the indicated actions you must take to achieve a "Strongly Agree" rating and take those actions.

Brand Positioning Add-Valuator

Competitive Framework	Don't Agree (0)	Agree Somewhat (3)	Strongly Agree (5)	Indicated Actions
1. It is not merely a "Standard of Identity" statement.				
2. The Literal Competitive Framework lists all actual and potential competitors.				
3. The Literal Competitive Framework is expressed as more than category or segment.				
4. It contains a Perceptual Competitive Framework label that is expressed in "quotes."				
5. The Perceptual Competitive Framework suggests meaningful brand differentiation.				
6. The PCF sets up a relevant, meaningfully differentiated benefit that is competitive.				
Total Score				

KEY POINTS, PRINCIPLES & PRACTICES
Summary

✓ Identifying the brands and products your brand interacts with and sources volume from in your positioning statement is merely the starting point; it is (literally) the brand's Literal Competitive Framework.

✓ The greater opportunity for most brands is in creating an ownable Perceptual Competitive Framework for the brand. Consistent with the definition of Brand Positioning, crafting this additional framework dimension enables the brand to better control the way its consumers or customers *perceive* the brand relative to its main, literal competition.

✓ Communicating the Competitive Framework (both its Literal and its Perceptual dimensions) can take any number of forms. The most commonly used are the brand's: merchandising location; packaging architecture and graphics; designator (typically seen on the package near or below the logo); line extensions or new indications; and advertising/communications.

✓ A practical way to explore Perceptual Competitive Framework options is via the tree diagram that starts out quite narrow and expands to broader and broader categories or classes of products. Using model brands such as Jell-O and Gatorade, you can visualize their conscious framework evolutions over time. And you can also see how these brands have used product improvements, line extensions, and packaging innovations to communicate their broadened frames.

✓ A simple but effective way of articulating the complete Competitive Framework in the positioning statement is to break it into two parts, starting with *"Is the Brand of _____"* (Perceptual CF) and concluding *"Competing Mainly with _____"* (Literal CF).

✓ Key principles to double-check after articulating the two-part Competitive Framework are these: There should be a "telling noun" (like "equipment" or "satisfier") anchoring the perceptual dimension; the literal dimension should include the biggest volume "interactors" with the brand; and the perceptual frame should "set up" and lead logically to the brand's benefit(s). There should be a natural linkage between these two positioning elements.

(The answer to the question posed on page 94 is Kleenex®.)

THE PERCEPTUAL FRAMEWORK: "PISTONS" FOR YOUR POSITIONING

For some time now, we have been advocating a two-dimensional expression of the Competitive Framework within a Brand Positioning Strategy Statement: Literal and Perceptual. It has always been customary to include the Literal Competitive Framework in a brand positioning statement so as to make clear what products the brand competes with and intends to source volume from. But the notion of adding a Perceptual Competitive Framework is something quite new to most marketers. As the term implies, this dimension of the CF aims to establish a distinctive, differentiating *perception* of what the brand is—even within a set of parity-performing products and brands.

One of the examples we like to use in illustrating this principle at work is the Just for Men hair-color brand. If you're a guy looking to wash away some gray and you shop the men's grooming shelf in most drug stores, you'll likely find Just for Men alongside its literal competitive set, including brands such as Clairol for Men and Grecian® Formula. And if you were to take the trouble to read the labels and ingredients within these three brands, you would conclude they are all pretty much the same products—with one important exception that shows up on the Just for Men packaging and in its advertising: Just for Men says it is "more than a hair color, it's a *hair rejuvenator*." This brand has for some time now been aiming to create the perception of being something more than and better than its immediate competitors, of clearly being within the literal set, yet transcending the boundaries of that set.

The more you study examples of brands that are consciously trying to establish a perceptual framework like this, the more you really appreciate what a hard-working positioning element the Perceptual CF can be. Like the pistons inside your car's engine that "fire" within the six cylinders to power the vehicle, the Perceptual CF can power a Brand Positioning; here are "six cylinders" that the Perceptual CF can "fire" within:

1. *The Perceptual CF can drive perceived differentiation.* This is the intent in the Just for Men positioning, for sure. It is also the intent in the Olay Regenerist Brand, which claims to be "not just skin care, but revolutionary *cell care*." You can see in this conscious juxtaposition of the accepted category or competitive set (skin care) and the all-new "label" (cell care) how the brand wants to position itself as better than the other set players. In its package it may look like all the others—cream in a bottle—but its formula allows Regenerist to regenerate cells, unlike the others.

2. *The Perceptual CF works to "set up" the brand's positioning Benefits.* Another way of saying this is that when the target understands instantly what the brand wants to be perceived as, the "what that means for me" (or benefits) follow logically and naturally. Take, for instance, the perception that Nokia has invested so much in—both in product design and in brand communications—its desire to been seen as the "people connector" of mobile phones. By being the leader in fashioning phone shapes, sizes, and colors, the brand not only took over worldwide market share leadership but gave consumers everywhere designs they "connected" with personally.   And, of course, the brand simultaneously launched the "Connecting People" ad campaign, showing cell consumers all the ways that Nokia could put them in touch with their family and friends. This "people connector" perception made the design and functional positioning Benefits all the more clear.

3. *The Perceptual CF can add use occasions.* Who in the United States by now does not know that Bayer Aspirin is not merely a pain reliever but also a "heart-health maintainer"? Again, this brand made a conscious decision several years back to broaden what it stood for by leveraging clinical data that proved aspirin therapy could prevent heart attacks. Within a very tough literal competitive set of brands such as Tylenol, Advil, and Aleve, Bayer became the "only leading pain reliever that could actually save your life." So, without any change to the product itself, the brand changed its perception to become both a pain reliever and a heart-health supplement—and in the process picked up significant new occasions for consumption. (In this example, you can actually see all three "pistons" we've mentioned so far at work: differentiation, benefit set-up, and new use occasions.)

4. ***The Perceptual CF can serve as a brand positioning "mantra."*** When the perception is well seated (usually following years of consistent communications via promotion, packaging, advertising, and so on by the brand) it is not only nearly impossible for consumers to forget but, even better, virtually impossible for competitors to copy. Recently, while working one of our Positioning and Communication Colleges with marketing clients, we conducted a mini-quiz and asked listeners to identify a brand only on the basis of hearing its (inferred) Perceptual CF. Upon hearing "The Between-Meal Hunger Satisfier," there was near-unanimous identification of Snickers. But of course! What other brand could possibly own the words "hunger satisfier/satisfaction"? This is a perception so well established that it almost "completes" the brand name itself.

5. ***The Perceptual CF can help the brand bond even stronger with its target.*** We have long admired the way McDonald's long ago escaped the somewhat negative perceptual frame of "fast food" and actually invented a highly positive one to replace it: "Family Fun-Food Destination." How has it done this? Well, first, it had a vision of what perception it wanted to create; then it set about doing tangible things to make the new perception real for the target. Recall that McDonald's was the first "fast food" outlet to provide playgrounds on the premises; it also pioneered the Happy Meal; and, of course, many of its ad campaigns spoke directly to parents and their younger children of the good times McDonald's could offer. Sure, we all know that the food at McDonald's is still fast, but, especially if we have kids, we also know it's a great (and less expensive!) fun alternative to zoos, theme parks, and arcades.

6. ***The Perceptual CF can sometimes act as an effective "brand designator."*** The Olay brand also provides a good example of this perceptual framing at work—via its moisturizing/cleansing mini-towels labeled Olay "daily facials." Up against a competitor on-shelf like Ponds, with a parity-looking product, this on-package "designator" as a "daily facial" promises much more than the Pond's designator of "moisturizing and cleansing towelette." Not only does the Olay designator differentiate the sub-brand, but also, because the nomenclature is part of the trademark, it is also ownable. Yet another hard-working piston for implementing the Olay Brand Positioning.

We hope that these positioning "pistons" will inspire you to develop and add a Perceptual Competitive Framework to your brand's positioning. Although it may be the most underappreciated positioning element (versus, say, the Benefit or Reasons-Why or even the Brand Character), the closer you look at it, the more you realize that the Perceptual CF works harder for a Brand Positioning than any of the others. And well it should, because a positioning is, after all, the "way we want the target to perceive, think, and feel about our brand relative to the competition."

CHAPTER FIVE

"So, what's in it for me?"

—*Customer*

Chapter 5

Giving Your Brand Meaning with Benefits That Result in a Compelling Pay-Off

The *Benefit* is the third essential element in developing our Brand Positioning Strategy Statement. The Benefit is often the principal driver in the customer's purchase decision. It's the customer's payoff for purchasing and using your brand of products and/or services. It addresses the customer's questions "So, what's in it for me?," "What does this mean for me?," and "Why should I purchase your offering?" Indeed! These are questions the marketer must address and for which she must have appropriate answers that are relevant and meaningfully differentiated from those of our competitors.

Neither Features Nor Attributes

It seems as though many marketers are feature crazy. What is a feature? It's a part of a product that is offered as a special attraction. A feature is a characteristic. It tends to be but is not necessarily physical in nature. It can represent a specific design or an ingredient, or it may be something that is not physical but that certainly is a characteristic, such as payment terms.

Much of what passes for marketing or sales communication are features, not benefits. Features support benefits. They make benefits more credible to customers (more on this in chapter 6). Featuring "features" is at best tactical. It is not strategic. In fact, it can serve to dilute the true meaning of the brand by focusing on merely one aspect of the product and missing the totality of the brand experience and its meaning for the customer.

Many of us are familiar with the story of the elephant and the six blind men (which originated in India and varies in its telling depending on whether it is being told by Sufis, Hindus, Jainists, or Buddhists). Each of the six blind men came in contact with one part of the elephant and described that which he believed was before him. The first blind man grabbed hold of a leg. He stated that it was unquestionably "the trunk of a tree." The second fell into the side of the elephant. "Oh," he ventured, "this is a wall." The third felt up and down the elephant's tail. "No, no, you are both wrong" he said knowingly. "What we have before us is neither tree nor wall. It is rope!" The fourth blind man got hold of an ear. "I think this is a giant fan," he said. The fifth felt the elephant's trunk, which was squirming back and forth, and shouted that he was holding "a snake." And the sixth blind man grabbed hold of a tusk, which felt round and sharp. "No, no, no," he exclaimed. "You are all wrong. This is a spear we have before us." Confusing features with benefits and sounding off about the features is like the blind leading the blind. It neither tells the whole story nor communicates the *brand meaning* to prospects.

Features tend to relate to the product. Benefits must relate to the brand. It's the difference between the parts and the whole. Features are on the lower end of the pyramid that goes into making the product. Benefits sit upon it to establish the brand.

Features are relatively easy to replicate. If you introduce what you believe is a unique feature today, your able competitors will match and may even trump it tomorrow. It amounts to nothing more than escalation of trivia without giving meaning to the brand. Because features are short lived, so are their impact on customer perceptions and the value of the brand. Features are at best transactional. Brand meaning is transformational in creating experiences and establishing relationships.

Benefits

The positioning Benefit provides customers with a basis for choosing your offering. It gives your brand a special meaning. Therefore, it *needs* to be competitive and to *relate to the brand*. Moreover, it should be the most meaningful customer benefit you want to and can own in the minds and hearts of your customers.

Let's take time to examine something we mentioned about "needs" and relate it to the *brand*. Gatorade serves as a good example of offering a benefit related to the brand. Gatorade is an isotonic beverage used to quench thirst and replenish what your body loses through sweat during competition. Yet, Gatorade promises, or leads one to infer a promise, that it will make one a champion along the lines of a Michael Jordan (wow, could he sell Gatorade during his playing days!). That's because Gatorade, the brand, is endorsed by many major athletic associations (such as the National Basketball Association). We also witness alpha athletes consuming Gatorade in cups branded with the trademark, an iconic lightning bolt symbol, along the sidelines when they come out of the game for a rest. It is not a benefit promise that can be supported by the product itself, whose liquid is not markedly different from that of its competitors and which is certainly not formulated from professional endorsements.

Not only must benefits be relevant, but they also need to differentiate your offering from competitors. Failure to do so will lead customers to commoditize your product. As we've stated earlier, that is not a good thing. Once you are classified as being the same as all the rest, then customers will make their selection on the basis of price. If you are not a high-volume, low-cost producer, you are going to bleed margins and profits. Gosh, that's ugly! However, while you may not be able to differentiate on the basis of product, you may be able to do so with the brand by managing customer perceptions of it, as Gatorade has successfully done with its endorsements. By the way, we don't consume "endorsements." We consume (or buy into) what it suggests (the "promise" of the brand which is found in the Benefit of the Brand Positioning Strategy Statement) for enabling us to gain a competitive edge, achieve superior performance, and be a "winner."

Types of Benefits

There are a number of benefit types. Each of these benefit types affords the marketer an opportunity to differentiate the brand. There are *product*, *customer*, and *emotional* benefits. Gatorade provides us with an illustration of the three types of benefits.

- *Product* — Quenches thirst and replenishes lost minerals
- *Customer* — Enables you to play harder, longer
- *Emotional* — Gives you a competitive edge to be a "winner" like your favorite alpha athlete

Notice the difference among the benefit types. The *product benefit* gets at what the product does. In the case of Gatorade, it "quenches thirst and replenishes lost minerals." The product benefit is probably the most frequently used benefit type in positioning and marketing communications. Sometimes it's the only benefit you need; for example, when your product is establishing a new segment or category, it can provide meaningful differentiation. It can also be enough when the product benefit enables different customers to take away a customer benefit that is particularly meaningful to them (from among an array of potential customer benefits). Unfortunately, its frequency of use is most likely a function of the lack of sophistication of the marketer. The product benefit is the lowest-order benefit and, in far too many cases, is generic. Accordingly, there is a high likelihood that it, by itself, will fail to evoke brand loyalty.

The *customer benefit* addresses the reward inherent in the product benefit to the customer. In the Gatorade example, the customer benefit is being able to "play harder, longer." The customer benefit builds a bridge for customers in translating the product benefit into something more meaningful to them. Additionally, it can serve to differentiate one product from another. You may arrive at the customer benefit by simply addressing either of the following two questions regarding the product benefit: "So, why is that important to me?" and "What's in it for me?"

The *emotional benefit* is, in reality, another form or classification of customer benefit. "Feelings" and "beliefs," as opposed to performance factors, define it. We can identify an emotional benefit by the presence of the words in quotes. For Gatorade, it is the "feeling" that one has a competitive advantage (whether it is real or not) and/or that one "feels" like a winner (which again is a matter of debate). (Michael Jordan has been a winner, but you, me, well, let's see the scoreboard before we rush to any conclusions.)

The prescription brand Fosamax, which has been used in the treatment of osteoporosis, put the *focus of sale* in its early direct-to-consumer (DTC) print advertising on an emotional benefit. The first of a three-page spread ran the copy "Since I found out about my osteoporosis, I've been afraid to walk to my mailbox when it rains." Imagine, the targeted consumer-patient is afraid to perform a simple, everyday task—undoubtedly, for good reason. If you are familiar with osteoporosis, you know that bones can break easily. In this case, the consumer-patient is probably an elderly woman of some 70-years of age who fears not just a broken bone but, perhaps, the irretrievable decline in health that such an accident can bring to one who is unable to mend quickly and/or completely. At the extreme, this decline raises the specter of death. The Fosamax advertising urges the target consumer-patient to "Fight Your Fear." While the copy carried in the ad spells out both product and customer benefits, the focus of sale is clearly an emotional benefit. Fosamax promises not only a way to rebuild bone and bone strength (*product benefit*) so that the consumer can do what she wants and likes to do (*customer benefit*) but, importantly, also restores the consumer's "confidence" and enable her "to overcome fear to live her life" (*emotional benefit*)!

We find that many marketers confuse product and customer benefits with emotional benefits if the messaging has been delivered in a way that evokes emotion. We can take a product benefit and deliver it in an emotional way. That does not make it an emotional benefit. The emotional benefit relates to how the customer is to "feel" about the brand. It is not concrete but, instead, a perception of feeling, such as confidence, reduced anxiety, contentment, and so on.

Emotional Versus Functional Benefits

The Benefit can be functional (product or customer) or emotional. Regardless, the Benefit should provide the product or service you market with a competitive advantage in the marketplace. It must either give the customer a reason for choosing your brand in preference to someone else's product or brand, or nurture loyalty, and/or immunize the customer against the lure of competitive pricing promotions.

When a functional benefit is shared by a competitor, regardless of whether it is a product or customer benefit, the brand's emotional benefit may provide the compelling *point of difference* that wins the customer and creates brand loyalty. We refer to emotional benefits as "higher-order" benefits.

If you think back to your basic college psychology course, you are likely to recall the teachings of the eminent clinical psychologist Dr. Abraham Maslow. Accordingly to Dr. Maslow, we all have a *hierarchy of needs*. At the lowest rung of the ladder is the need for survival. Said another way, give me food. Give me clothing. Give me shelter. These are physical needs. When needs on the lowest rung are satisfied, we move up the ladder to the next rung. At the top of the metaphorical ladder is "self-actualization." This is a state in which an individual is at peace with herself and gives herself the freedom to pursue interests free from the control of the value judgments of others. This "self-actualization" is not physical. It's purely emotional.

Maslow's Hierarchy of Needs*

SELF-ACTUAL-IZATION
Morality, creativity, spontaneity, problem solving, lack of prejudice, acceptance of facts

ESTEEM
Self-esteem, confidence, achievement, respect of others, respect by others

LOVE/BELONGING
Friendship, family, sexual intimacy

SAFETY
Security of: body, employment, resources, morality, the family, health, property

PHYSIOLOGICAL
Breathing, food, water, sex, sleep, homeostasis, excretion

*An adaptation of his 1943 paper
A Theory of Human Observations

Needs and benefits are two sides of the same coin. Benefits pay off needs. So, if you subscribe to Maslow's theory that emotional needs are the highest-order needs, then it follows that emotional benefits are the highest-order benefits. What's more, attainment of an emotional benefit may suggest realization of lower-level product and customer benefits.

Mariner, the outboard motor company, ran a classic campaign that promised a compelling emotional benefit. One print ad showed some poor sap in a fishing boat with the headcover off his outboard motor. The boat is tied up to the dock while he tries vainly to start the outboard motor. Obviously, he does not have a Mariner outboard engine. In the background we see a procession of men with their boats on an adjacent ramp, impatient to begin launching into the water. On the dock, we see the buddy of the erstwhile fisherman, arms folded over his gut with foot tapping, anxious for the motor to catch and the boat to push off. We are given insights into what might be going through the fisherman's mind ("Shouldddda, shouldda, couldda, couldda . . . shoulddda boughttta a Mariner"). The ad creates the impression that we can be confident Mariner engines will "save us from incredible embarrassment" (*emotional benefit*). Additionally, the emotional benefit *leads us to believe* that Mariner engines are dependable (*product benefit*) and will give the owner many more hours on the water to enable him to enjoy his fishing (*customer benefit*).

Getting Emotional about Emotional Benefits

There are a few additional points we need to make regarding emotional and functional benefits. The first is to go beyond the product benefit to capture a customer and emotional benefit when creating the Brand Positioning Strategy Statement. If you stop at the product benefit, then you have created a product positioning (which is acceptable for line extensions to a brand), not a brand positioning strategy. Product positioning strategies fail to create a blueprint for a special experience, and make an emotional connection with customers. Therefore, these are easily neutralized by competitors and, as such, are short lived.

The second point relates to the brand's advertising communications. However, if your product has a real performance advantage over the competition, then go with the product benefit in your advertising, not the emotional benefit. Hammer away at the product benefit until it has been firmly established in the minds of prospective customers. The experience your customer enjoys will lead, over time, to an emotional benefit and connection.

Third, learn to play these benefit types as a professional musician plays a musical scale. If one has a meaningful product benefit that competition can't match, play the product benefit for as long as growth remains strong. When competition is able to deliver a comparable product benefit, move up the scale to play the customer benefit. You guessed it. Lead your competition to capture an emotional benefit to ensure that you remain ahead of the growth curve and at least one step ahead of competition in the minds of your customers.

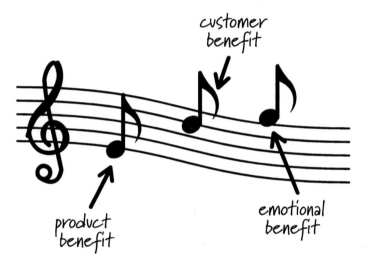

The key here is the perception we want to create in the minds and hearts of potential customers. It is the feeling the customer gets about your product or service that differentiates it in a meaningful way from competitive products. This is the positioning Benefit. The benefit played in the advertising and your other marketing-mix elements merely stimulates the takeaway intended in the positioning strategy and serves in the achievement of important marketing objectives (such as penetration or switching, to name just a couple).

One final point, the fourth one: Be realistic with your promise of emotional benefits. Marketers exaggerate the impact their brand will have on the (quality of) life of their customers. A night guard to keep teeth from grinding promises its users a "feeling of freedom." Are they for real? C'mon, we can do better than that! It is pure nonsense. While we laugh at them, we need to look to our own stable of brands within the company's portfolio. There will undoubtedly be some, and we hope yours is not one, that offers an emotional benefit promise of "getting your life back." (Where did everyone's life go these days?)

As it relates back to marketing communications, the really great advertising plays all three benefit types in the same spot or print ad, like the aforementioned Mariner ad, to create an impression of superiority. Master Lock used to air one TV spot per year—during the Super Bowl! At nearly $3 million per 30-second pop in current dollars, it had better be good! Many years ago, it aired a spot in consecutive Super Bowls that showed various toughs attempting to break into areas secured by a Master Lock of one type or another. Classical music played in the background as a counterpoint to the mean-spirited action. The ad communicates the three benefit types: Master Lock branded products hold up to the various attacks (*product benefit*); they keep our belongings and property safe (*customer benefit*); and they make us feel secure and protected from what may lurk out in the dark, mean streets of Anytown USA (*emotional benefit*).

Benefit Linkage and Relationships

In selecting the Benefit, there are a few linkages of which you need to be aware. While these linkages are self-evident, our experience working with marketers across a wide variety of categories throughout the world suggests they are worth mentioning.

1. *The Benefit must be consistent with the physical attributes of the product or service.* The Swiss Army Knife is a good case in point. Even if we haven't owned one, we are familiar with its versatility. What makes the Swiss Army Knife so versatile (product benefit) and makes us so resourceful (customer benefit)? It's the product's physical attributes. Each Swiss Army Knife incorporates a wide variety of tools. There's a ruler, a small scissors, a corkscrew, and much, much more. The Benefit flows from the product's physical attributes.

Unfortunately, one of our clients failed to understand this vital relationship between product attributes and the Benefit. The client was attempting to relaunch a sports beverage that had failed to achieve expectations. Unlike the market leader, Gatorade, our client's product contained carbonation, albeit a low level (i.e., lower than soft drinks). However, carbonation is not a desirable feature for a sports beverage. Sports enthusiasts do not want carbonation in their sports drink because they can't slam the beverage down to quickly relieve thirst and replenish essential elements lost through sweating. Also, carbonation is gas. Who wants or needs gas when you are involved in strenuous physical activity? Despite our advice that they eliminate the carbonation or pursue a different customer target and positioning strategy, the client chose to go head to head with Gatorade. Consequently, it failed to establish a meaningful or enduring franchise. Once it understood the futility of its launch and of subsequent relaunch attempts, it purchased the Quaker Oats Company, in large part to acquire Gatorade.

2. *The Benefit will change depending upon the competitive framework.* The Benefit and the Competitive Framework in the Brand Positioning Statement are also interrelated. If we go back to the often-used classic Jell-O example (which is shown on the next page), we find that the benefits will be different if we put the product into a dessert competitive framework (i.e., it's light, non-filling, fruity) rather than a gelatin (i.e., is preferred).

Competitive Framework - Benefit Linkage

The (Competitive Framework)	That (Alternate Benefits)	The (Competitive Framework)	That (Alternate Benefits)
Brand of Gelatin	• Is highest quality • Is preferred	Dessert	• Is fruity • Is inexpensive • Is light • Is refreshing
Packaged Dessert Mix	• Is fruity • Is refreshing		• Is nonfilling • Is for kids • Is for old people • Is fun
Light Dessert	• Is fruity • Is inexpensive • Is versatile	Way to end the meal	• Is light • Leaves a good taste in mouth • Is nonfilling • Is sensible • Makes you feel good

So, it is important to define a Competitive Framework against which we can deliver a meaningful point of difference to establish a competitive advantage. Certainly, the customer must be accepting of the Competitive Framework that you offer if you are to plumb its potential corresponding benefits. If the customer is not, then he will throw out your entire proposition and reject your product.

The Perceptual Competitive Framework should also be consistent with the Benefit. They must link! The Perceptual Competitive Framework draws from the Benefit and, at the same time, sets-up the Benefit.

3. ***The Benefit and Target Customer group are also interrelated.*** A Benefit that translates to a meaningful point of difference may be established with a certain kind of person. Jif® Peanut Butter has long been the choice of "choosey mothers." The key copy words have been "Choosey mothers

choose Jif" for decades. Who doesn't want to be perceived as "choosey" when it comes to taking care of the family?

Excedrin, "The Headache Medicine," is another example. When Bristol-Myers Squibb owned the brand, it employed communications that featured and called out to people who believed they suffered from frequent and/or severe headaches, the kind of headaches that other pain relievers just can't remedy (or remedy quickly enough). What does this target group lead us to believe about Excedrin? We think it suggests that Excedrin is a fast-acting, powerful pain reliever made especially for headaches. Not a bad take-away for Excedrin. (However, Excedrin, under new ownership, attempted to go beyond headaches to capture other pain conditions. We did not believe this was a wise move at the time, since it dilutes the meaning of the brand and its link to its customer base. Moreover, the company doesn't have the resources to compete with all-purpose pain relievers such as TYLENOL and Advil. The new ownership must have realized this also because they have returned to positioning Excedrin as "The Headache Medicine.")

Another long-running example is Hallmark greeting cards. The key copy words are "When you care enough to send the very best." In fact, the company has been using these key copy words since 1944. When you receive a Hallmark greeting card, you are made to feel special, since we all know the key copy words. Importantly, they brand the sender as someone who is "very caring."

Establishing a benefit through the use of a specific target group may be used to:

- Differentiate your brand from competitive products (after all, who uses your product tells me something about it);
- Create emotional customer identification (yes, I want to be perceived as one of those people); and
- Insulate the brand against the competition (you may have the same product attributes, but I have "badged" a select group of customers).

Single Versus Multiple Benefits

Imagine that you are the marketing manager for a new toothpaste product. Your product development manager (R&D) informs you her team has developed a multiple-benefit toothpaste to give you a formidable entry into this category. The new toothpaste eliminates plaque, contains fluoride to help prevent cavities, has a special ingredient to guard against periodontal disease, contains a whitener to keep teeth, well, white, and so forth. Now, what Benefit or Benefits are you going to select for your Brand Positioning Strategy Statement? Choose one from the following multiple-choice selection:

> ### What benefit(s) should you select?
>
> a) The one most important to consumers;
>
> b) The one my brand can win versus competition;
>
> c) The top 2 or 3;
>
> d) No more than 3;
>
> e) All of them; or
>
> f) Depends upon what I learn from market research.

This question is becoming more frequent. The response varies according to the conventional wisdom of the participant's organization. Thinking ahead to the advertising, some will say, "I'll select the one benefit the customer will most appreciate." Others state that they will find the one benefit that gives them a point of difference. Yet others will submit to picking the top two, but no more than three, benefits. Who's right? Who's wrong? We are about to tackle the question of the ages: single versus multiple benefits.

Before we address this question, however, let's pause to consider the wisdom of introducing a product with multiple benefits and not building them into the positioning and/or communicating them. If you are going to establish your new offering on only one product benefit, then why build additional benefits into it? After all, we can expect that these additional benefits will add to the cost of goods or services. And, what if you gain your competitive advantage from the additional benefits? Would you not, by failing to acknowledge the additional benefits, squander a unique opportunity to gain an advantage over the competition in creating brand loyalty?

What we have here is a dilemma brought about by communication concerns. As per the communications, this is a "probability" game. A single benefit improves the likelihood of *successful communication*. From the early days of television, many advertisers have measured the success of their advertising according to the memorability of benefits as evidenced by the recall score. The more benefits you shoehorn into a spot, the less the probability the customer will remember what you want her to recall. Stated another way, the probability for a successful communication (i.e., one that achieves a recall score equal to or better than the norm) falls as we add additional benefits. From this simple fact came the maxim to stick with a simple, single minded message. This was further translated to "stick with a single benefit." The maxim is reasonable, but the translation is a perversion.

On the other hand, there is *effective communication*. Effective communication persuades and motivates customers to think about your product and to take the action(s) you desire. This communication will in some way be one that leads to brand loyalty. The action could be to switch to your product, use more of it, use it more often, or pay a premium price. If your advantage resides within the multiple benefits, you could be abdicating the opportunity for effective brand building and communications in an effort to achieve successful communication (i.e., recall score).

In today's increasingly competitive marketplace, we may very well need multiple benefits to profitably win and maintain customers. What good is a memorable message (i.e., successful communication) if it fails to win customers (i.e., effective communication)? We need a positioning that will put us ahead of the competition. We need communications that are both successful and effective.

Additionally, in some categories that are heavily regulated, such as over-the-counter (OTC) medications, the marketer is required to establish his product as possessing multiple benefits (where multiple compounds or actions exist), and to communicate them. For example, Tylenol PM® is a combination analgesic and sleep aid. It cannot be one thing to one target and another to a different target. It must talk about pain relief and its ability to induce sleep. Why? The U.S. Food and Drug Administration (FDA) does not want people who have pain to take a combination product unless they also have a sleeping problem. They rightfully do not want people overmedicating. So, in this instance, like it or not, the marketer must communicate the multiple indications that are the product's benefits.

Improving the Likelihood of Successful and Effective Communication of Multiple Benefits

We may, and should strive to, improve the likelihood of communicating multiple benefits both successfully and effectively by (a) utilizing a single-minded proposition; (b) broadening the competitive framework; and (c) employing multiple executions.

- ***Single-Minded Proposition.*** This entails the alignment of benefits under the umbrella of a single-minded proposition. The single-minded proposition reflects the spirit of the maxim urging that the advertiser be single-minded and keep it simple without restricting benefits to a single one. The single-minded proposition increases the likelihood that the customer will remember, understand, and act upon the message. The single-minded proposition is communicated in the *campaign idea*, which we refer to as the "center of the plate" of your communications.

  Returning to the new toothpaste entry with multiple benefits, we may observe that this is a real case. In fact, the product promised many more benefits. You know the brand, and probably use it: Colgate Total. While it has several benefits—it fights cavities, removes plaque and tartar, prevents gum disease, whitens teeth, freshens breath, and lasts for 12 hours—its name, Colgate Total, communicates that it does it all! Additionally, this can be boiled down to express the brand's benefits in a brand positioning strategy as providing the "most complete and longest lasting oral health care."

  Another fine example is Vicks NyQuil®. This brand has run the same advertising campaign for more than 30 years now. It was launched by what was then Richardson-Vicks and was further fueled by its current parent,

Procter & Gamble. The campaign is anchored by a single-minded proposition that communicates the brand's benefits of providing multi-symptom cold relief and, at the same time, enabling cold sufferers to get to sleep so they can rest (and function normally the next day). The classic single-minded proposition goes something like this: "Vicks NyQuil. The nighttime sniffling, sneezing, aching, stuffy head, cold symptom relief, medicine so you can get your rest (and be refreshed the next morning)."

As per the litany of benefits, we do not believe it is important that the customer remember each and every one. We certainly don't! Instead, we are more concerned that customers come away with the impression that Vicks NyQuil is the best medicine for relieving all your cold symptoms and enabling you to get to sleep (its brand positioning Benefit). In this case, as in most, the general impression that reinforces the positioning is more important than the specifics.

- ***Building Upon the Competitive Framework.*** Everyone knows what an antiseptic does, or is supposed to do. It kills germs to prevent infection of wounds. We also know that antiseptics burn when applied to a freshly opened wound. U-g-h-h-h!!! The burning sensation is even more intense for children. (At least that is how it appears based upon the strong reaction the mere mention or sight of an antiseptic medicine brings to a child, or man child, with a fresh surface skin wound.) The mention of the designator "antiseptic" communicates the product's benefit of killing germs.

  A number of years ago, in Brazil, Johnson & Johnson introduced a combination antiseptic and anesthetic medicine for the treatment of wounds. The introductory spot showed a young boy who is about to have his wound treated with an antiseptic medicine by his mother. The room in which he sits turns into a scene from a horror movie. We see lights blinking on and off, hear the tearful child scream "NO!" to his mother, and see her emerge out of the dark with distorted and rather monstrous features. But, the product is Johnson & Johnson antiseptic with an anesthetic ingredient. Now, the screen grows calm. The mother is shown to be nurturing and tender. The boy grows docile and is thankful for the relief. What we have here is a broadening of the competitive framework. This is the antiseptic with an anesthetic. It's the antiseptic medicine that doesn't hurt—two benefits made more memorable and compelling by broadening the competitive framework.

- *Multiple executions.* We used to believe this was a luxury for those advertisers with deep pockets (i.e., loads of money to spend on advertising). But we have learned better. Even marketers with relatively small budgets may make use of this practice to improve the likelihood of successful and effective communications.

In this practice, each benefit is communicated in a separate execution. It works if the benefits are aligned and can be captured with a single-minded proposition. In this way, the spots are not disparate but are linked to build the intended brand positioning.

For years, Lexus has successfully employed multiple executions in its campaign "The Relentless Pursuit of Perfection." (Oops!) Each spot and print ad focuses on a specific benefit of Lexus automobiles. In one spot, we witness a world-class guitarist actually recording his music in the back seat of a Lexus as it speeds down a highway. The message is that Lexus gives you the quietest ride possible. The execution borrows from the single-minded proposition, while at the same time it strengthens it.

So, if you need to define your positioning with and communicate multiple benefits to establish a competitive advantage, don't shy away from the task at hand. The use of a single-minded proposition, a broadening of the competitive framework, and the use of multiple executions can improve the likelihood of your successfully and effectively seeding multiple benefits and an impression of superiority. It's not easy. It will be a challenge for your agency. But, look around in the world and you'll find the marketplace is replete with brands that have successfully employed these practices. As you watch television and read magazines, take note of the number of brands that are able to successfully communicate multiple benefits. The successful ones do it effortlessly. So don't let the fear of how you will communicate multiple benefits hamstring your using multiple Benefits to establish a meaningful brand positioning strategy.

Benefit Laddering Tool

Now it is time to put what we have learned to use. The Benefit Laddering Tool, shown here for Gatorade, enables us to identify and distinguish features from the potential product, customer, and emotional benefits provided by our brand of products and services. It is simple, but not always easy, to use. Try it for your brand using the directions that follow the Gatorade example:

Benefit Laddering Tool
Inferred Gatorade - Example

Emotional Benefit:

Makes me feel like I have a competitive advantage and I'm a winner.

Customer Benefit:

Enables me to play harder, longer.

Product Benefit:

Replenishes lost fluids and minerals.

Product Features:

- Liquid
- Wide-mouth jar
- 7% electrolyte formulation
- Endorsed by all professional sports organizations

1. We start by identifying all the product features. These are incontrovertible facts about ingredients, packaging, design, and so on.

2. Fill in the potential product benefit(s). What does your product or service do (e.g., replenishes lost fluids and minerals)? Utilize the product's features to identify what the product does. Think, too, about alternate competitive frameworks. Where does it lead you?

3. Next, identify customer benefits resulting from the preceding product benefits. So Gatorade replenishes fluids and minerals lost through sweat during competition. What does that mean to me as a customer of the category or

brand? Perhaps, it helps me compete at the top of my game. Or maybe it provides me with additional stamina to go the distance. Or it means I can play with more intensity. Go figure it out! Don't hesitate to inquire of your customers, your prospective customers, or even those of your competitors why the product benefits are important to them. In other words, what does it mean to your Ms./Mr. Customer?

4. Now we are going to translate customer benefits into emotional benefits. In the case of Gatorade, drinking it may lead you to *feel* like you're competing like a "pro." Or, it could be that you *feel* that you are invincible. The point is to probe what is going on in the minds of customers as it relates to their feelings and belief structure about higher-order benefits. Think about and apply this to your brand.

You should have a large number and wide variety of benefits. It's decision time. Howard Schultz, founder and chairman of Starbucks, said: "Customers must recognize that you stand for something." So, make your brand stand for an important and meaningfully differentiated something. Which of the benefits do you believe are most meaningful to your Target Customer? Which can you deliver given your product's features? Which can you use to differentiate your product from the competition? Which can you own? Don't stop here! Check out these hypotheses with customers. Find out what they can do to make your brand more competitive and more compelling in the marketplace.

Guiding and Checking Your Work

Now it's time to use the Brand Positioning Add-Valuator checklist tool to check your brand positioning Benefit to ensure it is technically correct and competitive. Assess each of the following seven points (which appears on the next page) by noting whether you "Don't Agree," "Agree Somewhat," or "Strongly Agree." Tally each box and step back to take stock of where you are with your Benefit choice. Importantly, identify the indicated actions you must take to achieve a "Strongly Agree" rating and then take those actions.

Brand Positioning Add-Valuator

Benefit	Don't Agree (0)	Agree Somewhat (3)	Strongly Agree (5)	Indicated Actions
1. Contains a single-minded benefit				
2. Goes beyond a product benefit to encompass customer or emotional benefit				
3. Creates "meaning" for the Target Group				
4. Addresses a relevant Target Group need (links to the target)				
5. The benefit proposition is either implicitly or explicitly competitive				
6. The PCP sets-up a relevant, meaningfully differentiated benefit that is competitive				
7. Is expected to drive brand preference among Target Group				
Total Score				

KEY POINTS, PRINCIPLES & PRACTICES
Summary

✓ The Benefit is the payoff for the customer. It provides her with the basis for choosing your brand of product or service. Therefore, it must be relevant to the customer, competitive, and ownable.

✓ In order to drive preference, the Benefit must not only be relevant but also be meaningfully differentiated from the competition. Differentiation can come in the form of differences in degree, such as "getting clothes cleaner," or in kind, such as delivering effective pain relief and "helping prevent a heart attack." Differences in kind are the result of Marketect thinking and usually lead to the most significant business results.

✓ Keep in mind that the three benefit types are *product*, *customer* (functional), and *emotional*. The *product* benefit gets at what the product does. The *customer* benefit addresses the rewards of the product benefit to the customer. The *emotional* benefit characterizes customer feelings and beliefs that grow from the *customer* benefit.

✓ *Emotional* benefits are higher-order benefits. Successful planting of an *emotional* benefit may suggest realization of lower-level *product* and *customer* benefits.

✓ When identifying the benefit, do not stop with a product benefit. It will result in a "product" positioning strategy as opposed to "brand" positioning strategy. Instead, include a customer and emotional benefit statement.

✓ However, if you have a meaningful *product* benefit that your competition cannot match, then play the *product* benefit in your first communication campaign. If your competition is able to deliver a comparable *product* benefit, move up to a *customer* benefit. When the competition is able to neutralize your *customer* benefit, consider playing an important *emotional* benefit. You want to stay head of your competition and ward off a slowdown in the growth curve.

✓ Allow the customers to feel the emotional benefit from the experience they realize in everything you do to support the brand.

✓ Your marketing campaign may utilize all three benefits types in the same or alternate marketing-mix elements.

✓ The Benefit needs to be linked to product features, Target Customer group, and Competitive Framework. Certainly, product features allow the Benefit as we witness with many brands. The Target Customer group may be utilized to establish a point of difference, as Pepsi-Cola has been able to achieve versus Coca-Cola with the "Next/New Generation." The potential set of benefits and the importance of each to customers will change with alternate competitive frameworks.

✓ A single Benefit improves the likelihood of *successful communication* (i.e., communication that achieves a recall score equal or better than the norm).

✓ *Effective communication* is measured by motivating customers to perceive your brand as you wish them to and then to take an action you desire (e.g., switching to your brand, purchasing more frequently, etc.). In today's competitive marketplace, we may very well need to communicate multiple benefits in order to create brand loyalty.

✓ Proven practices to improve the likelihood of both successful and effective communication of multiple benefits are to: (1) utilize the single-minded proposition; (2) broaden the competitive framework; and/or (3) employ multiple executions.

✓ Don't let concern for how you will communicate multiple benefits hamstring your using multiple Benefits to establish a meaningful brand positioning strategy.

✓ Employ the Benefit Laddering Tool to display potential benefits and to identify those that are competitive, meaningful and ownable.

DISPATCHES ™
Insights On Brand Development From The Marketing Front

PLUMBING THE DEPTHS OF EMOTIONS

Emotional connections are vitally important in creating brand loyalty. Why is it that consumers will pay a significant price premium (upwards of 60%) for JOHNSON'S Baby Powder? Is it the talc ingredient found in the product? Or is it the product's fragrance? The fact of the matter is that competitive baby powder products are made of the same ingredients—talc and fragrance. And, while the rational mind of the consumer chooses to defend the selection of JOHNSON'S Baby Powder with one of these product attributes, the subconscious mind, if plumbed, would undoubtedly reveal an emotional connection. It's the connection that matters when it comes to establishing "brands."

Dr. Abraham Maslow, the clinical psychologist, suggested the importance of emotions in his theory of the "Hierarchy of Needs." As you may recall from your studies, he postulated that humans have a hierarchy of needs, progressing from the most basic to the most sophisticated. He likened the hierarchy to a ladder we climb one rung at a time. We must first step onto the lowest rung, which deals with survival (give me food, clothing, shelter), before we can proceed up the ladder. The topmost rung is—yes, you have it, "self-actualization." (It's amazing how so many managers remember this regardless of how long they've been out of school.) Self-actualization is an emotional need. It's a feeling. It resides in one's head. So the eminent Dr. Maslow is informing us that emotional needs are the *highest-order* needs. And, remember, needs and benefits are two sides of the same coin. This suggests, in turn, that emotional benefits are the highest-order benefits. Ergo, we choose JOHNSON'S Baby Powder because it symbolizes the deep and abiding love we have for and share with our baby; we choose Starbuck's Coffee for a deserved self-rewarding experience; we buy Rolex watches to affirm our success to and status with others; and, maybe, we use Viagra because it helps us feel like a "whole man" again.

Accordingly, our brand positioning should (at some point in our brand life cycle) cater to an emotional need and pay off that need with an emotional benefit. But, as we have stated in past issues of *DISPATCHES*™, many of the emotional benefits we encounter in Brand Positioning Strategy Statements are just so much malarkey. Either the product hasn't earned it (one rung of the ladder at a time), or it's wishful thinking (that deceives no one but the marketers who have penned it), or it's over the top (in other words it's B--- S---!). Many more times, the proffered emotional benefit is innocuous. It just doesn't mean anything to prospective target customers.

Part of the problem traces to our rather limited vocabulary (do you find this surprising? astonishing?) when it comes to identifying and expressing emotions. Most often, the emotional benefit in the Brand Positioning Strategy Statement will read "confidence," "trust," "peace of mind," "control," or "feel like a (whatever; you fill in the blank)." It's just so-o-o-o shallow. Moreover, it is probably not grounded in the reality of the product, brand equity, customer experiences, and/or perceptions. A limited vocabulary also hampers our ability to identify and/or understand the emotions of our Target Customer and our ability to blueprint and establish the connection we hope to build through our marketing initiatives.

It's important for us, then, to expand our vocabulary when it comes to emotions. Our colleague Dave Roche recently provided us with a list of "the vocabulary of feelings" that provides a useful starting point, since "feelings" are, after all, "emotions." The source of this work is *Improving Therapeutic Communications—A Guide for Developing Effective Techniques*, by Hammond, Hepworth, and Smith. Actually, Dave came across this in his extensive reading on developing healthy relationships—the kind between partners. This, too, is apropos, since brands establish relationships with customers, but products do not. The vocabulary of feelings that Dave shared with us (which we believe may only be a partial listing) has 10 basic feelings (e.g., happy, fearful, lonely), which, in turn, contain a plethora of feeling states, which are further classified as "strong," "moderate" or "mild." The total number of vocabulary words is more than 300. A more precise articulation of someone who is "happy" could be "on cloud nine" (strong), jovial (moderate), or glad (mild).

We need to establish an emotional connection with target customers to create brand loyalty, and, in order to do so, we need to plumb the depths of emotions in drawing up our Brand Positioning Strategy Statements.

BOATS & HELICOPTERS:

1. *Expand your vocabulary of emotions.* This will assist you in identifying target customers' feelings and in articulating the emotional connection you need to establish. If you would like a listing of "the vocabulary of feelings," please e-mail us at *competitivepositioning@bdn-intl.com.*

2. *Get real with emotions.* Don't promise what you can't fulfill. The most valuable emotions are ones that the customer grants you through his experience with your brand. It is part of the brand equity. It's important to harvest these and to reflect them back to your target customer through your marketing initiatives.

3. *Connect on a subconscious level with customers.* In other words, don't be so direct. Don't tell customers what they should be feeling; let them feel it through the stimulus (i.e., communications, merchandising, packaging, public relations) you share with them.

4. *Be aware of where you are in the product life cycle.* While your BPS may point the way to an emotional benefit, be aware that it may take time to get there. Don't forget to communicate your product rational benefit in those cases where you have clear superiority over your competition.

We *feel relieved* to have this off our chests.

CHAPTER SIX

You know where the classic positioning term "Reason-Why" comes from, don't you? From that rightly skeptical consumer crying out in the marketplace wilderness, "Look, just give me one, good reason-why I should believe what you promise."

Chapter 6

Making the Benefit Believable
with the Reason-Why

Most marketers have little trouble understanding the point of *Reason-Why*; after all, it's one of the oldest and most basic of Brand Positioning elements. Every once in a while, you may hear a junior marketer make the mistake of suggesting that the reason-why exists to give consumers or customers (for prescription drugs) a reason-why to buy one brand over another. But, in the classic sense, reason-why exists for only one, quite different purpose: *to add credibility to the brand's benefit(s) or promise* (as noted in the chapter lead-in). In fact, most experienced brand builders subscribe to the principle that there should be at least one reason-why for each benefit in the Brand's Positioning Statement.

This principle seems to have stood the test of time. If you look back at brands that were pioneer advertisers in the early days of television, virtually every one of them—performance-driven brands and more recreational brands, like cigarettes and beverages—always took the time to highlight a particular, special feature *inside* their product, a feature that was intended to add credibility to the brand's main benefit. So a gum-mint brand like Clorets promised a benefit of freshening breath thanks to a special ingredient called retsin; a leading cigarette brand of those days, Lucky Strike, promised a benefit of full flavor, thanks to tobacco that was 'toasted' (a special processing) and thanks to 'fine tobacco' (which became almost as famous as the brand name itself when translated into the consumer acronym, 'LSMFT' ("Lucky Strike Means Fine Tobacco").

But it wasn't too long before brands began adding yet another kind of benefit credibility, going *outside* the product for an endorsement. Perhaps the "Greatest Reason-Why Story Ever Told" relates to one such brand that is often mentioned in graduate school marketing textbooks—Crest toothpaste. Crest is usually credited with being the first mass-market brand to seek and secure a meaningful professional endorsement—that of the American Dental Association. But that endorsement came a few years after the Crest brand had launched. In the very beginning, the brand promised an important new benefit among toothpastes: a significant reduction in cavities. And, consistent with the times, the brand made this benefit credible by focusing on a proprietary ingredient called stannous fluoride. No other brand in the American market at the time had this ingredient, and the clinical data showed convincingly that stannous fluoride resulted in a sizable reduction in the number of cavities. Yet, even with such an impressive story to tell, Crest achieved only a strong second-place share, somewhere in the mid-teens. It turned out that for it to become market leader, it needed more credibility.

So, the brand did something unheard of—it took the clinical data to the American Dental Association and requested a formal, professional endorsement of the brand and its cavity-reduction benefit, a kind of "seal of approval," if you will. You may have read about this request and seen that the ADA wasn't so keen at that time on endorsing Crest or any other commercial product. But Procter & Gamble's Crest team was persistent and the data were compelling. The rest of the story you know: The American Dental Association gave the Crest Brand the first (and, at the time, only) professional endorsement; it went something like this:

> *Crest has been proven to be an effective decay-preventive dentifrice when used in a conscientiously applied program of oral hygiene and regular, professional dental care.*

With this powerful and differentiating credibility, the Crest brand effectively had two types of Reason-Why in its Brand Positioning Strategy: (1) the *intrinsic* ingredient feature of stannous fluoride – which the brand team translated for the consumer as "Crest with Fluoristan"; and (2) the *extrinsic* endorsement of the ADA. And, with both of these supporting a meaningful, differentiating Benefit, the brand achieved market share leadership (a position it held for many years, until the launch of Colgate Total, another toothpaste brand with a meaningful, differentiating Benefit).

Although Crest's two-pronged positioning Reason-Why happened almost 50 years ago, it remains a solid model for many brands today. Gatorade has its "science of sweat" formula and many professional athletic endorsements to support its implied better replenishment benefit; Tylenol has its 100% acetaminophen ingredient (for gentleness on the stomach) and its "More Hospitals Recommend Tylenol" endorsement to support its safer pain relief benefit, and so on.

Intrinsic and Extrinsic Reasons-Why—Some Compelling Options

Although the Crest, Gatorade, and Tylenol brands have all used similar intrinsic and extrinsic Reasons-Why (ingredients and endorsements), there are a number of other options a brand might consider as support for its positioning Benefit(s). Among the most commonly used intrinsic ones are (in addition to ingredients): *design, processing, mode or mechanism of action, source of materials,* and something called the *"absence of negatives."* Among extrinsic Reasons-Why are (in addition to professional endorsements) things like *clinical studies and preference tests, self-created endorsers,* and *borrowed interest from the "trademark equity" bank.* Let's take a cursory look at a few examples.

- *The ingredient wars.* While we have already looked at some brands that have used longstanding, "strategic ingredients" to bolster their positioning's benefit credibility, it's important to note that finding (or just the being first to deliver) the next new ingredient remains a driving positioning factor in a number of categories. Take skin care, for example. It was not that long ago that retinol, with its ability to reduce fine-line wrinkles, was the "darling" ingredient throughout the anti-aging segment of skin care. And, in effort to keep improving the "fine-line reduction" benefit, virtually every major skin care brand began increasing its concentration of retinol, as much as FDA dictates would permit. Now, like stannous fluoride in toothpaste, retinol is pretty much a given, what some marketers call a cost-of-entry feature.

More recently within skin care, leading brands have been trying to outdo each other in the benefit area of sun protection—not protection from sun*burn*, which is caused by UVB rays and has already long been equalized among brands by various levels of "SPF" ingredients. Rather, skin care brands have been aiming to better protect against more recently understood UVA rays, which penetrate deeper into the skin to destroy collagen and certain proteins, thereby harming the skin's firmness. One of the first U.S. brands to add an ingredient against UVA rays was Neutrogena, with its patented Helioplex® formulation. Not to be outdone, however, L'Oréal developed and patented its own anti-UVA ingredient, called Mexoryl™. In fact, as a 2006 article in *Advertising Age* headlined: "L'Oréal Wins Big as FDA OK's Coveted Ingredient." The article went on to explain how securing a compelling new ingredient could impact the brand's marketplace potential:

> L'Oréal has won approval to bring to the U.S. a sought-after sunscreen technology that could give it a huge competitive edge in other categories, including makeup and moisturizers.

Of course, many new ingredients that support an "improved" better benefit are not necessarily all that differentiated in the effects they produce, regardless of how cleverly brands have named them. Even so, many consumers have been well trained by marketers to associate a new (or previously overlooked) ingredient with better performance. Ingredient news can easily grow a category, too. Remember when adding calcium to products like orange juice and cereals and cheese was big news—because of all the press about the rise of something called osteoporosis? Some reports showed that adding calcium to orange juice accounted for nearly 75% of that category's growth for a few years—and calcium is hardly a differentiated ingredient.

But whether it's truly differentiated or not, here's the bottom line: An ingredient that *readily links to a real or perceived, differentiated benefit* can be very powerful for a brand's positioning. For most brands, too, giving that ingredient a trademark-registered, memorable name (like Helioplex®) that also *links to a given brand* is also a powerful positioning tactic.

- ***Designing brands.*** Of course, ingredients don't work as well in every category. Sometimes the product compound is simply too complex—as would be the case with many over-the-counter medicines and prescription drugs. And sometimes, too, the product does not comprise ingredients but components—as would be the case for most devices. For brands like these, design features provide an excellent source of credibility for the positioning benefit. But, as with ingredients, marketers who can craft a clever, memorable way for customers or consumers to link these design features with the brand and its benefit often come out ahead.

One of the most commonly claimed positioning benefits within the analgesic category has to be "faster pain relief." You could argue that the claim has been made so many times over the years as to make it, well, hard to believe. But, just as with laptop operations and broadband Internet service, speed seems to be a benefit we can never get too much of. Within the past several years, most of the leading U.S. pain reliever brands have bolstered their positioning with added speed of relief. The first of these was Advil, which launched the Liqui-Gel™—a design feature that involved a liquid-filled capsule. Accompanying this feature was a benefit claim that appeared in print ads this way: "Faster and stronger on tough pain than Extra Strength Tylenol."

Despite the direct attack, it took the Tylenol brand a few years to attempt to neutralize the Advil benefit with its own patented design feature: holes. Or, more specifically, laser-drilled holes. In its early print ads, Tylenol stated: "Only Tylenol Extra Strength Rapid Release Gels™ have laser-drilled holes—designed to release powerful medicine, even faster than before." In that short and sweet body copy, the Tylenol brand not only gave its patented design feature a memorable name, Rapid Release Gels™, but also directly linked the feature to the new and improved benefit of faster relief.

One of the last big brands to enter the faster-relief fray was Excedrin. It called its entry Extra Strength Excedrin Express Gels™ (though this was a late entry, you have to admit that the "Ex" repetition in "Express" goes pretty well with the brand name). Though the brand did not claim a specific advantage over another competitor, as Advil did over Tylenol, the website headline *did* leverage the brand's heritage in headache relief: "Extra Strength Excedrin Express Gels™, the headache medicine with a fast-release ring. Headache relief starts in 15 minutes."

Observing the similarities in each of these brand's benefits, design features, and nomenclature, you might skeptically wonder, "Where's the differentiation in Brand Positioning, if anywhere?" But keep in mind that these product design moves occurred over time; Advil had its Liqui-Gel™ a few years before any other brand had something remotely similar. Plus, Advil made the linkage between the feature (liquid) and the benefit (speed of relief) wonderfully simple. You need not have majored in physics or chemistry to grasp that liquids absorb in the body faster than solids. The other point of this three-brand comparison is this: Almost no design feature (or ingredient, for that matter), can support or suggest a differentiating benefit forever. Marketers must be in the constant mode of looking for and developing that next meaningful feature.

- ***"Processing" can sometimes be a good thing.*** Nowadays in the United States, we've come to think of "processed foods" as something more and more to be avoided. The implication of too much processing is that too many good things—usually from Mother Nature—have been removed or, at least, watered down. But sometimes the unique way a particular product is processed can actually be a good thing, as when it serves as a reason-why for a differentiating benefit within a brand's positioning. Perhaps the masters of unique-process reasons-why are the beer marketers. While few Americans could explain how the "beechwood aging" process works, a good many would know that only the Budweiser brand is beechwood aged—for a distinctively good taste. Although perhaps less well-known because of its significantly lower media spending over the years, Miller Genuine Draft is the only beer that tastes like real draft beer (in a bottle!) because it is "cold-filtered." Simple expressions of more complicated processing efforts can be a very powerful way to suggest a differentiated benefit—particularly in categories where, more often than not, brands benefits appear to be about the same.

Some years ago, there was a time when Tropicana (you know, the orange juice company whose "Pure Premium" version was for many years the only leading brand *not* processed from frozen concentrate) wanted to compete more directly with Coca-Cola's Minute-Maid brand in the frozen-concentrate part of the market. The company conducted numerous blind taste tests among both current Minute-Maid frozen-concentrate users and among brand switchers and found that the Tropicana frozen concentrate was significantly preferred for its fresher taste by both user groups. The dilemma for Tropicana marketers in these surprising results was this: Would any regular user of Minute-Maid actually believe such a benefit claim? So the company searched for a compelling, believable, yet simple way of explaining how it could be that Tropicana frozen had a fresher taste than Minute-Maid frozen. What it discovered was that only Tropicana processed all oranges used in the concentrate—from the grove to the canister—in one day, 24 hours or less. Quicker time from the tree to the can made for a fresher taste. Minute-Maid, because it was such a large-volume frozen-concentrate brand, had to ship concentrate from Brazil to its plants to keep up with demand, and that made for a lot more time-consuming process.

"Processing" may often be a negative, but when it comes to crafting a competitive Reason-Why, a brand's unique process might just fill the bill.

- **But how does it work?** One of the most commonly exploited reasons-why among drug marketers is mode of action, or, more simply, a uniqueness in the way a given drug works within the body. In the days when similar "class-effect" leading allergy medications like Claritin® (and its follow-on, Clarinex®) and Allegra were fighting for top market position, the Singulair brand launched with a different mechanism of action, implying a benefit of better control of allergy symptoms. In some of the Singulair ads to patients, the brand claimed the following: "Singulair works differently. While many seasonal allergy medications block histamine, Singulair blocks leukotrienes, an underlying cause of allergy symptoms."

You may remember a similar approach in yet a different drug class, the cholesterol reducers, by the Zetia brand. Like Singulair, it was also a later entrant, following on the success of huge blockbuster brands like Lipitor,

Zocor, and Pravachol. Facing a market with such well-entrenched and heavily prescribed brands, how might Zetia make a competitive impact? Simply, the brand aimed to educate consumers on a different way to fight cholesterol: "The most common cholesterol-lowering medicines, statins, are a good option. Zetia is different. Statins works mainly with the liver. Zetia works in the digestive tract, as do some other cholesterol-lowering medicines. But Zetia is unique in the way it helps block the absorption of cholesterol that comes from food."

Perhaps you can see from these two examples that one of the challenges of using mode of action as a positioning Reason-Why is in keeping the communication of that MOA simple, understandable, consumer-friendly— in other words, credible! On quick judgment, it would appear that Zetia's story is reasonably understandable and believable—most people could probably grasp that reducing cholesterol where the food is (the digestive tract) may be more effective than doing so in other places where the food isn't (the liver). On the other hand, how many allergy sufferers would have ever heard of leukotrienes, let alone understand them?

- *Go to the source.* There are some categories in which, quite frankly, there isn't much to be said about Reason-Why elements such as ingredients, design, processing, or mode of action— you know, categories like bottled water, in which the product is, well, pretty basic. How *do* the water brands try to differentiate their benefits? A good many of them still tout the uniqueness of their source, implying that better-tasting or more naturally fortified water comes from a tiny little village in the Alps than could possibly come from a major U.S. city's water supply. As the Evian brand once said in its U.S. ad campaign: "Every drop of Evian comes from deep in the heart of the French Alps. It's naturally filtered for over 15 years through pristine glacial rock formations. The result is a neutral ph balance and a unique blend of minerals, including calcium, magnesium, and silica." Though consumers rarely know many details like these about a given source, over the years certain one-of-a-kind locations have come to suggest to many consumers a better end performance.

Who doesn't know, for example, that the best champagne comes only from a small region in France (or, for that matter, that, to be legally labeled a "champagne," the brand *must* come from that region)? Or that to be rightly labeled a "chianti," a brand must also come from a defined region of Italy—identified on the label via a distinctive rooster emblem? If you think about it, across the world of beverages, a particular source has often been the main reason-why for an implied better benefit. One of the classic beverage reason- why stories we often relate in our positioning workshops is that of the Folgers Coffee brand, which, along with Maxwell House Coffee has been one of America's leading grocery store brands for years. Many years ago, in an effort to convince U.S. coffee consumers that Folgers had a "richer flavor" (than, say, its number one competitor, Maxwell House), the brand claimed that all the beans used in roasting Folgers were from the mountains—presumably the best place to source coffee beans. But to make the source reason-why stick in the minds of coffee consumers, the brand did something that, at the time, was unheard of: It trademarked the simple expression *"Mountain Grown®."* And it worked in communicating that the reason-why Folgers had a rich or richer taste was simply the "better source" of its beans. Pulling off such a trademarking stunt today would be problematic: Don't all coffee beans come from the world's mountainous regions?

- *What* **doesn't** *the product have?* Marketers are inclined to spend most of their positioning efforts *adding value* to their products, in an effort to meet consumer or customer needs better and to stay one step ahead of competition. But, as we have seen in recent years across numerous food, beverage, and even performance-driven categories like household cleaning products, sometimes adding meaningful value means taking something that is perceived to be harmful away. You'll often hear this expressed by marketers as shifting from the "presence of positives to the absence of negatives." And the absence of negatives can be a very powerful reason-why, particularly in support of a "better-for-you" (or for the environment) benefit.

Generally speaking, Americans have experienced a seemingly endless series of absence-of-negative fads, all in an effort to reduce our collective size (we are, after all, the fattest people on the planet). These fads really became mainstream with reduced-fat frozen entrees (like those from the Healthy Choice and Lean Cuisine Brands) and then snacks (like the Baked! line from Frito-Lay). Next came the lower carbohydrate entries, fueled in large part by famous diets, like Atkins. As you may recall, taking away carbohydrates was not limited to food brands—the major beer brands also participated, with line extensions such as Michelob ULTRA. Actually, you could argue that positioning a better-for-your weight management benefit— as supported by the absence of a big negative—was pioneered by the soft drink marketers. Didn't they bring us diet versions of their leading brands years ago? And all with their guns sighted on that biggest of calorie-inducing negatives, sugar! No wonder, even after all these years of replacing one "new and improved" artificial sweetener with another, we still need to exploit the negatives of sugar, masterfully done more recently by the Splenda Brand, which "tastes like sugar because it's made from sugar, but without the calories of sugar."

Of course, we need not focus on the many negatives of sugar or of processed foods. More and more today, the focus of marketers across the globe is on providing a "better-for-the-environment" benefit, as supported by reduced chemicals in the formulations and reduced nonbiodegradable materials in the packaging. Keep in mind that what often makes an absence of negative work is the "PR effect" surrounding it. In other words, the more publicity a given "negative" receives (like that surrounding trans fats, for example), the easier it is to leverage the absence of that negative as a reason-why in a brand's positioning. Thinking about the current onslaught of publicity surrounding global warming, just imagine what an advantage a brand might have if it could somehow promise less of it, backed up by a convincing absence of a causal negative, of course.

As a recap, here is a listing of some of the more common inside-the-product reasons-why:

Intrinsic Reason-Why – Examples

Brand	Benefit	Reason-Why	Type Of Intrinsic Reason-Why
Neutrogena	UVA protection	Helioplex®	Strategic ingredient
L'Oréal	UVA protection	Mexoryl™	Strategic ingredient
Advil	Faster pain relief (than ES Tylenol)	Liqui-Gels™	Design—Liquid filled
Extra Strength Tylenol	Faster pain relief (than before)	Rapid Release Gels™	Design—Laser-drilled holes
Excedrin Headache	Fast headache pain relief	Express Gels™	Design—Fast-release ring
Budweiser	Great taste	Beechwood aging	Process
Miller Genuine Draft	Real draft beer taste	Cold-filtering	Process
Singulair	Allergy symptom relief	Blocks leukotrienes	Mode of action
Zetia	Reduces cholesterol	Absorbs cholesterol from food in digestive tract	Mode of action
Evian	Purer, better for your well-being	Only from the Alps	Source
Folgers	Richer taste	Mountain Grown®	Source
Michelob ULTRA	Reduce weight gain	Fewer carbohydrates	Absence of negative
Splenda	Reduce weight gain	No calories	Absence of negative

- ***The "ADA" effect.*** We have already covered Crest's legendary capturing of the American Dental Association's endorsement. What we failed to mention was some of the "rest of the story," the aftereffects of that first-ever professional endorsement of a commercial product. One obvious aftereffect is that, before too long, other leading toothpaste brands sought and secured the same ADA endorsement (once they could also add stannous fluoride to their formulations and claim a similar reduced-cavities benefit). In fact, so prevalent is this once exclusive endorsement that, during some work in India, we picked up a tube of Colgate Total 12 that carried this endorsement:

> Colgate Total Toothpaste has been shown to be an effective decay preventive dentifrice...when used as directed in a conscientiously applied program of oral hygiene and regular professional care. (India Dental Association)

Given this now-global prevalence, one aftereffect of Crest's original move is that, eventually, a Reason-Why endorsement will be copied. In support of a Brand Positioning Benefit, then, such a Reason-Why becomes "cost-of-entry" and loses a lot of its oomph. That means that marketers who demand a truly competitive Brand Positioning Strategy must be on the constant lookout for new reason-why material, for new ways to secure extrinsic credibility for their products.

And yet, seeing a once-exclusive endorsement become cost-of-entry in one category doesn't mean it cannot be used exclusively again in another. In 2007, nearly 50 years after Crest's first ADA endorsement for toothpaste, Wrigley announced it had received an "ADA Seal" for its Orbit, Extra, and Eclipse sugarless gum brands. It turns out that a three-year clinical study conducted by Wrigley showed 8% fewer cavities in those who used those brands, and this followed a two-year study that showed a 38% decline. So Wrigley was effectively adding a new Benefit to the Brand Positioning Strategy of its three leading sugarless brands (improved oral health), supported by a first-ever—for gums, anyway—endorsement by the American Dental Association.

One other aftereffect of Crest's pioneering efforts in reason-why endorsement is that, to avoid being copied quickly, brands today have needed to be more *creative* in the endorsements they seek. One of the best examples of creative endorsement has to be what the Duracell brand has been doing over the past few years in the United States. Faced with never-ending "horsepower-race" benefit battles with other brands like Energizer, Duracell marketers made an unexpected positioning move: They secured a series of lesser-known (but highly relevant to battery consumers) users to endorse Duracell as their brand of choice. Perhaps you have seen the TV, radio, and print advertising campaign that has dramatized some of the following unique endorsements for Duracell:

Endorser-Reason-Why	Duracell Benefit
• Open-heart surgery hospitals	• Dependable postsurgical monitoring
• IMAX	• 3-D camera operations
• Rocky Mountain Rescue Squad	• Lighting caves to save lives
• T-Pass 3 (Firefighters' equipment)	• Sure communications in life-or-death fires

What has been particularly brilliant about securing these endorsements is that it has effectively made Duracell appear to be a more dependable choice than other leading batteries, even though the brand had made no such benefit claims to that effect. In other words, while the brand could not "win" with a differentiated benefit, it could gain an implied "win" with a differentiated, extrinsic reason-why.

- ***The necessity of studies.*** Let's face it, it's hard to beat a compelling clinical or consumer-preference study when it comes to supporting a "bigger, brighter, longer-lasting, faster-acting" or you-name-it benefit claim. In fact, any legitimate claim of differentiation virtually *requires* a credible supporting study before marketers can legally communicate that differentiation in the market. And, as marketers of prescription drug brands well know, it is impossible to secure a primary indication for a given drug without the clinical studies to back it up. You might even say that, to secure a competitive place in the market (a piece of ownable, marketplace "real estate"), drug brands must craftily design their clinical studies years ahead of market entry in order to have the supporting evidence to hold that competitive place. Take a look at a snapshot of the antidepressant drug market in the United States a few years ago:

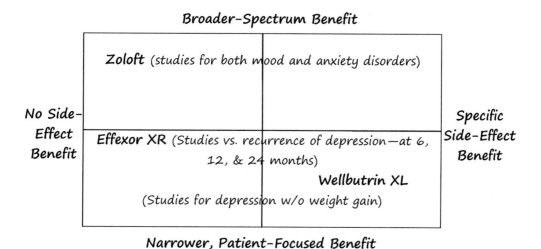

Other variations of studies, more commonly employed by fast-moving performance brands (like detergents and household cleaning products) and some food-beverage brands, are *in-use studies* and *blind taste tests*. Typically these require that a representative sample of consumers select one product as providing better results or as tasting better. As with clinical studies, however, none of these consumer perception or preference tests works if it is not credible. Among the most famous consumer taste tests ever conducted has to be the "Pepsi Challenge" that ran across the United States throughout the 1980s. It never lacked for instantaneous credibility because, whether the comparison was done live at grocery stores or captured live for TV advertising, the genuineness of consumers' surprise—even regular Coke consumers—at choosing Pepsi for better taste was jolting. Maybe that's a good rule of thumb when it comes to using a clinical study or other preference test as a reason-why in a brand positioning: It ought to provide "jolting credibility."

- ***Creating your own credibility.*** Just as creativity can be helpful in devising unique (but legitimate) external endorsements, it also comes in real handy for marketers looking to establish their *own* internal endorsement. For example, the Jeep brand created its own "Trail Rated™" system—a series of what it calls "five grueling tests with one objective: to make sure all Jeep 4x4's that wear the Trail Rated badge are proven capable on the toughest terrain on earth." So Jeep puts all its 4x4s through traction, articulation, ground clearance, maneuverability, and water fording tests to certify them as officially Trail Rated™. More to the point, *no other* 4x4 brand can be Trail Rated™ because, well, look who has trademarked the rating!

  Other brands have created their own benefit credibility using another technique; rather than making up their own endorsement or "seal of approval," they have literally built a separate entity, like a "resource center" or an "institute" that is best communicated via their website. Some years back, when the Excedrin brand focused its positioning benefit on better headache relief, the marketers at Bristol-Myers Squibb created the "Headache Resource Center." It may or may not have been an actual, physical location, but the effect was nevertheless a good one. As a consumer hearing Excedrin's claim to be "The Headache Medicine," you would naturally expect Excedrin to sponsor a facility to study better headache management and relief.

  But perhaps one of the most credible institutes of recent years has to be Gatorade's Sports Science Institute™. The brand is serious about supporting its leadership in athletic replenishment, and you can see just how serious it is by spending a few minutes at its website. The Sports Science Institute pages are loaded with helpful, even professional, articles and data about hydration, sports nutrition, training and performance (including sports psychology and endurance training), and medical conditions and sports injuries. Continuing to evolve an "equity" reason-why like this is smart marketing and even smarter brand positioning—it gives the brand something highly credible that another brand cannot copy or make "cost-of-entry."

- ***The trademark equity bank.*** Speaking of an "equity" reason-why, there may be none more valuable than an actual parent brand. In the broad world of baby care, for example, could any parent brand duplicate the efficacy credibility of Johnson & Johnson? Practically, this value comes into play whenever the Johnson's brand launches a new item; it must be credible (better) for baby because it's "From Johnson & Johnson." Consistent with this use, then, citing a parent brand as a positioning reason-why is sometimes referred to as *borrowing from the trademark equity bank.*

One caution should always be considered when thinking about using a parent or mega-brand as an equity endorsement: Does the parent brand truly have an unshakeable prowess it can lend to the endorsee? It's often easy for a company's marketers to imagine its parent brand has more real equity with consumers than it actually does. And, it goes without saying, any sub-brand that "borrows" equity from a parent should be able to "pay back" that borrowed interest with the overall value it adds to the brand's portfolio. When the Hallmark brand launches a new subline of cards, whether more serious or more humorous, the new line must add to Hallmark's longstanding benefit equity of "always caring enough to send one's very best."

The Main *Extrinsic* Reason-Why

Brand	Benefit	Reason-Why	Type Of Extrinsic RW
Orbit Sugarless Gum	Reduced cavities	ADA seal	Professional endorsement
Duracell	Dependable (long-lasting) performance	Preferred use	Series of professional endorsements
Effexor XR	Prevention of depression recurrence	6-, 12-, 24- month data	Clinical studies
Pepsi-Cola	Better taste (than Coke)	Sip test consumer preference	Blind taste tests
Jeep	All-terrain performance	Trail-Rated™ system	Self-created endorsement/seal
Gatorade	Athletic replenishment	Gatorade Sports Science Institute™	Self-created institute
Johnson's	Best baby care	From Johnson & Johnson	Borrowing from TM Equity Bank
Hallmark	Best feelings sent	From Hallmark	Borrowing from TM Equity Bank

Ensuring the Linkage of Reasons-Why with Benefits

With all the brand examples of intrinsic and extrinsic reasons-why we have looked at so far, it should be apparent that each is effective only to the degree it links with one of the brand's positioning Benefits. It seems easy enough to ensure Benefit - Reason-Why linkage, but so often marketers miss making a tight linkage by doing one or more of the following: *overloading the brand positioning with reasons-why that are legitimate but do not support any benefit; using a product benefit—instead of a product feature or attribute—as a reason-why; or failing to "cross-check" or, literally, to align each benefit with an appropriate reason-why.*

We've found a simple way to prevent all of these common misses from happening: expressing the positioning benefits and reasons-why side-by-side *and* drawing "linking arrows" to show how each reason-why actually supports at least one benefit. As we like to say, the most important part of the Benefit-Reason-Why table below is the *arrows*:

Benefit - Reason-Why Linkage

Benefit	Reason-Why
1. Has bakery-fresh taste you can enjoy each morning	A. Authentic bakery forms and textures B. Popular flavors that complement coffee and tea
2. And that you can eat without the worry of putting on weight	C. Nitrogen-flush packaging D. Low fat/calorie ingredients

As you can readily see in this fictitious snack-food example, each benefit has at least one reason-why to support it, and each reason-why is also a tangible product feature, not another benefit. We think displaying this portion of the

Brand Positioning Statement in this side-by-side manner is a sure-fire way to engineer in solid Benefit - Reason-Why linkage.

More Pointers on Articulating the Positioning Reason-Why

Besides displaying reasons-why next to their linked benefits, there are a few other things good marketers routinely do when articulating their brand's reasons-why—to make double-sure that they have true features and tangibles and not additional benefits. Generally speaking, using "lead-ins" like these will force the presence of true features and tangibles:

- *Contains* the following ingredients/elements
- *Designed* with these features/components
- *Operates* in this manner
- *Employs* this mode-of-action
- *Endorsed/Approved* by
- *Supported* by these data/clinical studies

Above all else, you want the brand's reasons-why to be so tangible as to be something demonstrable, something another person could actually examine, something that would stand as evidence in a court of law just when the judge bangs his gavel and demands, "Prove your claim!"

Checking Your Understanding: A Reason-Why Quiz

	Place a checkmark beside each of the items below that would qualify as a legitimate (as in a true feature or tangible) Reason-Why — for a snack brand. If an item is not a legitimate Reason-Why, what is it?
1.	Provides an intense flavor experience
2.	Made with only pure Belgian chocolate
3.	Presented in advertising by Sponge Bob
4.	Made according to a 1950s Gardetto's family recipe
5.	Delivers a smooth, creamy mouth-feel
6.	Has a supercool eucalyptus center that "gushes"
7.	Approved for school sale by the National PTA
8.	Replenishes more electrolytes than isotonic drinks
9.	Contains no trans fats
10.	Available at chocolate stores everywhere
	The answers are on page 162

Guiding and Checking Your Work

Here's a way to check your Brand Positioning Reason-Why to ensure it is technically correct and competitive. Assess each of the following six points (which appears on the next page) by noting whether you "Don't Agree," "Agree Somewhat," or "Strongly Agree." Tally each box and step back to take stock of where you are with your RW choices. Importantly, identify the indicated actions you must take to achieve a "Strongly Agree" rating and then take those actions.

Brand Positioning Add-Valuator

Reason-Why	Don't Agree (0)	Agree Somewhat (3)	Strongly Agree (5)	Indicated Actions
1. It is incontrovertible, tangible. It is not a "hidden" benefit claim. It is defensible in a court of law.				
2. It is one of two types: "intrinsic" (i.e., product feature or characteristic) and "extrinsic" (e.g., endorsement from recognized experts/ associations).				
3. Each Benefit has a corresponding Reason-Why.				
4. Each Reason-Why serves to add credibility to each Benefit claimed.				
5. The Reason-Why differentiates the brand.				
6. The mention of the Reason-Why evokes the Benefit.				
Total Score				

KEY POINTS, PRINCIPLES & PRACTICES
Summary

✓ Reason-Why is included in the Brand Positioning Strategy Statement to make the Benefit(s) credible and to provide "tangible evidence" of the Benefit claims the brand makes. In fact, the very best reasons-why are the ones that are so clearly expressed that they immediately call to mind the intended benefit they support.

✓ Accordingly, reason-why is *not* another product or consumer/customer benefit.

✓ Like benefits, reasons-why should be as differentiated as possible (even ownable!). Clever marketers can find ways to make a differentiated reason-why—like an advanced feature—imply a differentiated benefit, even at times when a differentiated benefit claim cannot be made

✓ Reason-Why typically takes one of two forms: something inside the product (*intrinsic*) or something outside the product (*extrinsic*). Among the most commonly used intrinsic Reasons-Why are the following: ingredients, design components, processing, mode-of-action, source of materials, and the absence of negatives. Among the most commonly used extrinsic Reasons-Why are the following: endorsements, clinical studies and preference tests, self-created endorsements or institutes, and borrowed interest from the "trademark equity bank."

✓ Many brands today aim to include both types of reason-why in their brand's positioning for maximum competitiveness. But whether including both types or not, the general rule of thumb is that for each Benefit there should be at least one Reason-Why.

✓ Linking Reasons-Why with their respective Benefits demands a conscious effort. An excellent way to accomplish this is by displaying each—in almost bullet-point fashion—side by side. It is also a most helpful check to literally draw arrows to show which Reason-Why goes with which Benefit.

Reasons-Why that "dangle" (because they do not link to any benefit) add no real value to a brand's positioning.

✓ Reasons-Why must be so tangible, so demonstrable as to stand up in a court of law.

✓ Finally, at least once each year, Marketing should explore with R&D potential new Reasons-Why to be developed—as insurance in the event a current RW gets copied by the competition. This checklist can help in identifying some unexplored options:

Reason-Why Tool

Brand Benefit(s):_____   _____

Reason-Why options:
--Ingredients: --Source of materials:
--Design: --Absence of negatives:
--Process: --Endorsements:
--Mode of action: --Clinical studies/tests:

(ANSWERS to Reason Why Quiz on page 159: 2, 4, 6, 7, 9; 1, 5, and 8 are benefits; 3 is merely an executional device—Sponge Bob is no expert on snacks, anyway; 10 is a distribution fact.)

DISPATCHES™

Insights On Brand Development From The Marketing Front

REASON-WHY RECONSIDERED

So much attention has been paid to Dove's "Real Beauty" marketing campaign over the past few years that we've almost forgotten about one of the most well-known (and best leveraged) positioning reasons-why anywhere: "1/4 moisturizing cream." This simple ingredient—that no one else owns—has enabled the Dove brand to expand successfully with *differentiation* into so many skin care and related categories, like deodorant and shampoo. We think this one example serves as a good reminder of the power of reasons-why, and it has caused us to reconsider some of the fundamental RW principles.

Before we review those, however, let's first recall that reason-why is a critical part of a brand's positioning because it serves to make the brand's benefits believable. Whether in the classic form of an ingredient (per Dove) or as a design element or a mode of action/operation, or in the form of research/clinical data and expert-body endorsements, each reason-why must link directly to at least one of the brand's benefits. Reason-why is not about *why* someone should buy your brand, though, if differentiated and well linked to a meaningful benefit, it might well cause someone to choose your brand over another. In general, a good rule of thumb most marketers subscribe to is that for each benefit there should be at least one reason-why. It makes for tighter credibility.

RW Principle #1: A Reason-why works hardest when its mention—on packaging, in communications, in merchandising materials—immediately suggests or implies the benefit it supports (even when the RW stands alone). Dove's "1/4 moisturizing cream" immediately suggests a nourishing mildness for skin that will leave it soft and looking natural. The "breathable sole" in every Geox shoe suggests drier, more comfortable feet for the wearer. Evian water is purer and tastes better because it comes from, well, Evian. And, as many allergists know, Singulair reduces allergy symptoms in their patients because it works differently from other allergy meds—others block histamines, but Singulair blocks leukotrienes. Regardless of the type, these various reasons-why are already so well marketed that they tend to elicit the benefits each supports at first mention.

RW Principle #2: A Reason-Why works hardest when it is not merely another benefit. Benefits make promises; Reasons-Why support those promises. Benefits promise one of three things: what the product does (product benefit), what that translates to for the customer (customer benefit), and/or how that all makes the customer feel (emotional benefit). Real reasons-why do none of these things; rather, they stipulate something *tangible* that will support each of these things. Quite literally, a real, productive reason-why is something that a customer could actually see and touch—an ingredient, a design element, a research study, a signed endorsement. As we often remind our clients, should a judge in a courtroom bang his gavel and demand of a brand manager making a claim, "Prove it," the reason-why should be admissible as tangible evidence.

RW Principle #3: A Reason-Why works hardest when it provides the brand with a differentiation that the benefit cannot. So often in our marketing efforts to have our brand perceived as a better choice, we overlook the "suggestive power" of a compelling reason-why. When the Schick Quattro razor was introduced a few years ago, it had no legally supportable promise of benefit to make to male consumers, such as a "closer shave" or a "smoother shave." But it did have one thing that, at the time, Gillette did not have: an extra blade (four versus Gillette's three). And, because razor marketers have trained American consumers so well to believe that "more blades are better," the perceived differentiation for the Quattro took hold. True, it was not a permanent differentiation because Gillette eventually followed with the five-bladed Fusion—but the suggestive power of an added blade did help Quattro to a successful launch. Sometimes, though, the perception of "having more of some feature" does last, as in the case of the Volvo brand. No matter where you go in the world, people immediately cite Volvo's dominant benefit as safety; although Volvo has no more air bags than other leading sedans these days, many perceive that it does.

RW Principle # 4: A Reason-Why works hardest when value can be added to it over time. In recent months, the Campbell's *V8®* brand has done this very thing. Long known as a "better-for-you" beverage because of its real vegetable juice content, the brand has always been free of cholesterol and saturated fats. But these absence-of-negatives reasons why didn't bring much to the party until the brand's recent acquiring of an American Heart Association endorsement. Per the copy in one of the current print ads, "Something good just got better." This endorsement value, added to the already healthy Campbell's *V8* ingredients, makes the brand's better-for-you benefit stronger. And did you see just a few weeks ago that Wrigley's has secured the American Dental Association endorsement for the sugarless gum brands (a first in the gum category)? Again, everyone knows the cavity-preventing benefit of sugarless gum, but now there is an even better reason to believe in its efficacy with the value-added ADA endorsement.

RW Principle #5: A Reason-Why works hardest when it is not COE (cost-of-entry). We already noted that the ADA is now endorsing sugarless gum—a first for that category. But the same cannot be said for the toothpaste category, where an ADA endorsement is a cost-of-entry reason-why and has been for many years. Another often-cited endorsement is "dermatologist recommended." The Neutrogena brand might claim that it owns this endorsement, but if other brands can also use it (or something very similar), it is really more COE than ownable. The truth is that virtually every reason-why that is now a cost-of-entry (like the fluoride ingredient in toothpaste to prevent cavities) was once a differentiating reason-why. But, as they say, all good things must come to an end, so it is always a good idea to be prepared for the day when your brand's differentiating reason-why becomes a COE. We like to see our clients' brands pursue an ongoing effort to find new and improved reasons-why—in partnership with their R&D teams. There *is* a creative way to completely avoid the "COE effect": Develop your own reason-why endorsement, such as Jeep has done with its "Trail Rated" system and seal. No other SUV can possibly be "Trail Rated" because Jeep has trademarked the nomenclature.

CHAPTER SEVEN

"Image is everything."

—*Andre Agassi*

Chapter 7

Developing a Winning Personality to Connect with Customers through Brand Character

---

Now we come to the fifth and final element of a sound brand positioning strategy—Brand Character. And, while it is the final element, it is in no way to be interpreted as the least. It is, perhaps, the most influential element of brand image. As the quote taken from Andre Agassi, the former tennis great, appearing in a Canon camera television spot, suggests, image is exceedingly important. It is also manufactured, as evidenced by recent confessions of countless celebrities (sports, entertainment, and politics). Brand Character provides us with an opportunity to create and establish a winning personality for our brand entity.

What It Is

As you have learned from an earlier chapter, "Competitive Framework" deals with *what your brand is* as a category or classification of products. Is your Hewlett-Packard a printer or a multitasking small business tool that contains fax, copier, scanner, and printer all in one? Is Jell–O the brand of gelatin or the anytime treat? Is Gatorade a sport beverage, a thirst quencher or the ultimate liquid athletic equipment?

"Brand Character," on the other hand, addresses *who* your brand is as a personage. It reflects the very personality you create for your specific brand. It represents the complexion, temperament, and spirit of the brand. As such, it is a strategic element of positioning and the brand.

What It Isn't

Brand Character should not be confused with "tone," which is frequently done by marketers and ad agency people who should know better. Tone denotes mode, style, or manner of expression for a given execution. Tone is an executional element, not a strategic one.

Stated another way, Brand Character gets to the very values of the brand's personality, whereas tone captures a particular mood. It is curious that the Spanish language has two expressions for the verb "to be." One is "*ser*," and the other is "*estar*." "*Ser*" is used with something that has permanent characteristics, whereas "*estar*" is used to relate something that is temporary in nature. So, if we were to say, "Juan *esta* borracho ahora," we are communicating that he is drunk now. On the other hand, if we were to use the *ser* form of the verb, as in "Juan *es* borracho," we are communicating that he is a drunkard. The first is synonymous with tone, the second with brand character.

Imagine someone who is a very serious-minded individual but who engages in a bit of whimsy from time to time. The personality, or character, is "serious minded." The specific mood at a given point of time is one of whimsy. It is temporary. Brand character is part of the personality make-up of the individual, whereas the other, tone, reflects an episodic moment.

Keep in mind that if all the communications for your product reflect the same tonality, your customers and your potential customers will come to perceive that tonality as the brand's personality. A campaign for an OTC product that is executed with humor may lead customers to perceive the product as something not to be taken seriously and, consequently, as being not very effective. So, it is very important to define the personality you want to establish for a brand in the positioning strategy and to review executional submissions in all your marketing-mix elements to ensure they are in synch with that personality. Otherwise, the marketer risks having execution define personality, which is a case of the proverbial "tail wagging the dog."

Importance of Brand Character

Brand Character is an important strategic element in the Brand Positioning Strategy Statement. It serves to:

- ***Differentiate brands with common features and benefits.*** Take the two soft drink giants, Coke and Pepsi, for example. During the 1970s, Coke battled with an image (in this case read "personality" or brand character) it perpetuated and which many consumers perceived as conservative, stodgy, republican, old, and so on. Needless to say, this image was not very attractive to the youth of America, which has the highest per capita consumption of soft drinks among all age-related demographic cohorts. Pepsi, on the other hand, enjoyed an image of being youthful, fun, active, and adventuresome, among other personality traits. Think about it. If you were to engineer the Brand Character for a soft drink, which would you choose? Coke of the 1970s? Hardly. If you know anything about soft drinks and the consuming core, you would choose Pepsi. So did America's youth!

  The brand character of Coke came about as a function of its position in the marketplace and of campaign executions whose tonality was "baseball, apple pie, and Chevrolet"—a piece of Americana. Pepsi's brand character was crafted to set itself apart from brand Coca-Cola in a way that would be positive with heavy soft drink consumers; make a weakness of Coke's ubiquity and resultant imagery; and be difficult, if not impossible, for brand Coke to occupy. Basically, it came down to creating the Brand Character Pepsi could own and making it the focus of sale.

  No one TV spot captured these differences in brand character between the two soft drink brands better than Pepsi's *Shady Acres*. This spot serves to use Brand Character to differentiate Pepsi from Coke. It starts off with a party of septuagenarians and octogenarians dancing to rock 'n' roll music. We also view old people tossing Frisbees and roller-blading. They are drinking Pepsi as they "party-hearty." The location is Shady Acres, a retirement community that portrays its elderly as being young at heart and in deed.

  The commercial cuts to two route salesmen who are offloading cases of Coca-Cola. One says to the other, "Wait, I thought Shady Acres was to get the Coke and the frat house was to get the Pepsi." The other responds, "Coke, Pepsi, what's the difference?" and shrugs his shoulders.

The spot then cuts to the Frat house where a very stuffy young man is calling out "I-22" for a game of bingo while he sips Coke in a can through a straw. The music playing in the background is classical (sounds like a minuet)—and lulling others to sleep. We hear snores coming from his frat brothers who are asleep in deep, stuffy chairs.

Once again, the spot cuts back to Shady Acres as a young-minded octogenarian man dances, holding a can of Pepsi, to rock 'n' roll music with a fiery septuagenarian woman.

The difference is clear; the imagery for Coke is old-fashioned, stuffy, conservative, everything a young person does not want to be identified with, or as. On the other hand, the Pepsi character is active, fun, young at heart, outrageous, or everything a young person would aspire to be, personality wise! The difference is not only clear but also meaningful. The difference is not what is in the can (i.e., the liquid) but the brand character. And, what a difference it is! (Pepsi effectively positioned itself while at the same time positioned Coca-Cola in an unflattering light.)

- ***Give customers an additional reason to choose your brand.*** We like buying from people we like or who are like us in mindset and values. When you establish your brand as aspirational, likable (i.e., as reflecting a personality or set of values that you appreciate) or helpful, you encourage customer affiliation and a potential positive relationship. In making the brand more attractive and appealing in character to the target, the marketer invites customers to join the brand. After seeing *Shady Acres*, who would want to join Coke? On the other hand, all party-loving teens would certainly want to be affiliated with Pepsi and the brand character it communicates. It comes down to what you stand for and whom you attract with that stance.

  Apple has a distinctive and very cool personality compared to PCs (i.e., personal computers). Apple has personified the Mac in a compelling television campaign as a cool, savvy, and hip person and PCs as rather stodgy, square, boring, and somewhat nerdish. Consumers want to identify with the Mac and not the PC character. In fact, in Great Britain there was a time when people would ask if you are a Mac or a PC. This wasn't a question of what you had and used but who you are personality wise. That's Brand Character.

One of the most successful trademarks to be built upon brand character is perhaps Nike. Nike epitomizes the positive values of sports through marketing its products lauding the exploits and personalities of alpha athletes, such as the incomparable Michael Jordan. As we stated in chapter 5, who doesn't want to be like Mike? He's not just a winner but a hero! He is competitive, a leader, a positive role model, "numero uno," genuine in a world of phonies, a gentleman, articulate, and downright lovable—and no less likable. (But, then, what would you expect me to say about Michael? This author is from Chicago and a loyal Chicago Bulls fan, even during this long, dark post-Jordan era!)

This Brand Character for Nike is one with which every sports-minded individual would like to affiliate, whether a fan of the Seattle Supersonics or the Chicago Bulls, a youth of America or of Lebanon. Nike has successfully established an enduring brand character to differentiate its products from those of its competition. Yes, Nike may enjoy some technological product advantages from time to time, but the majority of its consumers are either unaware of the value of the technology or, believe it or not, don't even use the product for its intended sport.

The Pepsi, Mac, and Nike brand characters are not fortuitous. They didn't just happen. They were engineered. Pepsi, Mac, and Nike just did it!

Importantly, the Brand Character is not just a collection of words, the sounds and meanings of which are created to please senior management. Instead, they are words that articulate an enduring personality, one envisioned and embraced by senior management to embody the brand. What's more, the Brand Character is reflected in product design, benefits, and all elements of the brand's bundle (i.e., marketing-mix elements such as package design and promotion). In fact, Michael Jordan and other Nike athletes of today (such as Lebron James and Kobe Bryant) get involved in the actual design and testing of products that bear their endorsement.

Understanding Brand Character—A Tale of Two Campaigns

When we introduced Reach Toothbrush, while one of the authors was the Product Director at the Johnson & Johnson Company, we articulated the Brand Character we hoped to establish for the brand. Back in 1977, we were among the first marketers to recognize the importance of brand character and to employ it in competitively positioning a product. This is evident in the introductory TV commercial for the brand, *The Inventor*. In this introductory spot, we see a male presenter who is in his mid-50s, dressed in a white shirt and bow tie. The presenter (the inventor) looks the camera (or viewer) in the eyes while he holds up a standard toothbrush and asks, "They invented fluoride toothpaste to help fight cavities; why hasn't someone invented a better toothbrush?" Then he proceeds to ask questions about design, such as "What if they angled it like a dental instrument so it could clean hard-to-reach back teeth?," as he transforms a standard toothbrush into a Reach Toothbrush. When we ask marketers to define the Brand Character from a review of the TV spot, they respond, "Professional, advanced, therapeutic, scientific, credible," and similar terms. Now, for the next question: "If this is the Brand Character and you are leading Product Research and Development, what would you work on?" Your answers are probably similar to marketers', which consistently register:

- Advanced designs that lead to superior cleaning and therapeutic efficacy;
- Clinical studies demonstrating superior cleaning and/or cavity-fighting efficacy;
- Endorsement from the American Dental Association;
- New products directed at specific dental care problems (e.g., a toothbrush for people with orthodontics); and
- A youth version of the adult brush.

You would be thinking about the therapeutic role of the Reach Toothbrush brand. The introductory spot ran for several years (it worked!). It was replaced by a campaign referred to as *"Mr. Reach."* The campaign features an animated character, Mr. Reach, who has a flip-top head (to demonstrate the brush and way it cleans). Voice-over is used to establish the situation for Mr. Reach. The announcer voice-over is distinctly British, but somewhat lighthearted in tone.

When marketers are shown a spot from this campaign and asked to define its brand character, they respond with "approachable, fun, whimsical, lighthearted," and similar words. Now, let's ask the same question we raised with *The Inventor* spot: "If this is the Brand Character and you are leading Product Research and Development, what would you work on?" The answers to this question are predictable:

- Fun shapes and designs;
- Character endorsements and icons on the handles (such as Disney or Loony Tunes characters);
- Fun colors;
- Neon colors.

These activities do not reinforce the brand's superior efficacy and advanced (at the time) dental instrument design. They do not support the therapeutic value of the brand. And, those initiatives mentioned above were the kind of actions taken. The company introduced neon, glow-in–the-dark colors. In effect, it undermined the superior efficacy and therapeutic imagery of the Reach Toothbrush. Why? Your guess is as good as ours, but we believe it was probably because a revolving-door marketing team didn't fully appreciate the value of Brand Character as a strategic element of the brand positioning strategy, and allowed a creative idea (albeit a very engaging one) to supersede strategic direction.

Today, the Reach Toothbrush brand has lost its way. In the past couple of years, it introduced a cosmetic brush for the brand whose heritage, as we have pointed out, is and has been therapeutic. The product had a very short life. We believe the brand may have a short life too, or not a very healthy one. The brand is suffering.

Through all these examples, we hope we have made it clear that Brand Character is a strategic element of sound, strategic brand positioning. Change the Brand Character and you will have a profound impact on the brand's positioning—and it may not be for the best!

What Makes for a Legitimate Brand Character

The Brand Character is not about the Target Customer. If you were loyal to a particular toilet bowl cleanser, you, as the target customer, would not wish to see yourself reflected in the Brand Character. Instead, Brand Character should take one of two directions: 1) something or someone that is aspirational that you wish to be part of (which is really about "badging" as "I am what I drink"); or 2) the relationship of the brand to the Target Customer.

The previous example of Pepsi, as depicted in *Shady Acres,* is the use of Brand Character to encourage badging. It is clearly aspirational. On the other hand, the example of Reach Toothbrush at its introduction reflects the relationship of the brand to its targeted customer, as being "a home dental instrument."

So the source of Brand Character should be defining not the target's personality but, instead, something that is aspirational and that will lead to badging, or something that reflects the relationship or role the brand plays with the Target Customer.

Getting at Brand Character

In defining a brand's character or personality, the marketer needs to use words that describe someone's personality. After all, in defining a brand's character, we are really describing its personality. So, the words one uses must be words you would use in talking about a friend's, a family member's, or even your own, personality. Therefore, we use words such as "approachable," "charismatic," "friendly," "authoritative," "intelligent," "enthusiastic," "knowledgeable," "discriminating," and so on. Anytime you come across a word to describe brand character that does not identify a personality trait or value, throw it out! It doesn't belong in the Brand Character statement. For example, we may find the word "efficacious" as one of a litany of adjectives in a Brand Character statement. Now would you say someone is "efficacious?" NO! You might say your friend is productive, efficient, hard working, or diligent but certainly not efficacious.

Exercise #1: Identifying Brand Character

Let's put what we have learned about Brand Character to work. Pick a category, be it cars, perfumes, notebook computers, whatever your wish. Look through a few magazines (e.g., *Newsweek*, *Good Housekeeping*, *Men's Fitness*, *Money*) and pull out ads for brands in the category you have selected. Select two brands and define the Brand Character, as it would appear in their Brand Positioning Strategy Statements, for each.

Remember: The words you use must be words you would use in talking about a friend's, a family member's, or even your own, personality. Anytime you come across a word to describe Brand Character that does not identify a personality trait or value, throw it out! Replace it with an alternate word that you would clearly use to describe someone's personality.

Word choice is extremely important. Not only is it important to ensure that each word identifies a personality trait; it is also important to ensure that all the personality traits are in harmony. Once again, we are in search of *integrity*, in this case integrity of character. In the few cases where we do find clients that have defined Brand Character, we often find that the words used are contradictory. For example, we often see the words "caring" and "authoritative" together in the same Brand Character statement. Perhaps, they can coexist (as in a dictator of some benign country), but we believe they are often found together because those attempting to sell a specific brand character are catering to the biases of their management. In other words, the specific word choice is being influenced by what the authors of the Brand Character statement believe their management wants to see. Sometimes words like these are just picked up from an existing Brand Character statement, using what has been there.

Also, marketers may respond negatively to a perceived brand's character and trash it. It's doubtful that the architect of the brand's character wanted to turn off prospective customers. Instead, it is the individual viewer's reaction, how the character strikes him. But the Brand Character may not have been developed for those who do not find it compelling. Jean-Paul Gaultier is quite a controversial designer. For his perfume bearing his name, the packaging may lead some people to assume that the character is trashy or vulgar. But, to its target, this same package design may communicate a totally different brand character, one that is appealing to them. They may see the brand as avant-garde, bold, somewhat rebellious, or independent. Therefore, when reviewing a brand's personality, it is important to see it from the perspective of its intended Target Customer within the context of the brand positioning strategy.

What you view consciously, using your left, analytical brain, customers absorb subconsciously, through their gut. So, when assessing a brand's character, it is also important to put yourself in the target customer's shoes and let your gut identify the Brand Character.

Developing Brand Character

Identifying an existing brand's personality, its Brand Character, is not a difficult task. On the other hand, developing a Brand Character for one's own brand typically is more problematic. Marketers find it difficult to create the Brand Character and, when that task is complete, to gain agreement to that identity from diverse groups of people (e.g., the advertising agency, internal support groups, senior management).

The first step is to be clear on the brand bundle, since that, and not the personality of the Target Customer, is what the Brand Character reflects. Imagine for a moment that you are marketing a toilet bowl cleanser. Do you think for a moment that the consumer would like to see her personality reflected in the product? As we stated earlier, "No way!" Instead, the Brand Character should be consistent with what the product can do for her. Assuming the product performs well, it should have a Brand Character of being "powerful," "highly efficient" and, maybe, "tough."

The Perceptual Competitive Framework provides the best handle on the brand bundle, since it gets at what we hope the brand to be. Given the knowledge of "what" it is, then we are ready to begin defining the "who."

In defining the "who," we have found it helpful to *move away from abstraction and start with the concrete.* Here is one way how we do it:

- ***Identify a celebrity who best characterizes your brand.*** One of the most productive techniques is to identify a celebrity who you believe best characterizes your brand. We are *not* referring to a spokesperson, or endorser. Instead, we are asking you to address the following question: *If your brand were a person, who would it be?* This could be any person. But, any person may not be known to those with whom you want to co-create the Brand Character, or whom you want to convince that it is the right one for your brand. If we suggest in this first step that our brand is Arthur Goldberg, you are very likely to ask, "Who the heck is Arthur Goldberg?" However, if we were to say our brand is Robert De Niro, we start on common footing, since you know who he is. You may disagree with our choice, but we have established common ground for our dialogue and for the creation of the Brand Character statement. So we start by asking, *"If your brand were a celebrity, who would it be?"* In this way, we are taking the task from the abstract to the concrete so that everyone involved may participate and understand.

- *Define the personality characteristics of the chosen celebrity.* If you were to agree that the Brand Character is best exemplified by Robert De Niro, we are ready to go to the next step, which is to define those of his personality characteristics that match the brand. We might agree that it is not Robert De Niro as we think we know him, but Robert De Niro in a specific role, such as Don Vito Corleone, in the movie The Godfather.

    What do we do if there is not general agreement about Robert De Niro in his role as Don Vito Corleone? Simple. He has played many roles. See if you can find one that fits. Find out where the disagreement lies. The misunderstanding my not be in the specific celebrity, but in the personality characteristics. Or, go ahead, suggest another celebrity. These actions lead to new contrasts, new word choices, and, therefore, alternate celebrities to make concrete what is typically managed as an abstraction. Through this dialoguing process the team of creators shouldn't have too much difficulty in getting concrete and agreeing on a celebrity and, more importantly, a set of personality characteristics for the brand.

- *Identify personality characteristics you wish to establish for your brand consistent with the product features and brand bundle.* This is not a process of wishful thinking. One does not just choose a celebrity because one would like to be like him. Instead you choose a celebrity because the personality characteristics resemble those of your brand. If we are marketing something that is fine and elegant such as Fendi silk scarves, Robert De Niro will not be appropriate – particularly as Don Vito Corleone. Instead, we might choose the iconic Audrey Hepburn or, in today's age, Heidi Klum. Their personality characteristics, associated with being elegant, classic, sophisticated, and surrounded by luxury, more closely match the product and its features, benefits, and imagery. They match how we want the customer to feel about the brand. If the personality characteristics do not match the intended brand bundle, then you need to find a celebrity whose characteristics do match. Also, everyone has a multitude of personality characteristics; the marketer's challenge is to select those few that best match-up and create the Brand Character you wish to establish.

There are other ways to approach development of the Brand Character besides the use of a celebrity. Some marketers have had success by selecting an animal and defining its personality characteristics and values. We have experienced significant success with using magazine brands. This is particularly helpful in selling others, since it allows for visual contrasts. Another technique is to borrow from other, well-known, established brands from other categories. In borrowing from other brands, we start by identifying the brand whose brand character we believe we share. We then go on to identify those characteristics of that brand that we believe are applicable to our brand. Yet another technique is to identify a specific role or archetype in society that is familiar to all (such as the "girl next door" or the "compassionate mother").

The key to all these techniques is to start with the concrete, someone or something everyone knows. In this way, the marketer will be able to establish common ground and begin a meaningful dialogue to enhance the development of Brand Character. Celebrities, animals, magazines, other established brands, societal roles—choose the one that works for you!

Exercise # 2 - Developing Brand Character

Try using the celebrity technique plus one other of your choice from those previously presented (i.e., animal, magazine, other brand or societal role) to create a Brand Character statement for your brand. Make sure you link specific personality characteristics with the brand bundle (its product attributes, features, and/or benefits.)

Brand Character Tool

```
┌─────────────────────────────────────────────────────────────┐
│  Celebrity:                                                    │
│         Personality Characteristics                           │
│      •                                                         │
│                                                               │
│      •                                                         │
│                                                               │
│      •                                                         │
│                                                               │
│      •                                                         │
└─────────────────────────────────────────────────────────────┘
```

Toward More Meaningful Articulation of the Brand Character

We need to get beyond use of mere adjectives. It seems as though every brand uses the same words to describe its brand's personality. Johnson's Baby Brand Character is caring, trustworthy, authoritative. The Brand Character for Marlboro cigarettes is caring, trustworthy, authoritative. Okay, so we are exaggerating. But there are just a few words and related synonyms that capture virtually every brand's Brand Character (as they express it); everything is presented as caring, trustworthy, authoritative, a leader, contemporary, and youthful.

It is much more effective to employ a narrative. For example, Tide Laundry Detergent is "the perfectionist you can count upon to do the job right." Viagra may be the "empathetic, nonjudgmental marriage counselor who assists you in developing and enjoying a loving relationship with your partner."

We can take the articulation of Brand Character even further to make it more appropriate and clear, even to the point of making it incapable of being misunderstood. A young, highly creative product director with whom we worked believed that the focus of sale for his brand should be Brand Character. He found his brand in a situation similar to that in which Coke found itself in the 1970s. His brand had a very old-fashioned image. It was a brand one's father or mother used, not oneself. While his advertising agency agreed that the

Brand Character needed to be updated, it was not able to come to a common understanding of what that Brand Character should be.

Frustrated by the failure of numerous attempts to co-create a Brand Character statement or to gain agreement to a proposed character consisting of several adjectives, the creative product director developed a three-minute film to illustrate the Brand Character he believed should define the brand. The film was made up of clips from TV ads (from a multitude of brands from diverse categories), supers of words, and jazzy and sophisticated but very hip music. Everything he used in the film was taken from existing material. He created nothing new but the resultant pieced-together film.

Coming onto the scene well after the product director had been faced with the challenge and developed the film, we were very impressed by this example of defining and communicating Brand Character. We were impressed with his initiative, creativity, and his use of available materials to make his words come alive, to make them concrete. We were particularly impressed with his use of music. Think about it. Music is yet another way to express Brand Character or personality. Back in our days in the soft drink business, new campaign development was marked by a creative concept ("naked idea"), key copy words, core dramatization, and music (which went beyond the melody to include lyrics).

You may not have to go as far as this talented and creative product director did. You have enough techniques with those we gave you. But articulate your brand's character in a three-dimensional form consisting of pictures or, better yet, film, and music and you will have a more compelling way to define, communicate, and make understandable throughout your organization the desired Brand Character you wish to establish.

One Final Note

Established brands such as the one managed by our product director client typically have a difficult time in adapting and revising their Brand Character. The reason is that, through years of marketing, or mismanagement of marketing, they already have a brand character (as perceived by the marketplace). The further one departs from this existing perception of brand character, the more likely the attempt will fail. So, what do you do when your brand is at point "B" and you need to get to point "Z"?

First, you need to recognize where you want to get to—point "Z." You are the architect of the brand, and one of your roles, as we have mentioned, is to create the strategic vision and platform for the brand. If you need, want, and aspire to get to point "Z," then first you need to recognize it and convince your management of this goal.

Second, *chart* and *manage* your way to point "Z" *over time*! Do not try to do it in one leap. It takes time to wean potential customers from their current perception of your brand (particularly if it is the result of years of false starts, mistakes, mindless execution of tactics, or mere neglect). If you move too quickly, if the change is too radical, they will not believe you. At best, you will confuse customers. At worse, they will outright reject this new notion and your brand.

Making significant changes to Brand Character requires you to know where you are going, to identify and manage your way over there, and to understand that potential customers will need time to get comfortable with the changes. It will also take commitment and constancy of effort. Finally, the emerging new Brand Character will be communicated via each element of the marketing mix, not just advertising. My grandmother counseled me (again, one of the authors) not to just listen to what people say but to observe what they do. What they do is more telling regarding their true character. Similarly, an evolution or change in the Brand Character is very likely to require formulation changes, new packaging architecture and/or graphics, trademark modification, endorsements, line extensions, addition of new services, and so on. Brand character comes from more than what you say. Potential customers perceive it by everything that you do.

Guiding and Checking Your Work

Let's use the Brand Positioning Add-Valuator to check your Brand Character statement to ensure that it is technically correct and competitive. Assess each of the following four points by noting whether you "Don't Agree," "Agree Somewhat," or "Strongly Agree." Tally each box and step back to take stock of where you are with your Brand Character statement. Importantly, identify the indicated actions you must take to achieve a "Strongly Agree" rating and then take those actions.

Brand Positioning Add-Valuator

Brand Character	Don't Agree (0)	Agree Somewhat (3)	Strongly Agree (5)	Indicated Actions
1. Narrative description (or, better yet, 3-D portrayal) of a person or thing.				
2. Fits the brand's bundle and/or capitalizes on the brand's equity.				
3. Addresses an aspirational badge or the relationship of the brand to the Target Group.				
4. Serves to meaningfully differentiate the brand from the competition.				
Total Score				

KEY POINTS, PRINCIPLES & PRACTICES
Summary

✓ Brand Character is a strategic element of brand positioning and most influences imagery and the relationship to the target customer.

✓ Brand Character deals with *who* your brand is as a personage. It defines and reflects the personality of the brand.

✓ It should not be confused with tone, which denotes mode or style of expression. Tone is an executional element. Brand Character is a strategic element.

✓ Keep in mind that if all the product's communications or, at least, the most impactful ones reflect the same tonality, your customers and your potential customers will come to perceive that tonality as the brand's personality.

✓ Brand Character may be used to differentiate products with common features and benefits.

✓ It may also provide customers with an additional important reason to choose your product. It encourages customer affiliation and a potential positive relationship.

✓ Successful brand characters are engineered.

✓ The Brand Character is not a description of the Target Customer.

✓ The source of the Brand Character is either aspirational, to encourage badging, or a reflection of the relationship of the brand to the Target Customer.

✓ The successful brand character is reflected not just in words but in all elements of the marketing mix. It gains meaning from everything you do, from product formulation, to packaging, to servicing.

✓ Moreover, at the same time, Brand Character influences everything you do. Marketing-mix elements such as product development and design, and line extensions, will be informed, and influenced, by the Brand Character statement.

✓ In defining the Brand Character, use words that you would use in talking about a friend's, a family member's, or even your own personality.

✓ Anytime you come across a word to describe Brand Character that does not identify a personality trait or value, throw it out! It does not belong there.

✓ It important not only to ensure that each word identifies a personality trait but also to ensure that all the personality traits are in harmony.

✓ In developing the Brand Character statement, get beyond the abstract and start with something concrete.

✓ One of the most productive techniques is to identify a celebrity who you believe best characterizes your product and intended brand bundle. We start by asking, *"If your brand were a celebrity, who would it be?"*

✓ Next, define the personality characteristics of the chosen celebrity.

✓ Then, identify personality characteristics you wish to establish for your brand consistent with the product features and brand bundle. Everyone has a multitude of personality characteristics. The marketer's challenge is to select those few that best match up and create the Brand Character you wish to establish.

✓ Another technique that may be employed in going from the abstract to the concrete in developing Brand Character is the use of animals, magazines, other brands, and societal roles.

✓ Remember to link specific personality characteristics with product attributes, features, and/or benefits. The brand characteristics are more than wishful thinking.

✓ Go beyond the use of adjectives and state the Brand Character as a narrative.

✓ Better yet, articulate the Brand Character in a three-dimensional form. Use photos or film and you will have a more compelling way to define, communicate, and make understandable the desired brand character you wish to establish.

✓ Making significant changes to the brand's character requires you to know where you are going, to identify and manage your way over there, and to recognize that it will take time for potential customers to get comfortable with the changes.

✓ The emerging new Brand Character must be communicated via each element of the marketing mix, not just via advertising.

✓ Brand character comes from more than what you say. Potential customers perceive it by everything that you do.

DISPATCHES™
Insights On Brand Development From The Marketing Front

GETTING CHARACTER REFERENCES
FOR YOUR BRAND

Of all the brand positioning elements, Brand Character remains perhaps the toughest to understand readily and to express clearly among ourselves and to others within the company. It's not so much that we, marketers and our colleagues, don't get the concept that a brand's character is, essentially, its personality (its "who-ness," rather than its "what-ness"). No, most of us understand that. What seems to make articulating this "who-ness" so difficult is simply not having an adequate language at our disposal. We fall back time and again on what seems to be the universal "sameness" language for expressing the Brand Character—a string of four or five adjectives, such as "leader-like," "caring, "popular," and "trusted." While such "universal" adjectives often reassure the corporate chieftains (how could they not?), they do nothing to help brand builders differentiate their brand's personality from the others in the category.

What's needed are new, more telling ways—new reference points, really—for making a brand's differentiated personality intelligible to everyone who has a hand in building the brand. Here are some suggestions for those reference points, some "character references," if you like:

1. *The One Word.* If you were forced at gunpoint to utter only one word—noun, adjective, verb, you name it—that would distinctively capture your brand's personality, what would that word be? Even better, what one word would your most loyal customers utter most often? While we don't know this for certain, a good guess at what Energizer battery users might utter is "energizing" (or, perhaps, "energetic"). On the other hand, you might expect Duracell battery users to say something like "dependable." The important thing here is the distinction between these two; each brand has ownership of a differentiating personality trait.

2. *The Versus.* They say that a person is known by the company she keeps, but it's also true that she can be known by the company she doesn't keep—in other words, by who she is not. Translating this approach to our brands, it's often helpful to express your brand's character versus that of another, contrasting brand's in a format that says who your brand is and who it isn't. So, for example, we might say the brand character of Virgin Airlines is "cheeky" (to use a British term) without being "smug" like British Airways. In this way, Virgin's impudent personality is a positive, fun-filled one. Or we might assume that Nokia's character is like that of a "trendsetter," whereas Motorola's is like that of a "journeyman" (i.e., one who is always reliable, if not colorful).

3. *The Thought-Bubble.* You've seen in comic strips and books how sometimes a character's thoughts are made known to the reader via a text-box "bubbling" up from his head. What if you sketched one of your typical, loyal brand users with one of these bubbles? What short, positive expression—revealing how the user truly feels about your brand as a person—might it contain? The Charles Schwab loyalist might be thinking, "Here's a straight-shooter, someone who never has hidden agendas or ulterior motives, the only one without a poker face." A different way of expressing the brand's personality, but one that differentiates it (from Fidelity Investments, T. Rowe Price, and the others) nevertheless.

4. *The Party.* Some of the beer brands have been known to use this technique at focus groups with their consumers. The premise is that there is a wild party going on and your brand just showed up as the latest arrival; consumers are asked to describe what happens now to/at the party. It's an indirect way of expressing a brand's personality impact. So, what DOES happen when your brand shows up? Maybe when Wal*Mart shows up, the music switches to twangy country-western mixed with schmaltzy patriotic tunes and everyone orders a Busch beer. But when Target arrives, the music abruptly goes to alternative, and it's Kahlua B-52s for the house. In these shifts, one can discern two very different brand personalities: Wal*Mart as the down-home, "block party" partier; Target as the cool and convivial partier.

5. *The Analogy.* One of the most surefire ways to express a brand's characters is by embodying it in someone or something else that nearly everyone knows—a celebrity, a comic book character, a radio station type, or some icon-like brand from a totally unrelated category. For example, Campbell's Soup might be the oldies station, whereas Progresso Soup would be the classical station. Or, you might describe Kitchen-Aid appliances as Rolls-Royces and Kenmore (the Sears brand) appliances as Chevrolets. These kinds of analogous descriptions provide fertile images so that just about anyone can picture the distinctive personality traits that separate one brand from another.

What should be clear from working with these kinds of "character references" is that articulating and communicating a brand's character really means bringing the brand to life. And it's nearly impossible to give life to a brand—as if it were a real person—when all you have at your disposal is dead language. We often talk of (and have written previously about) making the extra effort to give your brand a "3-D Brand Character"—which means expressing it in at three distinct ways: words, pictures, and sounds. Using some of these character references will help you get those added dimensions.

BOATS & HELICOPTERS

1. First thing, make the identification and articulation of a truly differentiated (i.e., differentiated within your category) Brand Character a live project on your brand. Assemble the right resources to get it done—such as your agency's creative team, your package design creative personnel, and your more creative market research types.
2. Next, set only one ground rule: no string of overused, categoric adjectives allowed.
3. State the Brand Character as a narrative or, better yet, in a 3-D format such as a short film clip.
4. Set up some qualitative research and work through some of the character reference exercises presented earlier.
5. Once you have the character expressed just about right, do the most important thing of all: Identify what specific product, packaging, advertising, merchandising, promotion, and other initiatives you will have to implement to continue fostering your differentiated character in the minds and hearts of your target users.

Give your brand a character reference!

CHAPTER EIGHT

"Wax-on, Wax-off; Brush-up, Brush-down."
—Mr. Miyagi

Chapter 8

Pulling Together a Strategically Appropriate and Actionable Brand Positioning Strategy

Now it's time to pull together your Brand Positioning Strategy Statement for your brand that's strategically appropriate and actionable (i.e., technically sound).

Wax-on, Wax-off

In the movie *The Karate Kid*, a gang of thugs is terrorizing Daniel, a teenager new to their high school. Unfortunately, his tormentors are dedicated students and enthusiastic practitioners of Karate. Which means that Daniel takes a lot of abuse. Physical abuse! In an effort to put an end to his torment, or just to survive for the moment, he challenges one of his assailants to a match at a future Karate tournament. His only salvation is to learn Karate and learn it fast.

Mr. Miyagi, an elderly Okinawan-American who has befriended Daniel, offers to teach him the empty-hand way of self-defense. Mr. Miyagi takes Daniel to his home, where he puts the rather nervous and frightened teen to work reconditioning his deck and wooden fence. He instructs Daniel in a technique to "wax-on" and "wax-off," to recondition the deck wooden floor. He shows Daniel how to "brush-up" and "brush-down," to paint the fence. After a few days of this backbreaking, muscle-aching work, the frustrated Daniel rebels and confronts Miyagi. He tells Miyagi he is tired of being his personal slave. He needs Mr. Miyagi to teach him Karate, not to take advantage of his availability and work him to exhaustion.

Mr. Miyagi responds by demanding that Daniel show him the technique used to wax-on and wax-off. The boy goes through it halfheartedly. Mr. Miyagi demonstrates and has Daniel imitate the technique with focus and precision. He also barks out an order that Daniel show him the technique he taught him to brush-up and brush-down when painting the fence. Once again, Daniel makes scant effort to execute the technique properly. So Mr. Miyagi shouts for the boy to focus. When Miyagi gets the response he is looking for, he throws a flurry of quick punches and kicks at young Daniel, who deftly blocks each one with the wax-on and wax-off, brush-up and brush-down techniques he has learned and applied over the preceding days in his labors.

Up to now, with each exercise we have undertaken, we have been engaged in waxing-on and waxing-off, brushing-up and brushing-down. Unto themselves, the exercises are highly productive but limited their importance. Put the results together, and we could have the start of something big. We have everything we need to pull it all together into a competitive Brand Positioning Strategy Statement.

If you have been diligent in participating in the exercises using the tools presented in the previous chapters, you can easily piece together a draft Brand Positioning Strategy Statement. So use the format we created, which is provided on the next page, to create a Brand Positioning Strategy Statement for the product or service you are responsible for marketing. This format is more detailed and sophisticated than the classic model to assist in developing a well thought out and competitive positioning strategy. As we have stated from the beginning of this book, it will not lead you "what" to think but, instead, assist you in "how" to think. It will leverage "what" you think to capitalize on your unique knowledge, experiences and talent. As you pull together the various elements you completed, be prepared to edit, edit, and then edit again. This is an iterative process!

Brand Positioning Strategy Statement

To *(Target Group):*
- Demographics
- Psychographics
- Patient—Condition/Lifestage/Targeted Occasion
- Attitude about Condition, or treating it, etc.
- Current Usage and Dissatisfactions
- Telling Behaviors
- Needs (Rational and Emotional)

_____ *(Brand Name)*

is the brand of _____ *(Perceptual Competitive Framework)*

competing mainly with _____ *(Literal Competitive Framework)*

that_____
                            (Benefit)
because_____.
                    (Reason-Why Support)
The Brand Character is _____
                            (Brand Character)

In order to assist you, we have two examples that we have inferred. The first is for a prescription product, Lipitor, and is aimed at health care practitioners (HCPs). This is a Pfizer brand whose patent will be expiring in the near future. It is also one of the largest, if not the largest, prescription brands, with sales at its peak in excess of $12 billion worldwide. The second is for Gatorade, a fast-moving consumer good (FMCG). The Gatorade positioning we share here is pre-"G," (or stated another way, just for its base product on which the brand was built). Use these examples as models. Imitate them in pulling together your Brand Positioning Strategy Statement. We will call your attention to those areas that we find most troublesome to architects of the brand positioning strategy and articulating it.

Inferred Lipitor Brand Positioning Strategy Statement—Example

To *(Target Customer):*
- **Demographics-Psychographics:** *"Goal-oriented" GPs, Internists, Cardiologists, Endocrinologists, and Lipidemiologists*
- **Patient-Condition:** *Treating adults, typically 35+ with hyperlipidemia and multiple risk factors (some combination of family history, high blood pressure, age, high BSL, low HDL, smoking, etc.) for CAD and ACS (heart attacks and stroke).*
- **Attitudes regarding treating condition:** *These physicians are concerned that, left untreated or not properly treated, the condition could lead to serious complications and premature death. They believe the key to successful outcomes is to get key lipid numbers to healthy goals for these patients and thereby avoid CAD and ACS.*
- **Current Usage and Dissatisfactions:** *They currently prescribe diet and exercise as first-line treatment, followed by statins when the former fails. They are frustrated that, no matter how much better the lipid profile becomes, they still can't reach the desired levels for their patients with diet and exercise alone and/or with other statins.*
- **Telling Behaviors:** *Refer patient to dietician. Provide counseling to change lifestyle.*
- **Needs**
  - **Rational:** *Achieve heart-healthy lipid goals for more of their patients; and*
  - **Emotional:** *Self-Assurance that they are doing their best to reduce their patients' risk for CAD and ACS.*

<u>Lipitor</u> *(Brand)* **is the brand of** *(Perceptual Competitive Framework) Proven Heart-Healthy Lipid Goal Achiever and CAD Risk Averter competing mainly with (Literal Competitive Framework) cholesterol-reducing agents such as Vytorin, Crestor, and Zocor.*

That (Benefit): *you can trust Lipitor will help you achieve heart-healthy lipid goals for more of your patients (particularly when combined with diet and exercise) and* *significantly reduce their risk factors for CAD and ACS (i.e., heart attack and stroke).*

Because *(Reasons-Why Support)* Lipitor is:
- *Clinically proven to reduce LDL-C: 39–60% and TG: 19–37% and to raise HDL-C: 5–9%*
- *Clinical studies demonstrate it reduces the risk of revascularization by 42%, Nonfatal MI by 45%, and Stroke by 48%*
- *The #1 prescribed cholesterol-lowering agent*
- *Your experience with Lipitor*

The *(Brand Character)*: *Lipitor is a trusted, honest, achievement-oriented companion whom you can always count on to help you achieve your goals. He is totally reliable and won't let you down regardless of the situation.*

Starting at the top of the Lipitor statement with the Target Customer, carefully review the Demographics and Psychographics. The demography is composed of health care practitioner labels such as "internists." This may seem like a broad target, but the key operative is the psychographic "goal-oriented," which is highlighted by placing it in quotes (and you should denote your psychographic target by placing it in quotes also). The psychographic label, which denotes a specific segment mindset, runs through the demography to provide focus. One does not have to go into more depth than shown in the Lipitor example. However, you may choose to include more information about the target (e.g., married, children, social involvement) to add texture and, in that way, enhance everyone's understanding of the Target Customer.

Next comes the Patient-Condition when working in the health care sectors (regardless of whether we are dealing with pharmaceuticals or medical devices). Health care marketers need to define not only the HCP but also the patient target for whom the brand will best meet the target's specific needs. Ultimately, all pharmaceuticals and medical devices are used to serve the patient population. Even if a device will ease the stress of performing a procedure, it can be expected to benefit a patient type in some way.

When articulating the attitudes of the HCP, it is critically important to ensure that these are relevant to the psychographic segment you have chosen and that they, ultimately, tie to giving your brand meaning. In the inferred Lipitor case, these attitudes reveal insights into what makes these HCPs "goal oriented." It helps establish the relevant, meaningfully differentiated values of Lipitor, which are to help this HCP target to achieve healthy lipid goals for more of their patients, particularly those patients at high risk for CAD and ACS.

When it comes to defining current usage, be specific. Don't be reluctant to name "names" of products your target is currently using to treat the patient and the condition. The dissatisfactions are quite important and deserve your attention. List them. These will lead to the needs that your brand strategy will seek to exploit.

The telling behaviors are about what else your target does in dealing with the patient and condition. Again, these need to be relevant to the target (both HCP and patient). They help provide insight into the thinking, level of commitment, and even values of your target.

As with needs, please don't stop with rational needs. Include emotional needs, too. Get inside the head of your HCP target, and express the emotional need inherent in meeting the rational, functional needs with your offering.

Check that you have both a Perceptual and a Literal Competitive Framework. The literal framework is more than your class of drug or standard of identity. It represents the market in which you compete, however you define it. The Perceptual Competitive Framework is a label for "what" you ultimately wish your brand to be perceived as being that clearly marks it as different from all other entries in the market in which it competes. The Perceptual Competitive Framework label is a noun, not a verb. If it is a verb, then you are probably stating a benefit and need to correct it. While the Perceptual Competitive Framework leads to the Benefit, it is not a benefit. Think of this as naming a new segment. In this case, it is a segment of one—your brand.

Benefits must match the needs. After all, the brand must fulfill the customer's needs via the Benefit. The benefits you choose to put in the Benefit section must be competitive. In other words, they spell out your uniqueness (not in features but in promise) and drive customer preference for your brand. Look to see that you have articulated the Benefit as we recommended, borrowing from the Benefit Laddering tool. You should have a product, customer and emotional benefit (just as you should have a product, customer, and emotional need in the needs section of the Brand Positioning Strategy Statement).

In the Reasons-Why section, give us nothing but the facts here. These are features and attributes of the product and brand. This is not a place to stash more benefit claims. If something reads like a benefit, then it doesn't belong here. A reason-why should be present for each functional benefit, what the product does and what the results are for the customer. Remember, these can help make the Benefit more compelling to the target customer. So don't use the same reasons-why as your competitors. Select those facts that not only support your benefits but distinguish your offering.

Now comes the Brand Character. If you are listing personality attributes such as "caring, authority, trustworthy," then STOP IT! This should be a narrative to aid in understanding the brand personality. This Brand Character should be not a reflection of the target but instead a reflection of the brand as it relates to the Target Customer—either aspirational, to encourage badging, or a way to reinforce the relationship of the brand to serving the customer.

One final note for all of you HCP marketers: This brand positioning strategy work needs to be started early in the development process of the compound, device, or equipment. For pharmaceuticals, we believe it should begin following phase 1 clinical trials. At this time you have some feel for what your compound can do, and yet it is sufficiently early to direct and influence future product development and clinical activity to drive realization of a relevant and meaningfully differentiated brand strategy. The same goes for medical devices and equipment. Once an idea appears on the radar, it is essential for marketing to get involved and to represent the needs of the customer within the context of gaining a strategic advantage in the marketplace.

Now for the Gatorade review:

Inferred Gatorade Brand Positioning Strategy Statement—Example

To (Target Customer):
- **Demographics-Psychographics:** *Active athletes of all ages and performance levels who love to compete and who perceive themselves as "winners" like their alpha athlete heroes*
- **Patient-Occasion:** *Pre-competitive hydration, refueling during and following athletic performance*

- **Attitudes regarding occasion and competing:** *These athletes believe that proper hydration and refueling during sweating are essential in order to perform at one's best. All serious (i.e., world-class) athletes do it!*
- **Current Usage and Dissatisfactions:** *They currently rely heavily on liquid replenishment (especially water, juice drinks, other isotonic beverages) to perform at their competitive best but find that they often fail to provide the added energy to take them over the top to win. .*
- **Telling Behaviors:** *Emulate their favorite alpha athletes by patterning their basketball shot or golf swing after them. Brag about their success at the water cooler.*
- **Needs**
  - **Rational:** *Replenish essential fluids and minerals lost through competition to restore energy; and*
  - **Emotional:** *Feel like they have the competitive edge of alpha athletes.*

<u>Gatorade</u> *(Brand)* **is the brand of** *(Perceptual Competitive Framework) Ultimate Liquid Athletic Equipment* competing mainly with *(Literal Competitive Framework) other sports beverages, water, juices, and even soft drinks.*

That (Benefit): *Provides unsurpassed replenishment of essential fluids and minerals lost through competition to restore energy and provide you with the competitive edge of your favorite sports heroes to make you a winner.*

Because *(Reason-Why Support)*:
- *Gatorade's 6% carbohydrate "science of sweat" formulation;*
- *Clinically proven at Gatorade's High-Performance Laboratory;*
- *Official sports beverage of, and used by, all major U.S. professional leagues (e.g., National Basketball Association, Major League Baseball, National Football League).*

The *(Brand Character)*: *That fiercely competitive alpha athlete teammate who serves as a role model and provides all the know-how, encouragement, motivation, and assistance you need to bring out the winner in you.*

The Brand Positioning Add-Valuator Tool

Your work is not complete until you employ the Brand Positioning Add-Valuator tool. It will help you assess your Brand Positioning Strategy Statement and identify ways in which you may add value in ensuring that it is technically sound and competitive. This tool helps objectify your subjective judgment. It uses a rating and weighting system. But we are going for more than rating scores. The purpose is to identify both the areas of the Brand Positioning Strategy Statement that need improvement and the direction needed to strengthen the statement. Give it a try, and then go back and edit your brand positioning statement so that it is technically perfect! You'll find the complete Add-Valuator tool at our website, *www.competitivepositioning.info.* Good luck! You've come a long way to creating brand loyalty. Next is to reflect it in everything you do—Power Positioning.

KEY POINTS, PRINCIPLES & PRACTICES
Summary

✓ Build your Brand Positioning Strategy Statement from all the pieces you have assembled for each element, using the tools and undertaking the exercises offered in this book.

✓ Start at the top. Clearly and completely define the Target Customer group. Include a psychographic, and call attention to it by putting it in quotes.

✓ Identify a Perceptual Competitive Framework (PCF) label to serve to differentiate your brand and avoid marketplace commoditization. Also, use the PCF as a "North Star" to guide the development of the brand.

✓ The Perceptual Competitive Framework must lead to, and link with, the Benefit.

✓ The Literal Competitive Framework goes beyond the standard of identity or class of drugs. It includes products that represent your source of volume. It represents the market in which you have chosen to compete.

✓ The Benefit needs to be relevant to the Target Customer group. Additionally, the Benefit needs to be meaningfully differentiated from that of your competition. Go beyond the product benefit to identify a customer and an emotional benefit. These articulations of the benefits must be in alignment to ensure the brand promise is single-minded.

✓ The Reasons-Why must be incontrovertible in a court of law. They are undisputable proof that the brand can deliver on its Benefit promises. Reasons-Why must link to Benefits in the Brand Positioning Strategy Statement. Adding an extrinsic Reason-Why to intrinsic proof can help your promise be more compelling.

✓ The Brand Character Statement reflects the brand bundle and the brand's relationship to the Target Customer group. A narrative provides a more clear understanding of the brand's personality.

✓ Use each positioning element to inform the next.

✓ Also allow each element to enlighten your thinking regarding previous element inputs.

✓ Revise accordingly, and iterate your way to a Brand Positioning Strategy Statement that is technically sound and competitive.

✓ Use the Brand Positioning Add-Valuator to help make your Brand Positioning Strategy Statement technically sound. You'll find the Brand Positioning Add-Valuator at *www.competitivepositioning.info*.

CHAPTER NINE

So you think you have a competitive brand positioning?
Well, unless you have already "cross-checked" it
against the current positioning of your key competitors,
you'll never know for sure.

Chapter 9

Getting the Big Picture with the Positioning Matrix

As we have seen so far, crafting a unique brand positioning requires deep "spade work" and a fair amount of creativity—within *each* of the six elements of a Brand Positioning Strategy Statement. But being unique doesn't necessarily mean being competitive, which should be the goal for any brand positioning. How can you know, really, how competitive your brand's positioning strategy is without (as noted above) "cross-checking" the *inferred positionings* of your key competitors?

Ensuring a Competitive Brand Positioning

This notion of "cross-checking" (what good pilots do constantly with their various aircraft instruments, to keep the plane headed in the right direction) should be taken literally because the very best way to size up the competitiveness of *your* brand's positioning strategy is to lay it out right next to those of your competition. As you can see in the following matrix (which appears on the next page), this laying out of positioning statements is nothing more than a build on the basic structure of a classic Brand Positioning Strategy Statement—a format twist to display your thinking:

Positioning Matrix

Brand	Target Group	Customer Needs	Competitive Framework	Benefit	Reason-Why	Brand Character
Your Brand	Demographics: Psychographics: Attitudes: Usage & Dissatisfaction: Telling Behaviors:	Rational: Emotional:	Brand of (PCF): Competing With (LCF):			
Competitor	Demographics: Psychographics: Attitudes: Usage & Dissatisfaction: Telling Behaviors:	Rational: Emotional:	Brand of (PCF): Competing With (LCF):			

The simplicity of this displayed-thinking matrix tool is evident, but, once each square is filled in, the matrix becomes a highly analytical tool, as well. Of course, the value of any analysis you do with the matrix is directly proportional to the validity of the square inputs. Completing the matrix squares for your own brand should be the easy part, assuming you already have built your own brand positioning. Here are some pointers for the more difficult part—inferring the Brand Positioning Strategy Statement (in bullet-point fashion) for each of your key competitors:

- *Assemble a varied team of colleagues whose opinions you value and trust (e.g., from your creative agencies, from other category brands within the Company, from R&D, from Consumer Intelligence).*

- *Also assemble as many consumer/customer "touch-points" for each competitive brand as possible: packaging, package inserts, advertising, selling materials, website pages, promotional materials, product (!), and so on.*

- *Spend the better part of a day having these multifunctional team members complete their inferred take on what each competitor's brand positioning is.*

- *Pull together a consensus positioning strategy statement*

Once you have consensus positioning strategies for your key competitors, it's a good idea to put them aside for a few days, let them "incubate," so to speak, and then look at them again with fresh eyes (and maybe even with the those of other colleagues who didn't take part in the consensus build-up). Now you're ready for the analytical work—trying to objectively assess which brand in the category or class has the most competitive positioning platform.

This assessment requires at least two phases: the *judgment phase* and the *check-out* phase. In the judgment phase, you're still relying on intuition (as well as on any inside knowledge you may have regarding the strengths and weaknesses of your category). In the check-out phase, you're confirming and amending the collective judgments by hearing from category users—preferable loyal or regular users of each brand, who typically have the best grasp of their brand's current positioning.

Positioning Matrix Analysis—Judgment Phase

Over the years of assembling many positioning matrices with our clients, we have found that the most challenging aspect of the ensuing analysis is in laying aside your natural biases and *objectively* assessing your competitors' brand positioning strategies. Somehow we can always see the errors of our enemies' ways, but we have a much tougher time acknowledging shortcomings of our own. Maybe you've heard the occasional marketer say something like this about their number one competitor: "We hope they keep doing what they're doing because they are really screwing up." To help avoid natural biases like these, we think it's a good idea to assume—if only for the sake of argument— that your brand positioning is not currently the best, strongest, or most competitive in the category (a kind of devil's advocate posture).

Once you've done this, here are the steps we recommend to quickly get into the matrix and decipher its points of strength and weakness:

1. *Use the 5 Cs Checklist* against each inferred positioning strategy. This will enable you to determine how well each holds up *technically* on Clarity, Completeness, Cohesiveness, Competitiveness, and Choice-Fullness. By way of review, here again is our synopsis of the "5-Cs of Technical Competence":

5-Cs of Technical Competence

> **Clear**—language is incapable of being misunderstood
>
> **Complete**—contains all essential elements and parts
>
> **Competitive**—expresses differentiation; creates preference
>
> **Cohesive**—all the parts are well-linked
>
> **Choice-Full**—it's single-minded; not all things to all people

2. *Check the "natural pairs"* to see how well each acts as sides of the same coin. These pairs, which reflect one another, include Needs and Benefits, Benefits and Reasons-Why, and Target and Brand Character.

3. *Identify where differentiation lies.* In which of the squares does a brand offer a real or perceived, meaningful difference (relative to its chosen Target Customer, that is)?

4. *Judge which positioning appears most competitive* and then take a shot at articulating the implications for your brand (even if your brand is judged the most competitive).

To practice using these steps, here is a Positioning Matrix we inferred (which appears on the next page) after some recent work in Australia—for three leading toothbrushes: Colgate 360, Oral-B CrossAction, and Reach Clean & Whiten. After your analysis, which one would you select as being the most competitive?

Positioning Matrix—Advanced Toothbrush Category
(Australian Market—Circa 2007)

Brand	Target	Needs	Competitive Framework	Benefits	Reasons - Why	Brand Character
Colgate 360	Adult, manual brush users, who are "Clean Seekers"; usually floss and use mouthwash	A cleaner mouth (beyond teeth)	*Is the Brand of* Whole Mouth Cleaner *Competing with* manual and advanced brushes	Provides a whole mouth clean	--Clinical Study: more plaque removal --Clinical Study: 96% bacteria removal --Tongue cleaner	Outgoing, well intentioned, but does not take self too seriously
Oral B Cross Action	Adult, manual and advanced toothbrush users who are "Oral Health Intensives"; typically floss, use plaque wash, see dentist often	Better plaque removal —for healthier teeth and gums	*Is the Brand of* Advanced Plaque Remover *Competing with* manual and advanced brushes, plaque rinses	Provides better plaque removal* —for healthier teeth and gums (*than manual brushes)	--Patented "criss-cross" bristle design --The brush more dentists use	Professional and matter of fact; highly efficient
Reach Clean & Whiten	Younger adult, manual and advanced brush users, who are "Whitening Aware"; use whitening toothpaste but not much else	An (easy) whiter-brighter smile and clean teeth	*Is the Brand of* Easy Smile Brightener *Competing with* manual and advanced brushes, whitening pastes; probably not strips	Provides white, bright, clean teeth— easily	--Unique "micro-scrubbers" (to whiten) --Bristles (to clean)	Youthful, friendly; easy-to-know and like

Our choice for "most competitive" would be Oral B's CrossAction, which is single-mindedly focused on plaque removal for a very informed target and which has a "better than" claim in its Benefit. But what we think matters a lot less than what Australian toothbrush consumers think—which lead us to the second analytical phase, *check-out.*

Positioning Matrix Analysis—Check-Out Phase

There are many research methods available, from qualitative to quantitative, that allow you to learn from category users (1) what the current brand positionings are, (2) which ones have the most appeal, and (3) what manufacturers might do to strengthen them. But the trick always comes down to this: how to get normal, everyday consumers (or, for drug brands, customers) to respond to "a positioning strategy"? After all, customers don't typically think in terms of brand positioning strategy. You can show them "white-card concept statements," but these often fall short--especially in communicating viscerally (either the Emotional Benefit or the Brand Character).

A better idea may be to show them some *advertising*--the same advertising you and your colleagues studied to come up with the inferred category positionings, in fact. See if heavy category users (including regular users of each brand in question) play back the same kinds of Needs, intended Target Customer, Competitive Frameworks, Benefits, and so on.

But there is still another form of "stimulus" that seems to work well in getting normal consumers to articulate what they take as a brand's positioning—*a short-form print ad.* This particular stimulus consists of only a Benefit-Headline, a Benefit or Reason-Why Sub-Head, and a Target Character (sometimes Benefit, too) Key Frame Visual. These are typically put together by one or more creative teams, usually via stock art and computerized graphics. To develop these, though, the creative teams must literally use the consensus positioning statements that the multifunctional team inferred earlier as "blueprints."

These kinds of minimal print ads actually make it easy for consumers and customers to "take a quick read"; they invariably evoke both rational and emotional responses, as well. And from these responses, you get the answers you're looking for, especially about which brand positioning in the category hits the most hot buttons, has the most appeal, is the most competitive.

Positioning Matrix—Other Vital Uses

While we've used the positioning matrix so far to better understand the relative competitiveness within a given category, the tool is by no means limited to this use alone, nor should it be thought of as a "set format." In our consulting work with clients over the years, we have found so many creative ways to employ the matrix. Here are some of those ways:

Positioning Matrix - Other Uses

1. Prior to new campaign development, review the *historical advertising* for the brand...and "track" the brand's positioning evolution through these historical snapshots.

2. When developing a positioning for a new product, use the matrix format to create a wide range of potential positionings—from close-in to far-out.

3. When seeking to update or "push the boundaries" of a well-worn positioning (established brand), use the matrix to position "companies/brands you admire" and apply what they do well to your brand (for example, how might Google® position your brand?)

4. Use the matrix to map out the transition/iterations from "where we are today" to "where we want to take the brand's positioning tomorrow."

5. Lay out differences in your brand's positioning that exist from (a) geographic region to region, (b) one target-constituency to another, or (c), for drug brands, one indication against another.

6. Finally, use the matrix to "house" a mega-brand's portfolio to help ensure that all line extensions or sub-brands within that portfolio actually belong!

This last use of the positioning matrix is truly a vital one. So many brands today have sprawled well beyond their original boundaries and now comprise a far-reaching set of products and sub-lines. This has made managing the portfolio much harder—especially managing what *additional* products will become part of the portfolio in the future (as opposed to becoming entirely new brands in their own right).

We often say that having a Portfolio Brand Positioning Matrix is a lot like having a current "family portrait"—you know, similar to those panoramic photos you sometimes see in which generations of the same, sprawling family are all pictured together for a family reunion. Much like the family portrait, the portfolio matrix enables the viewer (in our case, the portfolio marketing manager) to easily identify what traits the individual product members share in common—the bases for *why* a given product belongs in the brand portfolio. Take a look at this inferred portfolio matrix for the Snickers brand (which appears on the next two pages) and see if you can identify those traits each extension or sub-brand shares as a Snickers.

Snickers® Portfolio Brand Positioning Matrix
(Inferred Circa 2006)

	Target	Needs	Competitive Framework	Benefits	Reasons-Why	Brand Character
Snickers (Peanut)	"Trapped" teens and adults, those who find themselves "tied up" or confined for long periods (as in school, offices, airplanes) and who "variety-snack" between meals	A dependable "staple" or "regular" snack that will always relieve between-meal hunger while also satisfying craving for real taste indulgence	*Is the Brand of...* Favorite Snack Satisfier ***Competing mainly with . . .*** other chocolate candy/bars, cookies, salty snacks, energy bars	*That...Is* the one that completely relieves between-meal hunger in a more satisfying, taste-indulging way	*Because...* Snickers is "packed" with roasted peanuts (with implied food value), caramel, nougat, and milk chocolate that other bars lack	The strong, burly, often-comical friend who is always around when you need a boost or need to be "rescued" (e.g., the hard-blocking fullback ahead of the star tailback)
Almond	"Trapped" adults mainly, who also prefer the taste of almonds over peanuts (or simply the variety of both); they like Hershey's Almond candies and snack between meals	A dependable, "regular" snack/ alternative that will always relieve between-meal hunger while also satisfying craving for almond taste indulgence	*Is the Brand of...* Favorite Almond Snack Satisfier ***Competing mainly with...*** Hershey's Almond candies, other almond snacks, cookies, etc.	*That...Is* the one that completely relieves between-meal hunger in a more satisfying, almond-taste indulging way	*Because...* Snickers Almond combines roasted almonds (with implied food value), caramel, nougat, and milk chocolate that other bars/ almond snacks lack	The strong, burly, often-comical friend who is always around when you need a boost or need to be "rescued" (e.g., the hard-blocking fullback . . .")

continued...

Snickers® Portfolio Brand Positioning Matrix
(Inferred Circa 2006)

	Target	Needs	Competitive Framework	Benefits	Reasons-Why	Brand Character
Cruncher	"Trapped" teens and adults who also prefer crunchier-textured bars and snacks; they like Nestle Crunch/ Hershey's Krackel and snack between meals	A dependable, "regular" snack/ alternative that will always satisfy between-meal "crunchies" while also satisfying taste indulgence	*Is the Brand of...* Favorite Crunch Snack Satisfier *Competing mainly with...* Nestle Crunch, Hershey's Krackel, other crunch snacks	*That...*Is the one that better satisfies between-meal "crunchies" in a more taste-indulging way	*Because...* Snickers Cruncher combines the crunch of roasted peanuts, and crispy rice, plus caramel, nougat, and milk chocolate that other bars lack	The strong, burly, often-comical friend who is always around when you need a boost or need to be "rescued" (e.g., the hard-blocking fullback . . .")
Marathon Energy Bar From Snickers	"Trapped" and on-the-go teens/ adults who eat various energy bars either between meals or in place of them	A dependable between-meal or "quick meal" way to sustain energy— but in a way that actually tastes great	*Is the Brand of...* Favorite Energy Sustainer *Competing mainly with...* PowerBar, Clif Bar, Gatorade, and similar bars; other candy bars	*That...*Is the one that sustains energy with better taste than any other bar	*Because...* Marathon from Snickers is packed with 16 vitamins and minerals plus protein; peanuts, caramel, and milk chocolate other bars lack	The strong (physical and character) friend who is always around when you need a boost or to be encour-aged

A couple of things seem readily apparent from this portfolio look at Snickers:

- Snickers Almond and Cruncher line extensions are a tight fit with the "parent" (Snickers Peanut)—as all three deliver squarely against what the parent has long stood for: *hunger satisfaction and taste indulgence.* Even the driving between-meal occasion matches up well for these three family members.
- But the Marathon Energy Bar from Snickers (admittedly, a sub-brand, not a line extension) takes the brand into an entirely new need-state: *energy replenishment.* Yes, the taste promise is still there, but you have to wonder whether, without the hunger satisfaction and fully indulgent taste, this bar is *really* a Snickers.

The Matrix and the Big Picture

In this chapter's title we've referred to "Getting the Big Picture." Laying out your competitors' inferred brand positionings is one way of getting a bigger picture, or perspective on things--namely on your marketplace and just where your brand fits in that marketplace. But this notion of a Big Picture goes beyond even this "fit" perspective. It has to do with putting forth the honest, analytical effort to judge just how strong--in the absolute and relative to other brands--your brand positioning really is.

As we have taken apart each of the six positioning elements, we have focused more on how to craft a *technically sound* Brand Positioning, one that adheres to rock-solid principles that, if followed, lead to a written positioning statement that is crystalline in its clarity. But, just as being technically accurate doesn't guarantee a piece of historical fiction will read as a great story, neither does crafting a technically correct positioning guarantee great sales. To get those, you need a *strategically sound* (as in "one that really competes') positioning, too.

So, be hard-nosed in your judgments once you've laid out your positioning matrix. For each of the six blocks, ask yourself some questions like these:

Judgment Questions

- What, specifically, is my point of difference in this element of my positioning?

- How solid is my footing here; could my differentiation be neutralized, even made obsolete? How?

- What if I *did* place one of these other category brand names into my positioning--would it work for them, too?

Using the matrix tool like this will not only visualize for you the *real* Big Picture; it will also set you up for the logical next step: transforming your brand's positioning into a *Power Positioning.*

One Last (but Critical) Positioning Matrix—The "Official" One

Once you have a competitive brand positioning, as qualified following the Big Picture look at the marketplace, there is one other positioning format that we strongly recommend you complete: your brand's "Official" Brand Positioning. What makes it official are two things: each positioning element is aligned with the marketplace data and consumer/customer research to support it, and the positioning is signed (as in approved) by the company president.

The official positioning format is relatively simple—the left side of the matrix spells out the six essential brand positioning elements, and the right side specifies the research "evidence" supporting it. This evidence typically includes things like: Usage and Attitude Studies, Segmentation Studies, Consumer/Customer Preference Tests, Diary Panel data, Brand Interaction Volumetric data, and various forms of qualitative research findings (from focus groups, in-depth interviews, in-home or on-premise observations, and the like).

The "Official" Brand Positioning Statement

Positioning Elements	Research-Support
Target (Demo-Psychographics/ Attitudes):	• E.g., Psychographic Segmentation Study
Needs:	• E.g. , Usage and Attitude Study
Competitive Framework:	• E.g., Brand Interaction Data_____
Benefit(s);	• E.g., Blind Taste Test
Reasons-Why:	• E.g., Clinical Efficacy Study
Brand Character:	• E.g., In-Depth Consumer Interviews
Approved By Company President:_____	

Having your Brand Positioning Statement completed like this is very powerful, not only because it reflects the "due diligence" in support of each positioning element (proving that, unlike what some of our nonmarketing colleagues sometimes suspect, we marketers do not "make this stuff up as we go along"). But it becomes a critical reference tool for each function in the company to check when making decisions affecting the brand—to make sure whatever decisions are made are consistent with the brand's positioning. Perhaps most powerful of all, though, is the fact that the statement, once signed by the company president, becomes "gospel"—at least until new marketplace data or research suggests an evolution of the brand positioning is indicated (more on that in the next chapter).

KEY POINTS, PRINCIPLES & PRACTICES
Summary

✓ Once you're satisfied that you have a solid brand positioning strategy for your brand, put it to the acid test by comparing it to your key competitor's inferred positioning strategies. To infer these, start by collecting as many of the consumer (or, for drug brands, customer) "touch points" as you can: packaging, package inserts, advertising, selling materials, website pages, promotional materials, product (!), and so on. Using these as stimulus, work with your multifunctional team brand team to infer the competitor's intended Brand Positioning Strategy Statement.

✓ As a team, use the "5-C's of Technical Competence" to conduct a first analysis of how *technically* sound each competitor's positioning is. As part of this, also check for the "natural pairs" within each positioning: Needs and Benefits, Benefits and Reasons-Why, and Target and Brand Character. These pairs should link together in an almost seamless way. Finally, run a "differentiation" check on each element of the competitive brand positionings. In which squares does the brand offer a real or perceived point-of-difference (relative to its chosen Target Customer, of course)?

✓ Work with your market research and customer intelligence experts to devise some methods for checking out how *current (ideally loyal) users* of each competitive brand understand their brand's positioning strategy? There are any number of good techniques to transform a strategic brand positioning into something consumers and customers can readily respond to—for example, you can simply show them some of the same "touch points" your brand team used or have a creative shop mock up some "mini-print ads" that bring a brand's positioning to life.

✓ Be creative in your use of the Positioning Matrix format! It can be arranged to show different geographic positionings, different Target constituency positionings, and, for drug brands, different indications under the same brand.

✓ If your brand either houses or is part of a "mega-brand," work with the full internal team to lay out a Portfolio Brand Positioning Matrix. This becomes the "family portrait" that demonstrates why and how certain line extensions, sub-brands, and sub-lines are logically and strategically part of the same parent or mega-brand. And it serves as the ongoing "direction finder" as the parent considers what new items to add to the brand.

✓ Finally, after completing your own Brand Positioning Strategy Statement and the competitive matrix, complete an "Official" Brand Positioning Strategy Statement for your brand—with all the hard marketplace evidence that supports each positioning element—and, most important, with the company president's signature!

POSITIONING THE BRAND PORTFOLIO

Despite the Ries & Trout dictum from 25+ years ago that line extending is a mistake, brands today continue to proliferate themselves via extensions. To appreciate the degree to which line extending is advancing, you need only read any week's *Brandweek* or *Advertising Age*. For example, the cover story in the March 6 2003 issue of *Brandweek* was entitled "Hershey's Snack Binge: Hershey is planning a slew of new salty snacks. But is the company over-indulging?" Inside you learn that each new item in this "slew" is either a line extension or a sub-brand of one of their big brands. In fact, their CMO ends the article by reinforcing the company's commitment to this course: "We're not going to be everywhere in snacking. We're just going where we can leverage our core competencies in core brands like Hershey's and Reese's which are very extendable."

In the years since Ries & Trout proffered their misguided dictum, of course, we have seen many, many examples of successful line extensions and sub-brands (failures, too!). Whether you are looking at something reasonably small, like Starbucks Frappuccino (more a sub-brand) or at something quite large, like Doritos Cool Ranch® flavor (a classic line extension), you would have to conclude though, that line extending *can* be a very effective way to grow a brand. The key question, then, isn't so much "Should the brand consider extending?" Rather, the more compelling question is "As we extend, who's minding the brand store?" In other words, how carefully is the brand team building the brand portfolio—and according to what blueprint?

We often reference architects in our training programs: We say that they are typically the profession responsible for (a) designing the plan or blueprint for the new building and (b) then making sure each day of construction that the building is being built according to specification. We think brand teams have similar responsibilities to design the plan for building the brand (the Brand Positioning Strategy Statement) and to ensure that all the monies invested and actions initiated for the brand are consistent with that design. In keeping with this thinking, we also urge our clients who are extending their brands—which is virtually everyone—to construct and continue to map out their "brand portfolios" in a Positioning Matrix format. Sometimes we call this format an "Umbrella Positioning Matrix," but it could just as rightly be called a "Brand Portfolio Matrix."

Even when we are not actively working with a client, we practice constructing these matrices by inferring the positionings of brands that have extended their portfolios—brands like Olay or Neutrogena in skin care and Snickers in snacks. To give you some tips on constructing your brand's portfolio matrix, let's take a look at what we've inferred recently for the Snickers brand. Our inferences are based upon a close look at as many brand "touch points" as we can get: advertising, website, consumer promotion materials, packaging/labeling information, and so on. First, we'll lay out our inferred "Base-Snickers" or "Umbrella Snickers" brand positioning; then we'll highlight some matrix-building tips in our Boats & Helicopters section.

Umbrella Snickers Brand Positioning

1. *Target:* "Trapped" teens and adults, those who find themselves literally or just feeling "tied up" of confined for long periods (as in school, offices, airplanes) and who regularly "variety-snack" between meals…
2. *Needs:* A dependable "staple" or regular snack that will always relieve the targets' between-meal hunger while also satisfying their craving for real taste indulgence.
3. *Competitive framework:* Snickers is the brand of favorite snack satisfier, competing mainly with other chocolate candy/bars, cookies, salty snacks, and energy bars.
4. *Benefits:* Snickers is the one that completely relieves between-meal hunger in a more satisfying, taste-indulging way.
5. *Reasons-Why:* It is "packed" with roasted peanuts (with implied food value), caramel, nougat, and milk chocolate that other brands lack.

6. ***Brand Character:*** The strong, burly, often-comical friend who is always around when you need a boost or need to be "rescued" (e.g., the hard-blocking fullback ahead of the star tailback).

BOATS & HELICOPTERS

1. First and foremost, any extension or sub-brand of this umbrella must fit within the demographic and psychographic boundaries of the umbrella. In most cases, the umbrella target is a fairly broad one, easing the fit of new items underneath. In our inferred Snickers, there is breadth demographically (teens and adults) and on a use-occasion basis. So, extensions like Snickers Almond and Cruncher, as well as sub-brands like Marathon (Energy Bar) from Snickers, should all be aimed at teens and adults (not kids!) who use snacks and bars between meals.

2. The closest-in extensions—like Snickers Almond—should have fundamentally the exact same positioning, with obvious exceptions such as "satisfying their craving for *almond* taste indulgence" in the Needs section; "Favorite *Almond* Snack Satisfier" in the Competitive Framework (and probably the specific mention of "competing mainly with Hershey's *Almond* Bar"); "relieves between-meal hunger in a more satisfying, *almond-taste* indulging way" in the Benefits section; and "combines roasted *almonds*, caramel, etc." in the Reason-Why section.

3. As for further-out, brand-boundary stretching sub-brands like a Marathon from Snickers energy bar, there is room for some adding to the brand portfolio *provided there is also some obvious equity sharing by the sub-brand.* Marathon is, after all, an energy bar—and this represents a totally new category for Snickers to enter. The sub-brand must meet the new needs of that category to survive, but it must also transfer over to that category some of the Snickers equity, or else why label it Snickers? In this case, Marathon meets the basic energy need (between meals, of course!) and adds something new: the Snickers "craving for real taste indulgence." You would also logically expect that the Competitive Framework section would look somewhat different: "Favorite Energy Sustainer competing mainly with PowerBar, Clif Bar, Gatorade, etc. bars and some other candy bars." The word "Favorite" is important because it represents the transfer of Snickers taste-indulgence equity.

4. The trickiest part of the Brand Portfolio Matrix to manage may well be the Brand Character section. Upon first thought, you could well conclude that *any* extension or sub-brand underneath the umbrella brand must evidence the exact same brand character—it's the core genetics that holds the "brand family" together. But, if you think about it some more, you can appreciate that, while family members often share certain, visible genetic traits (like eye color or baldness) that have a genetic basis, they each have their own idiosyncratic personalities. As a general rule, we think that close-in flavor, color, or scent extensions should have brand characters identical to those of their "parent." But, with stronger sub-brands or with any additions aimed at expanding the Target (such as the Mercedes C-Class of a few years back), there is room to add some new dimensions to the existing umbrella character. The key word is "add," because, again, if the new item is to be labeled part of the Snickers family, then it should also evidence some of those family traits. Our take on Marathon from Snickers, therefore, might go something like this: "The strong (physical and character) friend who is always around when you need a boost or to be encouraged." This borrows some from the inferred umbrella character but also adds the notion of "strong physically" and of "an encouraging individual."

We hope there is enough of a "teaser" here to incite you to lay out a Brand Portfolio Matrix for your brand. Even more important, once you have this as a guide, you can make better decisions about where to take the brand next—and where NOT to take the brand next.

CHAPTER TEN

*"What you do tells me more about
who you are than what you say."*
—Grandma Jennie Napoli

*"Strategy is war games.
Execution is war itself."*
—Leo Kiely

Chapter 10

Going Beyond Words to Establish
Power Positioning

So, we have painstakingly pulled together a technically correct and strategically appropriate Brand Positioning Strategy Statement. In doing so, we have transformed our product (or service) into a brand. Our brand positioning work is complete. Right? Wrong! The creation of brand loyalty and, consequently, our professional lives should be so easy. Unfortunately, our work is just beginning in transforming a product made-up of features and attributes into a brand that is built upon an emotional connection with its followers.

Power Positioning

An insightful young marketer participating in one of our Brand Positioning & Communication College programs, came up with this to say about brand positioning: "It is uniquely tied to your brand. If any other brand tried to use the same positioning it would be false." Inherent in this statement is the notion of an ownable, competitive brand positioning. What we have with our technically correct and strategically appropriate Brand Positioning Strategy Statement is merely a blueprint for the origins and development of the brand.

Now we need to convert this blueprint into the real article. It's time for us to undertake the stewardship of brand building. We need to practice "Power Positioning." Power Positioning is reflecting the brand positioning strategy in all marketing mix elements and adapting it, over time, to reflect changes in the marketplace. In that way, we are able to create brand loyalty. When we are successful in practicing Power Positioning, the brand's competitive positioning becomes the source of the marketing strategy and initiatives. At the same time, the brand positioning becomes a product of the marketing strategy and initiatives. It's like the law of karma—what goes around comes around.

It's What You Do

In order to own a competitive brand positioning in the marketplace, that positioning must be reflected in everything you do, not just in what you say within the confines of your organization, or in the business press, or in your advertising. Too many managers believe that positioning is all about what you say in your advertising and, consequently, that is the limit of their use of it. But this is extremely shortsighted. It's wrongheaded. Brand positioning guides everything you do in building a brand. An ownable and competitive brand positioning, Power Positioning is established through your actions. It originates from your product (i.e., tangible and intangible factors that make up the "whole product"), the competitive landscape, customer needs, and the capabilities of your company to execute with quality, precision and, let's not forget, creativity against the brand positioning strategy. It is the unique relationship you establish with customers through what you do, not just what you say, in making the positioning strategy come to life.

Power Positioning is reflected in all the marketing-mix elements. This includes product design, pricing, advertising, promotion, and so on. We refer to these marketing-mix elements as the "positioning planks" for the brand. The Brand Positioning Strategy Statement is the blueprint that informs everything we do in support of the brand. Each of the marketing-mix elements represents a plank we set down to make the blueprint a reality in building our brand. The ownable brand positioning is built plank by plank. The sum of these planks constitutes the whole of customers' perceptions regarding your brand positioning and their relationship with it.

The execution of each positioning plank and their integration will have a profound effect on how competitive and ownable your brand positioning is with customers.

OTC Case History

Bayer Aspirin serves as an insightful case history. For many years, we thought of Bayer as nothing more than another pain reliever, an old-fashioned one at that. Aspirin had been the primary compound for the relief of everyday types of pain until we learned of its role in Reyes Syndrome, which can prove fatal to children. So American consumers curtailed their use of aspirin and switched to other analgesic compounds, most notably Tylenol.

But then Bufferin® conducted a study that showed that aspirin could reduce the chances of a second heart attack. Doctors began recognizing the benefit of aspirin and recommended it to their patients who suffered from coronary heart disease and were at risk for a catastrophic coronary event. While Bufferin was the sponsor of the study, Bayer seized upon these findings and changed its brand positioning from a mere pain reliever to a "heart health protector." This is an inferred brand positioning strategy for Bayer Aspirin:

Inferred Bayer Aspirin Brand Positioning Strategy

To *(Target Customer)*:

- **Demographics-Psychographics/Condition/Attitudes**: *Adults 35+ who perceive they are at risk for CHD. They may or may not have already experienced an event such as a heart attack. They may also have other cardiovascular conditions such as high blood pressure, hyperlipidemia, or (pre)diabetes. These "medical health conscious" people want to promote health maintenance into their old age, avoiding (further) potential catastrophic events such as heart attack and stroke. They believe they have the power to be proactive in caring for themselves to enable them to live longer.*

- **Current Usage/Telling Behaviors**: *They use OTC analgesics for pain such as Tylenol and Advil, which do not provide them with protection against catastrophic events. They take supplements and watch their nutrition, without going overboard. They get a medical check-up each year and follow the advice of their doctor. They are highly likely to take preventive measures such as getting an inoculation against the flu, shingles, pneumonia, and other diseases. They tend to be up to date on all their medical needs and are fairly compliant.*

- **Needs *(rational, emotional):*** Effective pain relief and assurance of protection against catastrophic CHD events.

Bayer is the brand of *(Perceptual Competitive Framework):* The Wonder Drug, competing mainly with *(Literal Conceptual Framework)* OTC analgesics such as Tylenol and Advil; Plavix; cholesterol reducers; and other medications.

That *(Benefit/s):* Works wonders to provide unsurpassed relief from pain and protection against catastrophic CHD events.

Because *(Reason-Why):*
- No analgesic has been shown to be more effective in relieving pain
- Extensive clinical studies show Bayer can reduce the risk of heart attack by 32%
- Clinical studies demonstrate it can reduce the risk of recurrent stroke

The Brand Character is: The bodyguard who stays close to you and helps you avoid problems before they occur. The bodyguard will also help alleviate any problems that you may stray into. He is always on the lookout for ways to help you stay safe and feel secure.

The brand positioning differences between Bayer Aspirin and Bufferin are highlighted in the following chart:

Bayer Aspirin versus Bufferin

	Bayer Aspirin	Bufferin
Product:	Aspirin	Aspirin
Target:	Proactive, health-conscious catastrophe avoiders	Pain sufferers
Needs:	Effective pain relief and assurance of avoiding CHD	Effective pain relief
Perceptual Competitive Framework:	The Wonder Drug	Aspirin
Literal Competitive Framework:	Pain relievers, heart-healthy medications (e.g., Plavix, cholesterol reducers) and supplements	Aspirin and other pain relievers
Benefits:	Works wonders in providing unsurpassed relief from pain and protecting you against catastrophic CHD events.	Effective pain relief
Reasons-Why:	• Pain relief clinical studies • Heart health clinical studies • MD recommendations	• Pain-relief clinical studies
Brand Character:	Bodyguard	Generic, old-fashioned

While having a competitive positioning strategy is essential, it is not enough. It is a sound start. As Leo Kiely, Chief Executive Officer of MillerCoors, is fond of saying, "Strategy is war games. Execution is war itself." Now the strategy must be seeded and driven in the marketplace. It's time to go to war. You might be saying to yourself that Bufferin could have played on this same ground. But that's the point. It didn't. Bayer Aspirin did. And it went one step further. Bayer Aspirin executed its competitive brand positioning strategy in everything, absolutely everything it undertook. Now if Bufferin tried to occupy this same positioning, it would be running into consumers' perceptions that this is Bayer territory.

Here are some of the ways Bayer took ownership of its brand positioning strategy in the marketplace:

- *Product:* It introduced an 81-milligram product (this is the level the FDA recognizes as providing heart protection in the United States) that can be taken daily, as if it were a supplement. Additionally, it introduced a product that combines Bayer Aspirin with a natural cholesterol reducer. However, the FDA pressured Bayer into taking it off the market. Too bad. One of the authors of this book really liked and used the product, and hopes that someday soon it will be allowed to be reintroduced into the marketplace.

- *Packaging:* Bayer Aspirin made a number of changes to its packaging to reflect its heart-healthy brand positioning. It added the Perceptual Competitive Framework "The Wonder Drug" to the package label. Additionally, it changed its package claim from "Fast, Safe Pain Relief" to "Fast, Safe Pain Relief Plus the Lifesaving Benefits of Aspirin." It also put a heart symbol on the package front.

- *Professional push:* It encouraged doctors to "Prevent the event. Recommend *aspirin.*" Bayer Aspirin established that some 27 million at-risk patients are missing the anti-platelet benefit of aspirin. Is this a generic message? Well, yes, but, because Bayer is the only brand to promote this benefit, it is the brand most likely to benefit the most from doctors' recommendations.

- *Clinical studies:* Bayer Aspirin has sponsored and/or kept abreast of clinical studies that prove aspirin's lifesaving benefits, which it continues to evolve and promote.

- *Website:* Its website details "The Wonders of Aspirin" as it relates not just to pain relief but possibly to saving your life.
- *Advertising:* Bayer Aspirin has had a number of successful campaigns touting its pain relief and heart-saving benefits. Its campaigns featured the following key copy words: "Pain relief and so much more," "Take it for pain. Take it for life," and "Expect wonders."
- *Promotion:* Bayer Aspirin has sponsored the American Heart Association's "Go Red" campaign.

Bayer Aspirin delivered an effective one-two punch: a competitive brand positioning strategy followed by Power Positioning. As a result, the brand was able to not just stop but reverse a pernicious sales decline.

As Michael Eisner, the former CEO of Disney, states, "A brand is a living entity—and it is enriched or undermined cumulatively over time, the product of a thousand small gestures." These gestures must be in tune with the Brand Positioning Strategy Statement you developed. But it is also important that we apply the brand's positioning strategy *creatively* with each positioning plank. Here are a few considerations:

- *Product.* The most important positioning plank is the product itself. Marketers need to know their products, really know them from the perspective of the customer and within the context of competitors' offerings. We need to overcome corporate myopia. An important way to do this is to actually see the product through the eyes of customers. Some questions you should ask include: What needs does the product satisfy that other products do not satisfy or satisfy as well? What are the key features and benefits to customers?

    An existing product needs to evolve to maintain and/or grow a brand positioning in a dynamic, changing marketplace (and what marketplace isn't?). The marketplace changes can be inspired by demographic, regulatory, or competitive dynamics, to name just a few. A product as mundane as a laundry detergent became a powerhouse brand when Tide Laundry Detergent brand instituted something like 55 product changes in just the first 20 years after its introduction. These changes in Tide Laundry Detergent are, importantly, a function of a leadership mindset and best practices (among which are being "customer centric"). The Tide brand group has proactively sought to harness available technology to deliver superior performance to consumers against competition. The Tide Laundry Detergent brand dominates the laundry detergent category in North America. Sales of Tide are larger than sales of the next nine brands combined. Moreover, the brand has been able to extend its life cycle and leadership despite the fact that it is more than 60 years old.

But the product itself is not enough. We must get beyond the product we sell and think about the customer experience we deliver. A prescription brand for arresting the development of rheumatoid arthritis contains the same compound as, and performs similarly, to its competitors. But this one brand offers an important intangible to make its "whole product" offering more attractive. The intangible is a value-added service, which enriches customers' experience with the brand. Specifically, it handles the paperwork to qualify patients for the treatment and to ensure insurance reimbursement for its medical professional customers.

- ***Intangibles.*** Intangibles add value beyond the mere physical dimensions of your product. While intangibles are not material to the product, they are anything but immaterial in their contribution to establishing an ownable and competitive brand positioning. Intangibles provide us with the opportunity to meaningfully differentiate our products and services from competition.

The introduction and marketing of NutraSweet illustrates the importance of intangibles. NutraSweet is the brand name for aspartame, a white powder that is 20 times sweeter than sugar. But when customers such as Coca-Cola and General Foods Corporation (now owned by Kraft, Inc.) purchased and reformulated their products with NutraSweet, they received much more than its physical qualities. They purchased something akin to a seal of approval, a positive halo that served to encourage trial and repeat purchase.

Consider this: Consumers are exposed to two cans of Diet Coke. Both have the same formulations. Both are formulated with NutraSweet. The only difference is that one can has the NutraSweet logo on it, with its identifiable red swirl, while the other can of Diet Coke does not. Consumers are asked to taste the product from each can and rate their preference. Guess what? Consumers overwhelmingly preferred the taste from the can of Diet Coke with the NutraSweet trademark and logo on it—even though both formulations were identical. An intangible value, this branding of NutraSweet had tangible results.

At the time, the NutraSweet Company went beyond branding to provide its customers with additional nonmaterial value. It provided a strong and meaningful "scientific base" in people and experience. This translated to assisting customers in the development of new product and/or improved product formulations using NutraSweet.

Intel is another company that has increased the value perception of computers using a strategy similar to that of NutraSweet. The familiar "Intel Inside" message serves to reassure customers that they are getting the most advanced, most reliable, and best performance from their computers. An intangible, this branding of Intel has a very tangible impact on customer perceptions and on business results for those computer manufacturers building with Intel microprocessors.

Intangibles may take the form of servicing, warranties, terms, branding, or special relationships.

- **Distribution.** This is usually treated as a given, rather than as an important component of marketing and brand positioning. The Coca-Cola Company employed it prudently in its more than 100-year history in growing the soft-drink category with its strategy and practice of making Coca-Cola available "just around the corner from everywhere." The company moved beyond the pharmacy through a unique (at the time), complex, and highly effective bottling distribution system that made the brand available in vending machines and at grocery stores, hotels, offices and factories, ballparks and where ever people in need of refreshment congregate. The Coca-Cola Company also set up a separate distribution system to aggressively go after fast-food outlets, capturing the lion's share of this business. Moreover, the company went well beyond the confines of U.S. borders to establish Coca-Cola as a global brand.

  Starbucks is another interesting example. As the purveyor of fine coffee beverages and European experiences moved eastward, it carefully picked cities and locales to get started in new geographies. But the really interesting distribution strategy was to precede establishment of its own retail outlets with venues within Barnes & Noble Booksellers stores. This enabled Starbucks to be discovered by prime prospects, seeded demand, and created a positive halo for its stand-alone retail outlets that were to follow.

Amazon.com is yet another interesting example worthy of your consideration. Its business is built upon a new distribution network, the Internet. Its distribution system is integral to its competitive positioning in the market and to its value. Amazon.com is the largest bookseller in the world. Founded in 1995, the company has zero square feet of retail space and a market cap of $4 billion. The biggest physical bookseller, the aforementioned Barnes & Noble, founded in 1873, has 11 million square feet of retail space and a market cap of $2.4 billion. As brand builders, we need to think through how and where we distribute in establishing an ownable and competitive brand positioning.

Now we have Google. Google has $21 billion in ad sales. That's more ad revenues than all the magazines in the United States combined. It's about two-thirds of the ad revenues from all U.S. newspapers.

- *Authority opinions.* A legendary talk show host of late-night television announces one night to his millions of loyal viewers that there is a shortage of toilet paper. The next morning, masses of viewers take to retail stores to stockpile toilet paper. The net result is short-term out-of-stocks at retail and a shortage of toilet paper.

Oprah Winfrey establishes a book club that makes recommendations on what to read. This results in instant best-sellers. Ms. Winfrey tells her viewing public that she is cutting her beef consumption, and the industry goes into a decline and wages a failed suit against her. Again, Oprah Winfrey made her influence felt when she endorsed Barrack Obama over Hillary Clinton as the 2008 Democratic nominee for U.S. president. The rest is history.

This is the power of perceived authorities—key influencers. Want to know if a car is reliable? Check it out with J. D. Powers. Need to know what washing machine is the most reliable? Look it up in *Consumer Reports*. If you have difficulty appreciating the impact of authority opinions, including the opinions of celebrities, journalists, and newscasters, just talk with Coca-Cola executives who were with the company during the ill-fated introduction of New Coke during the early 1980s. Customer marketing is critically important. There is no denying it! But it is also important to market to (perceived) authorities when establishing a competitive and ownable brand positioning.

But be careful when taking this route. Pharmaceutical and medical device companies have long employed key influencers (which they refer to as Key Opinion Leaders or, for short, KOLs). While they value their selection of key influencers, one firm's choice is often neutralized by players from another firm. Let's call it a draw. If you are going to use authority opinions, select those that matter the most.

- ***Reputation.*** This is a critically important plank in establishing and/or reinforcing a brand positioning. Executives of the Johnson & Johnson Company know it well. They identify Johnson & Johnson as "A Company That Cares." In 1982 when product tampering was an issue for the Tylenol brand, Johnson & Johnson did all the right things for its legions of customers (retail trade, hospitals, and consumers)—which turned out to be the right thing for its reputation and business health.

  As customers, we all like to do business with people we like, people who like and respect us. It takes years to build the reputation of a company. Yet, this same reputation can be destroyed with just one wrong action. It is important to state the values of the company or brand and to provide a credo that clearly defines its relationship with customers and guides all future behavior. Johnson & Johnson has a credo. The company's chairman at the time, James Burke, claims he was guided by the company's credo (which, undoubtedly, was imprinted in his heart and soul) to deal with the Tylenol situation. It is critically important to live consistent with your credo. At the time, Johnson & Johnson most certainly did!

  It is also important to be meaningful. False bravado is not meaningful. You may be familiar with what we are talking about. A company introduces a new product that is, for all practical purposes, the same as existing competitors' offerings. When asked, "What is/are the anticipated factor(s) for success?" the management responds, "The company trademark." The landscape is littered with failures caused by this kind of corporate hubris. Reputations are earned by deed. In other words, speak with action! Don't overdraw on your goodwill account.

*Pro*sitioning versus Repositioning

Although rather frequent and significant changes in brand positioning strategies occur as new managers take responsibility for a brand, the conventional wisdom is that brand positioning should not change. It should be like the 10 Commandments, carved in stone. However, if we refuse to change our brand positionings, we are preparing to allow our brands to become obsolete, outpaced by new or more innovative competitors. Change is good. In fact, it is essential, provided that the change is geared toward realizing the brand's full potential and/or managing against important changes in the marketplace. Also, change needs to go beyond what we say to include what we do, as the Tide Laundry Detergent brand evidenced with its many significant formulation and packaging developments.

Basically, what we are talking about is adaptive, iterative, and proactive recreation of the brand over time. Evolution is the path. Revolutionary changes are unacceptable, except in dire circumstances. Imagine your brand has been supported with $20 million in marketing support for a positioning over each of the last 10 years. At this time, you have invested $200 million to advance a specific brand positioning. If a revolutionary change in the positioning strategy were to be introduced, it would negate the positioning you had previously seeded. You would be undermining the investment you had made in the brand. You would be walking away from, as opposed to expanding or deepening, the turf you occupied in your customers' minds. This might well lead to customer confusion and loss of identity.

Marketers are often involved in repositioning their brands. Repositioning is typically indicative of a brand that is no longer healthy and in a state of serious business decline. It's reactive behavior to continuing or worsening declines in sales, market share, and/or profitability. By the time most companies attempt to reposition a brand, it's too late. The brand's strategic health has deteriorated so much that it is difficult to restore.

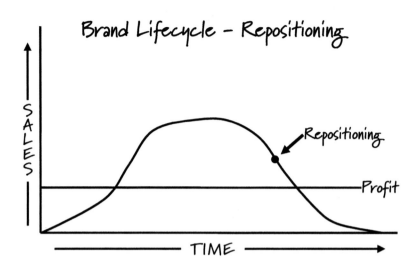

Attempts at repositioning generally lead to failure. Oh, sure, there are plenty of examples of successes. Those, such as the Bayer Aspirin and the MasterCard (discussed in chapter 3) case histories, are the ones we remember. But repositioning tends to be a case of too little too late. This can be traced to a number of factors, among which are weak commitment of management, as evidenced by limited support; extremely short time horizons for recovery; reluctance to change the product offering; and a stubborn hold on the very practices that led to the undermining of the brand's health.

We believe marketers should consider and engage in "*Pro*sitioning," a word we have coined that means "proactive positioning." *Pro*sitioning begins while the brand is still healthy, well before its business begins to decline. The time to engage in *Pro*sitioning is while the brand is still growing—but its rate of growth has slowed down. This will ensure that the needed proactive management begins before the brand's current positioning goes stale (i.e., is no longer as impactful as it was previously) in the marketplace.

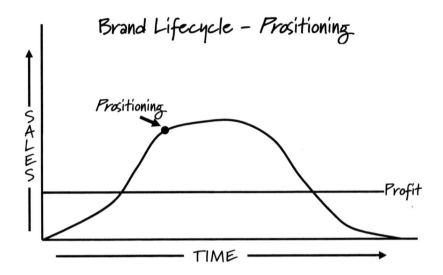

Among the many dynamics that trigger consideration of *Pro*sitioning are changes in customer demographics and/or psychographics; development and availability of new technologies; product improvements; sustainable competitive actions that threaten your brand; the entry of new products into the marketplace (especially those that re-segment the category); and new strategic customer insights that could benefit the brand if exploited.

*Pro*sitioning affords a brand with many advantages. First, it serves to extend the life cycle of the brand. A second advantage is that *Pro*sitioning serves to ensure the brand's strategic health and its relationships with customers. Third, successful *Pro*sitioning can serve to protect the brand against competitive inroads. Finally, it can help in avoiding the anguish, and likely the failure, of repositioning.

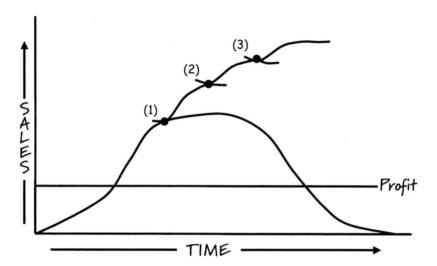

There are numerous examples of companies that have been successfully *Pros*itioned. Johnson & Johnson has transformed itself from a consumer giant into a leader in pharmaceuticals and medical devices, making it truly a health care company. General Electric has moved into financial services (oops at the time of this writing). Charles Schwab is no longer just a discount broker. And Pepsi, with its acquisitions of Tropicana Products and Gatorade, is truly a total beverage company. Among successful brand *Pros*itionings, we see the same examples over and over again. Starbucks, Nike, and Tide Laundry Detergent are examples that spring to mind. These are harder to recall, since they lack the drama that attracts the business press.

These companies and brands share some common traits. There appears to be a vision for the company and/or brand that goes beyond conventional category boundaries. Moreover, there's a willingness to repeatedly question the perception of what business the company is engaged in. This can come in the form of how managers view what they do (e.g., for Nike it might be to make athletic apparel that makes a statement) or what is in it for their customers (e.g., empowerment to "just do it" regardless of athletic proclivities and/or talent) or what company capabilities enable them to provide (e.g., inspiration). There is also sensitivity to future developments, whether they are related to customer attitudes and behaviors, marketplace dynamics, regulatory issues, technologies, or some other factor. Added to this list of traits is an openness to new strategies and a willingness to try them out in the marketplace. We also believe that insightful and strong "leadership" is another critical trait.

Yet, for all its advantages, *Pro*sitioning is an alien concept in today's corporate environment. Certainly, *Pro*sitioning takes a back seat in practice to repositioning. This traces to a number of factors, among which are:

- An absence of indicators to provide an early warning regarding the brand's strategic health and, consequently, a focus on business results, which lag behind brand health;
- A smug satisfaction with results (i.e., we're making our numbers) and a reluctance to challenge the status quo;
- A limited vision of the future and/or understanding of marketplace dynamics and its potential impact on the brand;
- Resource constraints (i.e., people, time, and/or money) and/or a lack of desire to seek out and test new strategies;
- Fear of failure; and
- Organizational issues, particularly politics, among others.

Another deterrent to *Pro*sitioning is a company's lack of understanding about how to go about achieving the new positioning, particularly if it is a stretch from the current positioning. But this can be solved by devising a plan designed to achieve the new positioning in sequential stages over a designated period of time, with each stage being defined by a major initiative, such as a product improvement, an acquisition, or introduction of a new technology. In other words, it can be achieved through engineering its evolution.

*Pro*sitioning is not a readily understood or welcomed concept. It requires a change in mindset from being satisfied and/or reactive to being proactive. But its advantages far outweigh its disadvantages. Consider *Pro*sitioning before you are forced to engage in repositioning to resuscitate your brand's squandered health.

*Pro*sitioning is an essential part of our concept of Power Positioning. Importantly, the evolution should be confined to select elements. Among some of the many reasons to consider evolution are these:

- ***Demographic changes.*** In chapter 2, we talked about our aging population. Every seven seconds, someone in this world turns 50-years old. We are aging. Don't think that skin care marketers haven't noticed. Skin care brands have embraced anti-aging formulations. And, in some parts of the world, skin care marketers are encouraging consumers to begin using anti-aging products when they turn 20-years of age.

  Dove introduced a line of beauty care products for mature women. But Dove's line is not anti-age but pro-age. Hence the line is called Pro-Age.

- ***New products in the marketplace, especially those that re-segment the category.*** How the customer perceives our brand derives not just from our positioning but from what competitive brands do to position us in the marketplace. The rise of smart phones has given way to communication devices, which have given way to the PDA, which has given way to information devices, which has given way to media devices, which have given way to hand-carried computers, which have given way to. . . . Certainly, many of these moves require product improvements and innovations. But, then, this is consistent with our concept that a brand positioning should be a vision, providing meaningful direction for the evolution of the brand to achieve its full potential.

- ***Product improvements/news.*** You add a fragrance to your soap and guess what? You are not longer just a "body cleanser" but a "body refresher" or "body enhancer" or some other dimension of customer need fulfillment. Or take the aspirin segment of the analgesic category. As mentioned earlier in this chapter, studies prove that taking aspirin on a regular basis can cut down the risk of heart attacks and stroke. It's news! So, the Bayer Aspirin brand is no longer just a pain reliever but a potential lifesaver or life extender. Whatever it is that your brand is, it is certainly more than it was before. It justifies evolution of the brand's positioning.

- ***Desire for new growth.*** ARM & HAMMER® Baking Soda brand realized new growth through the evolution of its positioning. It demonstrated use occasions to consumers that the consumer might not have been familiar with or hadn't taken to heart. The brand positioning reflected the versatility of the product. The result was new growth for ARM & HAMMER Baking Soda. The change in positioning also spawned the development of new products carrying the ARM & HAMMER trademark for specific functions (such as toothpaste for teeth whitening).

Swiss Army has expanded its business beyond knives to include articles such as watches. Basically, the company is seeking to sell additional merchandise to its franchise base of Swiss Army Knife customers. In this case, it is deliberately growing the equity value of the trademark to sell a wider variety of merchandise. It is engaged in evolving the positioning of its "umbrella trademark."

Power Positioning is the way to developing healthy brands. These are brands with competitive, enduring, and ownable positionings. In this way, positioning is truly the source of the marketing strategy and initiatives. At the same time, the brand positioning is a product of these same marketing strategies and initiatives! It is also accomplished through evolution of the brand positioning and marketing-mix elements consistent with the dynamics of the future marketplace to keep the brand fresh and healthy.

KEY POINTS, PRINCIPLES & PRACTICES
Summary

✓ The creation of brand loyalty requires more than a technically correct and strategically appropriate Brand Positioning Strategy Statement. We need to establish Power Positioning.

✓ Power Positioning is a competitive, enduring, and ownable brand positioning. It is reflected in all marketing-mix elements and evolves over time to adapt to changes in the marketplace and the realization of the vision for the brand.

✓ In order for a product to own a competitive brand positioning in the marketplace, the Brand Positioning Strategy Statement must be reflected in every marketing-mix element, its positioning planks, not just in what you say within the confines of your organization, to the business press, or in advertising.

✓ The sum of the positioning planks constitutes the whole of customer perceptions regarding your brand positioning and customers' relationship with it.

✓ The most important positioning plank is the product itself. Marketers need to know their products, really know them from the perspective of the customer and within the context of the competitors' offerings. An existing product needs to evolve to maintain and/or grow a brand positioning in a changing marketplace. A new product needs to be engineered to create meaningful differentiation.

✓ The "whole" product is made up of tangible and intangible factors.

✓ Intangibles are anything but immaterial in establishing an ownable and competitive brand positioning. Intangibles provide us with the opportunity to meaningfully differentiate our brand offering, regardless of whether it is a product or service, from competition.

✓ Get beyond the product you sell. Think about the *experience* you deliver.

✓ Distribution is another component of marketing and brand positioning. As brand builders, we need to think through how and where we distribute in establishing an ownable and competitive brand positioning.

✓ Company and brand reputation are a critically important plank in establishing and/or reinforcing a brand positioning. As customers, we all like to do business with people we like, people who like and respect us. It takes years of diligent effort to build the reputation of a company and/or brand.

✓ All the positioning planks need to come together as an integrated whole. This establishes the integrity of the brand positioning and is the basis for Power Positioning.

✓ It is wise to evolve the brand positioning. The evolution should be confined to select positioning elements.

✓ Avoid repositioning. Don't let your brand fall to a point where you are forced to reposition it.

✓ Engage in "*Pro*sitioning," a word we have coined that means "proactive positioning." *Pro*sitioning begins while the brand is still healthy, well before its business begins to decline. The time to engage in *Pro*sitioning is while the brand is still growing.

✓ Among some of the reasons to consider evolution include:

- – Demographic changes
- – The entry of new products into the marketplace
- – Product improvement and/or news
- – Desire for new growth

CHAPTER ELEVEN

Inspired by The Late Show with
David Letterman Top 10 List

Chapter 11

The 10 Most Critical Positioning Errors

Dave Letterman, host of *The Late Show with David Letterman*, popularized the "Top 10 List" with his inimitable zany sense of humor. In fact, books have been published with Dave's lists. You can view some of his Top 10 Lists on YouTube.com. What's the appeal? Well, they're outrageous takes on popular culture. Dave builds excitement throughout by starting with number 10 and counting down to number 1, which is the most ludicrous item in the list.

We thought we'd share our list of the "10 Most Critical Errors in Brand Positioning." Like Letterman, we'll count down from number 10 to number 1. Here we will list these *critical errors*, their *causal factors* and the *resultant impact* on brand marketing. However, unlike David Letterman's list, this one is not intended to tickle your funny bone (i.e., be humorous). Unfortunately, it's somewhat sad that these errors exist and are so prevalent.

Drum roll, please. (You have to play the drum role in your own head.) Here they are:

Number 10: Lacking cohesion throughout the Brand Positioning Strategy Statement.

In other words, the work just doesn't "hang" together. The pieces of the Brand Positioning Strategy Statement do not work in harmony to create a unified whole. It may be that the proposed Benefit does not link to the needs of the Target Customer group. Or the Reason-Why does not support the

Benefit. Or, perhaps, the Perceptual Competitive Framework is inconsistent with the Benefit promise.

There are many *causal factors* that lead to a lack of cohesion. Primary among them is fuzzy thinking. The resultant work mirrors the confusion present in the minds of the strategy's creators. Another causal factor is "management by consensus." The "someone" who should be making decisions is abdicating responsibility in favor of reflecting the divergent viewpoints of participating managers in the same strategy statement. Another factor is CPA, or "continuous partial attention." Appropriate attention is not being focused during the development of the positioning strategy to ensuring that the completed statement is cohesive.

The *resultant impact* of this critical error is a lack of clarity, which leads to poor execution. The Brand Positioning Strategy Statement serves as a blueprint for transforming a product into a "brand." If the blueprint is not clear, it is difficult, in fact nearly impossible, to ensure cohesiveness in execution of brand strategies and tactics among the various functional units (e.g., Product Research and Development, Promotions). So customers do not receive a unified, single-minded message through the myriad touch points to develop a clear understanding of what the brand should mean to them.

Number 9: Using Standard of Identity or Class (e.g., of drug) rather than Perceptual Competitive Framework in the competitive framework of the strategy.

The competitive framework indicates the market for the brand. As we have made clear, we distinguish between "literal" and "perceptual" competitive framework in our work with clients. The Literal Competitive Framework identifies where the brand will source volume—its competitive set. The Perceptual Competitive Framework signifies how we desire customers perceive the brand. It is the more important of the two in that it guides activities in an attempt to affect how customers perceive the brand in relation to the competitors noted in the competitive set, or Literal Competitive Framework.

Standard of Identity is the legal definition for what the product is. For example, the Standard of Identity for Walt Disney World may be an amusement park. But Disney World is so much more than an amusement park in the minds of customers. Class of drug identifies the type of compound. For example, Lipitor, which is prescribed by physicians to reduce their patients' cholesterol, is a statin. Many of Lipitor's primary competitors are statins, too. But to those physicians and the patients who depend upon Lipitor, with its extensive clinical studies and track record of success in preventing coronary artery disease and premature death, Lipitor is much more than a statin.

Among the *causal factors* in choosing Standard of Identity or competitive set over Perceptual Competitive Framework is a lack of appreciation regarding the importance of this element on shaping customer perceptions and guiding the management of meaningful differentiation. Marketers blindly repeat what their predecessors have done. It has become an automatic, thoughtless entry in the Brand Positioning Strategy Statement.

Another causal factor in health care sectors is the influence of legal and regulatory requirements. Marketers miss the point that the strategy represents not what you currently are but how you want to someday be perceived. They don't understand it is the North Star (or vision) to guide development of the brand. They don't understand that the marketer wants to use it to make clear what she expects from all resource groups to make it real through actions, not just words (e.g., getting the required clinical study results).

The *resultant impact* is two-fold. First, when marketers use Standard of Identity or plug in the competitive set to the Competitive Framework, they are contributing to commoditizing the brand in the minds of prospective customers. They're indicating that it is in the same class as every other offering. This communicates to customers that these products are all basically the same. Customers, in turn, will use this perception to simplify their selection decision. They will simply choose among alternative products on the basis of price (the lowest one), convenience, or habit. There is nothing to compel preference for a brand.

Second, it fails to provide guidance for the development of the "brand." The Perceptual Competitive Framework informs the development of strategies and tactics for all marketing-mix elements—including product development. As mentioned earlier, it serves as a "North Star" to navigate the brand to a unique place in the minds of customers.

Number 8: Using product claims for the Reason-Why.

The "Reason-Why" provides necessary support to make the Benefit promise believable. In other words, the Reason-Why is the substantiation for the Benefit. Product claims are just what they imply—claims! A product benefit claim lacks substantiation. Instead, it begs for substantiation.

The Reason-Why can be intrinsic or extrinsic to the product. Intrinsic Reasons-Why include elements such as design, ingredients or compounds, or mode of action (i.e., how it works), among others. Extrinsic Reasons-Why fall outside the product itself. Perhaps, the most notable Extrinsic Reason-Why is an endorsement from a notable organization such as the (fill in the country name) Dental Association. We need to ensure we are using bona fide intrinsic and/or extrinsic reasons-why to substantiate the Benefit.

Among the *causal factors* for using product claims for the Reason-Why, perhaps, the single most important factor is lack of sales(wo)manship. This is a way of saying that the marketer does not know how to close the deal to finalize the sale with the Target Customer group. Or it could be that the marketer does not possess the discipline of sacrifice in choosing from among a perceived multitude of benefits. So, he stashes product benefits in the Reason-Why section, naively believing that the Benefit promise is now single-minded. Another factor may very well be that the marketer does not currently possess a Reason-Why that differentiates the product from competition. It could be that all products share the same Reason-Why support. Or it could be the marketer is quickly dialing up to an emotional benefit that has not been earned through a meaningful set of experiences with the target group. In this case, the marketer is attempting to support an emotional benefit with product claims that tell prospective customers what the product does. Whatever the factor, it is just plain incorrect to use product Benefits as Reason-Why support.

The *resultant impact* is a lack of credibility of the Benefit. And, we all know that credibility is vitally important in creating brand loyalty. At the very least, customers will not distinguish a difference between the product offering and its competitors and will therefore fail to develop a strong preference for any one brand.

Number 7: Not being meaningfully competitive.

To be meaningfully competitive, we must be relevant to the Target Customer group as well as meaningfully differentiated from the competition. While many Brand Positioning Strategy Statements offer relevant benefits, they fail to establish meaningful differentiation. They tend to be different in "degree" (rather than "kind") and are indistinguishable from those of the competition. Potential customers perceive such statements as mere puffery. In other words, the customer doesn't buy the difference. It exists only in the mind of the marketer.

There are a number of ways in which we fail to be meaningfully competitive. For one, we confuse features with benefits. The positioning strategy proffers features without indicating the benefit to the customer. Another failure is to use "generic" benefits common to the category. While generic benefits are relevant, they do not differentiate one offering from another. Focusing on functional (either product or customer), rather than emotional, benefits also undermines our ability to establish a competitive positioning. A brand positioning should shape the meaning we wish to establish with the target group. If we use only product and customer Benefits in the Brand Positioning Strategy Statement, they can easily be replicated by competitors, neutralizing any competitive advantage. Employing emotional benefits, on the other hand, helps seed "meaning" and establishes a bond with customers. Yet another way in which competitiveness is compromised is to employ the same Reasons-Why as the competition to support the Benefit. (And many use the same Benefit *and* Reasons-Why as their competitors.) This fails to establish the credibility needed to drive brand preference.

The *causal factors* of not being meaningfully competitive trace principally to the mindset of the marketer and/or organization. They lack the mental metal to be competitive. Basically, neither the marketer not the organization is competitive. The marketing function does no more than make the product available to potential customers. These marketers and their organizations are content to just get their products into the marketplace. They support them primarily through sales force "push" without providing needed effort to "pull" them through with customers.

Another mindset issue is settling. While it may go unstated, these marketers evidence through their actions that they are resigned to selling "parity" products. And so they surrender, being content to perpetuate the sameness inherent in the marketplace. The lack of appreciation of the need to get beyond the physical aspects of the product and to create perceptions essential to the development of a brand entity is a stumbling block to being meaningfully competitive. If you cannot win with the product, then perhaps you should try to win with the brand. But this takes imagination and creativity, which appear to be rare gifts indeed.

Attention should also be given to relationships with internal regulatory and legal personnel who abort actions that, if undertaken, could contribute to establishing a meaningful competitive advantage. Marketers tell us that their regulatory and/or legal people will not approve a meaningfully competitive positioning because (choose one or more of the following) it's not in the labeling, or clinical/marketing research studies do not support it, or some governing body (such as the FDA or FTC) will take action against them. But the Brand Positioning Strategy Statement is not what you are today or what you are going to tell prospective customers. Instead, it is the blueprint for what you aspire to build over time through product improvements, incontrovertible evidence from clinical studies, new labeling, creation of alliances, and so on.

The *resultant impact* is a weak foundation for the development of a healthy brand and continued loyalty. Since there is no meaningful competitive advantage, marketers are driven to resort to poor practices. Growth is sought through "phantom" price increases. While the list price is increased, so is level and/or frequency of price discounting. This conditions customers to demand or shop for a deal. As a result, more and more sales are promotional sales. Or organizations get into a vicious cycle of rampant line extending and product proliferation (in many cases, beyond the boundaries of their positioning) in an effort to cycle growth over that of the previous year. Additionally, marketers begin behaving like politicians. (That's a frightening thought!) They seek an expanded base of customers by frequently switching messaging and what they stand for, attempting to be "all things to all people." (See error number 6 for more.) So, as a consequence of not being meaningfully competitive, the company compromises brand meaning, customer loyalty and even profitability.

Number 6: Having poor Target Customer group definition.

Whew, there are a number of ways in which a poor Target Customer definition is manifested. We see this all the time. One is the absence of a "complete" definition of the Target Customer group that reflects and shares an in-depth understanding of psychographics, attitudes, and usage behaviors and needs, among others. A complete definition shows we truly understand the target. Another is a lack of clarity. Marketers give us mere demographics or employ overused, rather meaningless descriptors such as "active people." Who isn't active today? Another overused descriptor is "technology savvy" as the defining characteristic of the target group for any product that has a technological component to it. Or how about "early adopters?" This is particularly irksome since one does not even need to market to these people. They will find your new offering. Moreover, they will be the first to exit when the next new thing comes along. So don't trouble yourself with them.

But the most insidious is not making a choice. What we are referring to here is the marketer's attempt to be "all things to all people." We can't be all things to all people and create a meaning for the brand that will drive customer preference and loyalty. Even if you could, which you can't, the offering would be vulnerable to those competitors that effectively segment the market. As Phillip Kotler, the respected professor of marketing, stated, "You're not marketing if you're not segmenting."

The *causal factors* contributing to poor Target Customer definition include a lack of appreciation of market segmentation. We watch marketers struggle with this concept regardless of whether they are mass marketers or specialists (such as marketers of medical devices and diagnostics or of pharmaceuticals). They understand it intellectually, but they are unable to feel it in order to obey and be driven by this principle of strategically selecting and better serving a viable and valuable segment of the population than their competitors.

Another factor, which is related to the previous one, is that marketers are not "customer-centric." Instead, they are selling products on a transaction-to-transaction basis. It's about "my product," rather than "What can I do for you today, tomorrow, and the next day, well into the future?"

Yet another causal factor is the fear of leaving something on the table (i.e., not maximizing the perceived sales potential). Specifically, organizations are fearful of overlooking or losing customers. Worse yet, they are loath to niche the product opportunity. The word "niche" has the same effect on marketers that garlic has on vampires. It causes them to scurry away. This fear is perpetuated by senior managers who demand more volume than the offering can bear. Or, at its best, it may be attributed to an overly ambitious marketer. Ambition can be a good thing, but what product has 100% of the market? It's not going to be your product! Let's be realistic and market our product consistent with the opportunity and company resources.

A related factor is defining the target segment so as to achieve a hyper-inflated forecast that is based upon some profound need of the organization. This need is probably tied to meeting investors' expectations. If investors are demanding a "blockbuster" and the organization desperately needs one, the sales forecast and the target population have to support the hope. Just as the forecast is fat, we believe there's a fat chance the company will achieve it with a fat target group. (For our international friends, "fat chance" is an expression that means "not likely!")

One more causal factor in this litany, and perhaps the most grievous, is a superficial knowledge of the target. This can result from a paucity of marketing research. But it is most likely driven by an absence of contact with the target and an inability to empathize with them.

The *resultant impact* of poor targeting is a weak brand positioning, pure and simple! The Target Customer group is the first element in the Brand Positioning Strategy Statement. If the target group is incorrect or is not clear or complete, the other elements that link to it will suffer greatly. The positioning at best will be suboptimal and at worst will be inappropriate to establishing a healthy brand. We've touched upon other consequences in the preceding paragraphs, such as lack of focus in managing brand development, absence of customer loyalty, missed forecasts, and poor communications (too many or the wrong messages).

Number 5: Blindly accepting the global Brand Positioning Strategy Statement, not localizing it.

Okay, here's where we risk losing some people. Here's where we provoke outrage among some of you, particularly senior managers. But hear us out. Seek to understand the meaning of this critical error.

Most organizations foist a global brand positioning on the world. The global Brand Positioning Strategy is headquarters' view of the rest of the world. (Think about the view of the world as graphically depicted on the front cover of New Yorker Magazine years ago. It basically showed the Pacific Ocean and Asia as a small area bordering at the edge of New York.) Unfortunately, far too often it is developed by managers who have little or no international experience and/or who lack the benefit of the local and cultural insight of their international counterparts. At best, the global Brand Positioning Strategy s expressed as a functional benefit. As mentioned in point number 7, such a strategy will probably not be competitive, and, even if it is, it can be easily neutralized by competition.

The brand positioning is the strategic sweet spot that balances the product/brand with the Target Customer group and the company capabilities with the competitive environment. Wouldn't you think this is likely to change according to the market? At the very least, the sweet spot for markets will vary due to differences in customer needs, competitive strengths, claim support, or company capabilities. This requires adjusting for local needs.

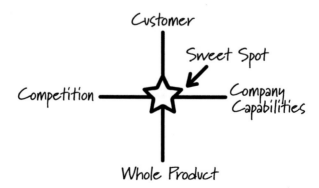

POSITIONING SWEET SPOT

Another issue with blindly accepting the global brand positioning strategy is the failure to internalize its meaning for a specific market. This resultant lack of appreciation for the global BPS makes it difficult, if not impossible, to achieve effective execution of it in the marketplace.

Among the *causal factors* contributing to blind acceptance of the global brand positioning strategy is a lack of appreciation for the need for a blueprint to manage going beyond product characteristics to create a brand entity. If global and/or local managers don't share an understanding of what it means to develop a global brand, the actual strategy work will fail to register at the local level.

Another factor relates to a word we used earlier: "foist." The strategy may be mandated by the global team but not actively executed by marketers at the local level. There may be a sort of quiet resistance to executing it in the marketplace. The market has the plan but doesn't really do anything with it that is meaningful. As a result, brand positioning just develops depending on customers' perceptions from tactical initiatives, competitive response, and so on.

The more savvy organizations have a global brand positioning strategy and allow for flexibility in messaging. But messaging is one of the primary avenues for communicating the brand positioning strategy. The reality is that it can overwhelm the global brand positioning strategy. In other words, the market goes its own way.

Time constraints may be blamed for a global brand positioning strategy that does not include adequate representation from international markets. We hear over and over again that "we just didn't have time to involve everyone." We are talking not about involving everyone but about getting a representation of different markets. We are encouraging you to share understanding in order to develop a more competitive positioning that will drive customer preference and, ultimately, create brand loyalty.

The *resultant impact* is rather predictable. Perhaps, you've experienced frequent changes (such as annual ones) in the brand positioning strategy. This is a function of new managers, who did not participate in the development of the original Brand Positioning Strategy Statement, coming on board after the fact and wanting to make an impact. Annual changes typically do not bode well. Frequent changes in brand positioning strategy are going to confuse the organization (think about your sales force!) and your customers.

The most significant impact is not seeding a competitive brand positioning strategy in the marketplace. It is exceedingly difficult to establish the intended brand positioning strategy without an understanding accompanied by faithful execution of it. Moreover, this lack of understanding drains energy from the organization and keeps it from focusing on generating really big ideas that will lead to a truly global brand.

Number 4: Not making sound strategic choices to ensure a single-minded brand positioning strategy.

The Brand Positioning Strategy Statement must be *single-minded*. This is *not* to say that there need be only one benefit. That might be simple-minded, particularly where one needs more than one benefit to be meaningfully competitive and to capitalize on the brand's unique capabilities. But if there is more than one benefit, the extra benefits must be consistent with the target group's expectations and the brand's capabilities to meet those expectations. Moreover, the Benefits must be in alignment. Specifically, they need to provide linkage from the product benefit to the customer benefit all the way up the Benefit Ladder to the emotional benefit. In this way, the Benefit in the Brand Positioning Strategy Statement is really single-minded. Alternatively, the benefits need to link to form a cohesive whole in creating a single-minded perception of the brand.

But being single-minded in the brand positioning strategy is not limited to the Benefit. It also includes the Target Customer group. As stated in critical error number 6, the brand cannot be all things to all people if you are to be able to create a meaning for the brand that will drive customer preference and loyalty. So don't even try it! Even if you could, which you can't, the brand offering would be vulnerable to those competitors who effectively segment the market to focus their strategy in serving the targeted market segment better.

Finally, let's step back for a moment and look at the meaning of the strategy itself. Is there one meaning? One intent? Or are there multiple meanings in the strategy? If, when you or others review the strategy, there are alternate interpretations of the brand's meaning (i.e., what the brand stands for in the minds of its readers), then you have a significant problem. There can be only one meaning. There can be only one interpretation. That's being single-minded! One travels one strategic road, not many at the same time.

Among the key *causal factors* for not making sound strategic choices to ensure a single-minded brand positioning strategy is the inability, or an unwillingness to take the time, to identify discrete choices regarding potential strategic directions. We need first to top-line potential strategic directions. This is the nature of creative intelligence—to be able to identify alternatives. We should never converge without first diverging to identify and weigh possible directions. We recognize that this is easier said than done, given organizational pressures, employees' desire to please the boss, group think, lack of imagination, and category infatuation (i.e., doing what every other product does in the same way because that is the way *we think* the business works). But if options are not entertained, the likelihood of achieving a single-minded, appropriate brand positioning strategy will be low.

Time constraints also limit our ability to make sound strategic choices or even entertain them. This is particularly perplexing, since brand positioning strategy development is one of the most important responsibilities of marketers. We have to choose to undertake this critically important responsibility despite the press of urgent but nonessential tasks such as responding to 40, 60 or more e-mails per day. There is absolutely no reason why anyone should be caught without the time to devote to thoughtful positioning strategy development unless, of course, you want to admit to poor management. Over-index your time on the job up front to conduct this important undertaking.

Let's pause for a moment to consider organizational management style as a causal factor for not making sound strategic choices. The culprit may be labeled "consensus management." Oh, you've heard of it. Chances are that if your brand positioning strategy is conflicted (i.e., not single-minded), then your organization probably relies on consensus management. In this case, everyone's view is appreciated, valued equally, and reflected in the strategy, regardless of its true merit or its impact in the marketplace. As a result, the proverbial camel emerges where the desire was to produce a horse.

The *resultant impact* of not making sound strategic choices to ensure a single-minded brand positioning strategy is mass confusion, inside and out. What we mean is that team members responsible for executing the positioning strategy inside the organization, as well as resource people outside the organization, will be confused. There is no clear, single-minded direction. People choose what direction they will execute, and there is no litmus test (in the form of a single-minded strategy) to ensure faithful execution of a given strategic direction. Outside the organization, customers will also be confused. They will receive multiple, nonaligned messages (through packaging, clinical studies, product developments, merchandising, advertising, promotion, and the like) such that no clear meaning will emerge to stick in the marketplace. Customers will not take the time or do the work to figure it out. Why should they if the marketer, for whom it all means so much more, hasn't done so?

At the very least, there is a dilution of resources. And, few marketers have all the resources they feel they need to successfully create brand loyalty. So they need to focus, focus, focus resources. Even if you as a marketer had all the resources you needed, which we bet you do not, why squander them?

Number 3: Not making the Brand Positioning Strategy Statement "official."

This is about *developing, fixing, and institutionalizing* the most appropriate strategic choice. It starts by doing one's homework in the form of marketing research to develop the most strategically appropriate choice. Marketers and their organizations often spend their limited funds to conduct marketing research that often goes unused. The marketing research that exists in the brand's library should be approached as one would approach creating a mosaic. From the pieces that exist, one should develop hypotheses and assess them with input from customers obtained through additional marketing research. This will ensure that the strategic choice is grounded in reality. It will also reveal if and where additional research may be needed.

But the strategy is not "official" until the most senior manager responsible for the health of the business approves it with her or his signature. If a brand is not healthy, the business will bleed, wither, and die. At the heart of the brand's health is the faithful execution of the brand positioning strategy. It is amazing to us that senior managers such as division presidents or country general managers are required to sign off on a mere $5,000 change part for the manufacturing line but are neither required nor compelled to do so for the Brand Positioning Strategy Statement. Think about it. The major equity markets throughout the world value companies in large part on the basis of the health and, therefore, the potential of "brands" to provide a predictable future growth stream of income, not on the number or quality of change parts. When a company pays a significant premium to acquire another, the decision is based upon the health and potential of the acquired company's brands. So, if senior managers desire to add value to the corporation, which they should, they need to be very much involved in brand positioning development and execution. Without their acknowledgement, commitment, and leadership (which make the strategy official), it is unlikely that the positioning strategy will drive brand development in the organization.

The *causal factors* for not having an official Brand Positioning Strategy Statement include a lack of appreciation for it. Lip service is given to brand positioning. But lip service is cheap. When it comes time to get behind it, operational issues and demands take precedence. This is probably a function of the top managers not really respecting the role of marketing and brand positioning because of the organization's inability to measure return on investment (ROI) for marketing. More than likely, these senior managers came up through the ranks via a discipline other than marketing. Alternatively, marketers have failed to establish a clear link between marketing initiatives and ROI.

Managers also tell us that they do not have the funds to conduct marketing research. Many therefore choose to fly blind. But they do not have to do so. At the very least, we can check the Marketing Research Department (MRD) library to review past research. Or we can check with colleagues in other countries for marketing research they have conducted. We can scour industry databases online for valuable info. We can purchase syndicated studies. We can scrape up some money to do qualitative research. Any marketing manager with a curious and inventive mind can choose to do something to nurture the development of hypotheses regardless of availability, or levels, of funding.

The time issue, or, more precisely, the lack thereof, raises its ugly head once again. This is the cop-out of all cop-outs. We have little patience for it at this point (in this book, in this chapter, and in our lives), and so should you! The stakes are far too great not to invest the time and attention needed to be competitive in creating brand loyalty.

The *resultant impact* of not developing an official brand positioning strategy is the absence of a long-term marketing campaign. Need we say more? The positioning strategy is not fixed. When a new product manager comes along, the positioning gets changed. In fact, the positioning strategy may get changed more frequently than that, even annually! When we use the term "fixed," we do not mean that the strategy doesn't evolve. There has to be room for adaptive growth. Instead, what we mean is having a basic foundation from which to build all aspects of the brand. Every initiative for every marketing-mix element is assessed not only on its ability to grow the business but also on its ability to establish the brand positioning in the marketplace.

Organizational discipline falls apart. There is no official, validated blueprint for the development of the brand. The brand becomes "the house that 'whoever' at the time happened to live in it built." Initiatives are chosen irrespective of what they communicate about the brand. A multitude of disparate messages vanish in the marketplace, having failed to create a clear meaning with the intended target group. When it is all said and done, there's very little curb appeal, and the value of the brand is thereby diminished.

Additionally, the absence of an official Brand Positioning Strategy Statement sends the wrong message throughout the organization. Its absence communicates that the statement is not really valuable and therefore is not worth the effort to create.

Number 2: Not executing all marketing-mix elements to be consistent with the Brand Positioning Strategy Statement.

This is what we have termed "Power Positioning." Despite what others may have you believe, brand positioning is about a lot more than what you *say* in your advertising. Brand positioning is about everything you *do* in creating meaning for the Target Customer group. We build our brand positioning one plank at a time—trademark, promotion, product development, clinical evidence, merchandising, packaging, authority opinions, advocacy groups, alliances, product intangibles, and so on. We don't just use it to guide advertising. In fact, there are a number of healthy brands that have established meaning and achieved enviable customer loyalty without the benefit of advertising.

Power Positioning is the execution responsibility of marketers. Once thoughtful planning has been completed it is absolutely essential that the strategy be faithfully executed in the marketplace. The best strategy will get you nowhere if it is not executed or if it is poorly executed.

The *causal factors* for not executing consistent with the brand positioning strategy include inconsistent understanding of the strategy. If people within the organization and external support groups do not understand or know the strategy, their creative efforts are not likely to hit the mark. Inconsistent understanding of the strategy can be traced to its development by just a few inner circle managers. It's important to not just develop an Official Brand Positioning Strategy Statement but to do so in collaboration with those managers who will be executing it. This ensures going beyond mere intellectual acknowledgement to a profound, shared understanding. And, lest people forget, it is important to evangelize the strategy throughout all corners of the brand team (internal and external resource groups) over and over and over again. Everyone needs reminders of what the brand will stand for in the minds of customers and prospective customers.

Another causal factor is archiving the brand positioning strategy as opposed to using it as a living document and checkpoint through which all ideas must pass. The strategy statement should not and cannot be retired upon its completion. It is not something we check off as having completed. It is more than a task. Instead, it must become an important filter through which all ideas must be screened to assess their potential to create a competitive brand meaning in the marketplace that drives customer preference.

The *resultant impact* of not executing all marketing-mix elements consistent with the brand positioning strategy is that the intended positioning fails to be seeded in the marketplace. And if it is not seeded, it does not develop and grow. It is a dream that goes unfulfilled.

Customers are confused about the meaning of the brand. As a result, they will take the easy route and commoditize your offering. The critical determinant of purchase behavior will become price—if one is even able to capture the customer's attention. It is not the stuff of brand loyalty.

The product offering exists, rather than thrives, from promotion to promotion. It is kept above water by news such as new features or line extensions. It is not built on a mutually beneficial relationship between brand and customer.

We have now come to the number 1 most critical positioning error (drum roll, please—ta-ta-ta-ta-ta a a—*boom!*):

Number 1: Not having, or being aware of, a Brand Positioning Strategy Statement for your offering.

This is it, folks. Perhaps you've already guessed and guessed it correctly. This is the proverbial ostrich with its *head in the sand*—being completely oblivious to or ignoring what is essential to creating brand loyalty and orchestrating customer perceptions for a brand, not a product, that drive preference as directed by the Brand Positioning Strategy Statement.

In our work promoting and teaching marketing excellence, we start each of our programs by asking if participating managers have a Brand Positioning Strategy Statement. It's disheartening, even appalling, to discover that no more than one-third of them, at best, lay claim to having one. It's altogether possible that a Brand Positioning Strategy Statement exists for their brands but that they are unaware of its existence. It's possible but unlikely. Nonetheless, we recommend that when they return to their offices at the completion of the program, they ask their bosses to share the Brand Positioning Strategy Statement that has been created or, if none exists, to create one.

The Brand Positioning Strategy Statement is the blueprint for the marketing and franchise building of the brand. When we use this word "brand," we are referring to more than the product. The product is nothing more than its physical characteristics or components. But the brand is much,

much more. The brand is a constellation of values and customer perceptions that forge a special relationship with the target group. For example, Johnson's Baby Powder brand is more than talc and fragrance. It is a mother's unconditional love for her baby and a desire to care for her baby in the best way possible. Lipitor is much more than a pill to lower cholesterol. It is an insurance policy trusted by health care practitioners to protect the lives of their at-risk patients from a coronary heart disease catastrophic event (such as heart attack and stroke).

If *no Brand Positioning Strategy Statement exists*, it doesn't mean that there is not a brand positioning. "How's that?," you may ask. Well, the brand positioning is *the way we want customers to perceive, think, and feel about our brand versus competition*. They will think something about the offering regardless of whether one has a Brand Positioning Strategy Statement or not. You may not know what they think, and what they think may not be what you want them to think about the offering (regardless of whether it is a product or service.) Chances are prospective customers will think of your offering as a mere product consisting of physical attributes, rather than as a brand. Chances are they will commoditize the offering in their collective minds to be like just about every other offering in the category! This does not serve to create brand loyalty in driving customer preference.

Among the key *causal factors* for not having a Brand Positioning Strategy Statement is executives' confusing, or limiting, its use to defining *what* to communicate about the offering, as in advertising. Therefore, the Brand Positioning Strategy Statement may be viewed as unnecessary if a Communication Strategy or Creative Brief exists for the offering. But the Brand Positioning Strategy Statement is about much more than what we say about the offering. It is everything we marketers, and our organizations, do to create and shape customers' perceptions regarding the development and establishment of a brand. It's not just about advertising. It's about what we do with each and every element of the marketing mix to create and reinforce the brand strategy.

Another causal factor of note is not making the Brand Positioning Strategy Statement, where it exists, "official." In other words, unless it is official, it is not understood or owned by the organization, as a patent is owned. Instead, it is seen as belonging to a small team of people or merely one person—its creator. As a consequence, many managers do not know of its existence. This is exacerbated when the creator of this unofficial brand positioning strategy statement moves on to another assignment or, worse yet, another company. Then no one holds the key to the brand and its development.

Not committing it to paper, institutionalizing it, is a causal factor similar to the one just noted. Entrepreneurs typically have a very clear brand positioning strategy in mind when they create and commercialize their offering. They may not refer to it as a positioning strategy. To them, it may be their vision or competitive advantage or mission in life. Whatever nomenclature they use, it is clearly a brand positioning strategy. However, it is all in their heads. It is manifested by their organizations as long as these entrepreneurs remain involved in the business. They know what they want. They communicate it verbally. And, importantly, they inspect every initiative the organization creates to fit with the strategy before it is introduced into the marketplace. But once the founder moves on and so-called professional management enters the scene, the strategy is lost not just to the organization but the world.

The last causal factor, which we merely touch upon here, is one that we have brought up in discussing other critical errors. It's the recurring issue of time. It seems as though many claim that they simply do not have the time to create, test, and adapt a brand positioning strategy. What a truly sad state this is. It's people taking action without thinking. It's building without a blueprint. It's a mess in the making. It's a disaster waiting to happen.

The *resultant impacts* of not having, or being aware of, a Brand Positioning Strategy Statement have been identified in previous critical errors. (Go back and pick them out. The very act of doing so will help nurture a higher degree of understanding.) But the most significant negative is essentially creating a product rather than a brand offering, with all the consequences inherent in this direction.

This is not to say that a product offering will not have strong sales or even favorable sales growth, particularly where the offering is the first of its kind, has a demonstrable product advantage that the customer can realize, and/or has organizational muscle to drive it. But its inherent health, the quality and longevity of its life cycle, will be diminished on a real or opportunity loss basis. This negative impact may be largely hidden, perhaps, for many years, just as the impact of termites is not realized until one's foot falls through the floor. But eventually it will be realized. New offerings that deliver a product advantage, or a new business or operational model, will expose and exploit that lack of sound health. The disease state may be diagnosed by increases in the percentage of promotional sales to total sales or in the level of discounting. However, the sickness may not be recognized (who would want to admit to it?), and, even if it is, it probably will not be traced back to its root cause—the absence of a Brand Positioning Strategy Statement.

The Brand Positioning Strategy Statement serves to direct the development of a competitive, ownable, and sustainable advantage. Without it, marketers find themselves adrift in a sea of similarity. Also, their organizations send confusing signals to prospective customers in the form of multiple, nonaligned messages (through packaging, clinical studies, product developments, merchandising, advertising, promotion and so on) so that no clear meaning can emerge, no less stick, in the marketplace.

What to Do about It

1. Develop a *single-minded*, strategically appropriate Brand Positioning Strategy Statement directed at a *well-defined target group*, and utilize it as the blueprint for the development of a *brand*, not a mere product, in creating brand loyalty. This is a priority. Do not pass "go," as they say in the game of MONOPOLY, until this task has been successfully completed. The development of the Brand Positioning Strategy Statement should be undertaken in collaboration with a multidiscipline team reflecting multifunctional expertise. Ensure that this collaborative strategy creates special meaning for, or gives meaning to, the target group. Product benefits just don't cut it. Think about the experience your brand can deliver.

2. Think well into the future to identify meaningful differentiation through the development of a *Perceptual Competitive Framework*. The Perceptual Competitive Framework should lift you above and out of this "age of sameness." It needs to provide you with a new way to map the marketplace so that customers will make your brand their clear choice. It will help ensure that your offering is perceived as being meaningfully distinctive, not as a

commodity. Moreover, it will guide the utilization of resources toward creating meaningful differentiation well into the future.

3. Become a servant of the people. Think to serve your target group. Yes, we are in business to make a profit. But the best way to profit in the long run is to serve your target customers better than competition. Before you can better serve them, you need to know them better than your competitors, too. Dig to discover customer insights that will unlock the way into your current and prospective customers' hearts, and lives.

4. Check out the strategy via a dialogue in the marketplace with prospective customers and adapt accordingly to iterate your way to success.

5. Make it "official." The only way to make it official is for the most senior manager in the organization (such as the CEO, CMO, GM, or Country Manager) to affix the corporate head's signature to it. Once it has become official, have it laminated. Share the strategy with all functional groups within the organization, such as sales, product research and development, and promotions. When we suggest you share it, we don't mean e-mail it out to everyone. We mean you should evangelize the strategy by presenting it to each functional discipline group. Go broad and deep. And, so that you or they do not forget about it, dust it off and return periodically to reiterate the strategy and identify what it means to everyone.

6. Localize the Brand Positioning Strategy Statement on the basis of customer needs, the competitive landscape, and company capabilities for a given market. More than likely, this will not so much entail a different positioning strategy for different locales as it will require a different place on the same line with the country that developed the "global" brand positioning strategy. The mere act of undertaking this will ensure a greater understanding of the brand positioning. Importantly, it will promote ownership, leading to more successful execution. By the way, those companies that insist on creating a brand positioning strategy that will fit every market the same way typically have a strategy so broad as to have no meaning. The act of localizing the strategy will drive specificity and, with it, meaning for the organization and prospective customers.

7. Use the Brand Positioning Strategy Statement to guide every marketing-mix strategy and initiative undertaken to establish the brand and to create brand loyalty (i.e., product development, clinical studies, selection of key influencers—absolutely everything!). Do not review proposed initiatives in a

vacuum. The brand positioning strategy is your blueprint for the marketing and franchise building of the brand. Check to ensure that each activity is consistent with the blueprint. If it is not, you must either modify the initiative or abandon it. Otherwise, the house you ultimately build will end up a Rube Goldberg concoction. Moreover, the intended brand positioning will not take root in the marketplace.

8.   Review and evolve the Brand Positioning Strategy Statement as needed. Let's face it—things change. There will be product improvements, new entries into the marketplace, further evolution of customer needs, and other changes. We need to anticipate and keep ahead of potential new developments by leading. Evolving the brand positioning strategy is essential to stay ahead of the competition, regardless of whether it comes from within or outside the category.

PROBLEMS WITH
POSITIONING PHARMACEUTICAL PRODUCTS

It's no secret that we at Brand Development Network International work in many sectors and in many parts of the world. One of these sectors is Big Pharma (i.e., the pharmaceutical industry). Our learning in the pharmaceutical sector is broad and deep. However, while invaluable, it's not always pretty. We learn not only from what they do correctly but from what they do incorrectly, as well. The need for Big Pharma to be more competitive has never been greater than in the current global and local market environments. But, actually, these companies and their brands are going in the opposite direction. Big Pharma is becoming less competitive in its positioning practices.

If you are a marketer from another sector, please don't delete this issue of *DISPATCHES*™ until you've read what we have to say. What we learn from working in one sector benefits the work we do for clients in other sectors, such as FMCG (Fast Moving Consumer Goods), skin care, medical devices, financial, and food and beverage. And, what we learn from our work in a given geographical area helps our clients in other geographies. Chances are that you too are facing a growing need to be more competitive. (Who isn't in this difficult economic environment?) It's highly likely that you may be dealing with these same "less than competitive practices" in the positioning of your brand, too. So read on!

Positioning Problems

We define Brand Positioning as *how we want target customers to perceive, think, and feel about our "brand" relative to competition.* This word "brand" is very important. It is about much more than the product, which is nothing more than physical attributes. Instead, a brand encompasses a constellation of values that forge a special relationship with the target. It is also important that targeted customers perceive our brand as different from the competition, minimally in degree but optimally in kind. And, the difference must be relevant to the target and meaningful against the competition.

But if you look at how pharmaceutical companies are positioning their offerings you will find an absence of relevant and meaningful differentiation. In other words, what you will find is a "sameness" that contributes to commoditizing entire categories. As a result, products aren't making their business goals, more new entries face failure (meeting minimal rather than overly inflated expectations), and, at the very least, companies are experiencing opportunity losses even as they rev-up their sales efforts. What's going on here? Unfortunately, there is not just one practice but many that contribute to this positioning problem. Here are some significant ones:

1. Focus on the compound, not the brand. When you consider a given pharmaceutical category such as proton pump inhibitors (PPIs), which work to turn off acid-producing pumps to prevent GERD (let's just refer to it as severe, chronic heartburn, the kind that keeps people up at night when they are supposed to be sleeping peacefully), you'll note that all the compounds work the same. They have the same mode of action and basically deliver the same results. In other words, all of the PPI products are interchangeable or at least are largely perceived that way by the vast majority of physicians. It really doesn't matter which one is prescribed. (We know you are going to argue this point, but, for crying out loud, show us the data!) By the way, this isn't a whole lot different if we are talking about different colas (in the soft drink category), or credit cards, or drug-eluting stents, or banks, or just about any physical entity. They are constituted with the same basic materials, work in the same way to do the same thing, and on, and on, and on.

So, with the focus on the compound, the physical product entity, how is one going to create relevant and meaningful differentiation? The answer is: You're not!

2. The need for consensus. Oh, this is getting ugly, particularly if you are doing "global" positioning. (And, who in Big Pharma is not doing "global" positioning these days?) You see, managers from various geographies who participate in creating the positioning find it difficult to agree on what is important. Understandably, each vies for what she believes works best for hers geographical market. In fact, it is difficult enough to get two countries to see eye to eye (i.e., agree) in the EU on a given positioning, let alone try to get two countries from different geographical regions (such as Europe and Asia) to agree. So, whatever small differences might exist between competitive products gets watered down. The end result is a diluted positioning that lacks compelling meaning to the target customer.

3. Regulatory and legal dictums. This is getting even more ugly now. Bet we are going to get in trouble for even suggesting this. But it's the truth. The regulatory and legal role is growing in importance. And, it is keeping marketers from being truly competitive. Now, we are not blaming your company's regulatory and legal personnel. They are doing what they are supposed to be doing. And, at least, they are being aggressive in fulfilling their role of keeping us marketers, and our organizations, from running afoul of the FDA and other regulators. However, they are not serving to keep us marketers or our organizations out of trouble because we have failed to meet our forecast or successfully competed in the marketplace. Instead, they are contributing to it and we are helping them.

How might we be helping them hinder our marketing efforts? Well, if we go back to factor number 1, focus on the compound, they will allow us to make only claims consistent with what the compound does with clinical studies and resultant labeling. That's it, and nothing more. Remember what we said earlier about the compound? It's basically the same as every other compound in the same class of drug. So how can we possibly expect our regulatory affairs and legal personnel to give their approval to competitive claims of differentiation that are not supportable? It would be insane.

On the other hand, they do not understand brand positioning and, therefore, what you are doing and how you are going to use it. To the regulatory and legal people, "product" and "brand" are interchangeable, just as we marketers might think that a tort and a tart are too. (Okay, so we are exaggerating about that last part, but you get the picture.) And, to them, positioning is what we say (i.e., specific claims about the product), not about the relationship we want to create with the customer. Nor do they appreciate that the Brand Positioning Strategy Statement is a blueprint for the future brand that you hope to build. It is a guide for all future activities that we need to engage in internally in order to realize the full potential of our offering in the marketplace. Unless we understand these crucial differences and help them understand it, we are doomed to *sameness*.

4. Reliance on faulty quantitative marketing research studies. Hey, we are not trying to point the finger at marketing research. As with the regulatory and legal folks, there are many true professionals in this field who are eager to help us establish success with new and existing products. But often the materials (e.g., white card positioning concept) that are tested with customers are indistinguishable from one another. Or, we rush to quantitative studies before we know what questions to ask or even what we should share with respondents. Or, we fail to appreciate that something that is very different may not immediately have appeal because it is, well, different from conventional expectations. Or we do not read the results from our target population segment because we have not chosen a segment for whom our proposition will have real meaning. Or we just ask the wrong questions and, therefore, make decisions on the basis of the wrong responses; we ask, "Do you like this?" (Who cares if your customer likes it? That is not a relevant question. Instead, we should be asking whether they understand the benefit to them. Is that benefit important to them? Is it meaningfully differentiated from competition? What is their likelihood of prescribing or using the product?)

Also, we've observed a lot of esoteric maps drawn up by consultants or by marketing research, that show where various products fit within a category. To be blunt, we just don't get them. They try to make something out of nothing. In other words, it just isn't real. And, if it could be made real (which is another story, one we could embrace), the likelihood of successful execution is slim. Sorry about, that folks. Read on!

5.   Sameness in execution. Sameness in execution negates any differentiation that you may have in the positioning strategy. There are three ways in which pharmaceutical marketers contribute to "sameness" in execution. The first is that the same message is communicated for all, or many, of the products in the same category. You know them! Everyone claims the product is "efficacious, safe, and tolerable." Sound familiar? Of course it sounds familiar. This is probably what you are communicating for your product offering. But it doesn't really say anything, does it? What does "efficacious" mean? (Oh, we know what the word means. We just don't know what it means for your product. Does "efficacious" refer to product speed of relief, quality or completeness of relief, duration of relief, *what*?)   And when many of the products are communicating the same claim, guess what? They all sound like they work the same! Where is your difference?

A second way that sameness in execution perpetuates sameness in positioning is that pharmaceutical marketers use the same marketing-mix elements to reach and attract customers. What do they use? They use the sales force; KOLs (Key Opinion Leaders); Medical Congresses or Conventions; CME (Continuing Medical Education), and so on. They may think they are in a groove, but, in actuality, it is more like a rut.

Finally, the sales force is armed with viz-aids that have reams of meaningless data and pseudo-claims. We say "meaningless" because they are about features and attributes, typically generic in nature, for which no meaning (or context) is established for the customer. Pharma companies leave it to their sales personnel to lift something out of the viz-aid that just might sell the customer. This something might not be consistent with the brand positioning. It is a copy point, rather than a strategic message. While one sales person may stress one copy point with a given customer, a competitive salesperson will stress a counter copy point. This just contributes to that sense of sameness that pervades each category. We're surprised medical professionals have time to listen to this. Instead, sales messages need to be tailored that are consistent with the positioning *and* with the behavior objective for the different customers (i.e., behavior types) within the target segment. (More on this in a future book.) In this way, the positioning is seeded while we motivate a desired behavior to make the sale.

BOATS & HELICOPTERS:

Here are some thoughts on ways Big Pharma marketers and, for that matter, all marketers can develop more competitive positioning strategies:

1. *Position the brand, not the product.* Think about how you would like your offering to be perceived beyond product attributes and performance. Think about the meaning or relationship you would like to establish with targeted customers. This will require you to identify a segment of the population that you want to serve better than your competition. It will also require that you look to the long term in directing the company's resources to building a special relationship with the identified target.

2. Diverge before you converge. Seek alternate strategic options. Encourage new thinking. Avoid the herd effect of converging prematurely. Play out your options. Give them a chance to breathe. Allow your staff to suggest yet other alternatives. Then, when you have identified the obvious and the not so obvious (and maybe even the unique), apply appropriate criteria to narrow your choices prior to engaging in any quantitative research. (By the way, one of the ways you may choose to narrow choices may be through the use of qualitative research.)

3. Think global, but act local. This is related to the previous point. The "brand" meaning or relationship you look to establish can be global, while the actual "product" performance factor or support should be local. If we are going to debate performance factor or feature importance on a market-by-market basis, there is little likelihood that an agreement will be reached that will satisfy all markets, no less provide the basis for a competitive, ownable, and enduring brand positioning strategy. It is not only the wrong place to start (see point #1), but it will force arbitrary consensus that will underscore the very thing we do not want to do—perpetuate sameness. Somebody, please, somebody, make the decision on a global brand positioning and let the local markets make the decision on what aspect of the product is to be stressed.

4. Get regulatory and legal people involved early. We know this may sound crazy, but you may find it helpful to encourage your regulatory and legal people to get involved in the actual positioning process and work sessions. Virtually everyone thinks he knows how to do marketing. (If you doubt us, ask your neighbor or, what's even more scary, your product research and development manager.) So, your invitation may be welcomed. They will learn that there is more to marketing than they know. Additionally, they will begin to appreciate the role of positioning and what you hope to achieve. Finally, you will get them problem solving, as opposed to merely acting as a watchdog whose role is to keep you from destroying the reputation of the company and getting them fired.

5. Get on track with marketing research. We can no more run our brands on polls than we can run our nations on them. That is what much of research has become—polling to determine "pass" or "fail." Let's see what we can learn to help us develop strategically appropriate, competitive brand positioning strategies. Let's use research or (better yet) "customer intelligence" to engage in a dialogue with customers that will enable us to learn, adapt, and iterate our way to success. And let us not abdicate our responsibility to marketing research for decisions that only we can make. While we are at it, we will need to clearly spell out our objectives, identify our target customer segment, develop a meaningful design, use appropriate materials to encourage sound feedback, and discover what is behind customers' claimed interest levels in our positioning.

6. Dare to be different. Drive home your relevant, meaningful differentiation through the employment of different vehicles and tactics. Avoid relying excessively on anything that makes you look the same as your competitors. Above all, do not make the same claims as your competitors unless you have the muscle (i.e., feet on the street, financial resources) to put them down in what is likely to become a costly battle of attrition.

7. Create meaningful sales messaging. Remember to develop specific sales messages that reflect the brand positioning strategy but are designed to elicit specific behaviors from the different behavior types within the same target segment.

AFTERWORD

"If each of us would only sweep our own doorstep,
the whole world would be clean."

—*Mother Theresa*

Afterword

Now we come to our final thoughts. We are delighted that you've made it this far with reading *COMPETITIVE POSITIONING.* Congratulations! But, this is not the end. Reading and accumulating information is not enough. We must put thought into action if we are to truly create a future of success as defined by building healthy brands that compel customers and create brand loyalty. As Robin Sharma states, "Ideation without execution is delusion." We can also say that planning without execution is leadership delusion. (And execution without planning is just plain leadership failure, or leadership insanity. Take your pick.) It is a false hope in the face of inevitable failure. We must act. And we must act now.

Create a future for the brand and a brighter future for your customers and organization by undertaking the development of a relevant, meaningfully differentiated Brand Positioning Strategy Statement that is designed to better serve your Target Customer than your competitors. For the Marketect, the Brand Positioning Strategy Statement is the blueprint for creating the brand. And we know that it is not enough to develop the blueprint. We must serve as faithful stewards to ensure that the brand is built to specifications through the practice of Power Positioning.

The Brand Management Organization

Brand management should be established as the guiding force for the organization. What is a good organizational model for brand management? The wheel. Simply stated, brand marketing, and specifically the brand manager, needs to be at the center of the wheel, directing and connecting the spokes of the organization—sales, marketing research, product development, and manufacturing (among all others)—in fulfillment of the brand positioning strategy. Anything less than this will, at minimum, undermine the degree of success enjoyed by the brand or, worse yet, the ability to build a brand. The exception to this is when the CEO serves as the de facto brand manager (as practiced by entrepreneurs such as Steve Jobs of Apple Corporation, Richard Branson of Virgin Airlines, and Howard Schultz of Starbucks—all Marketects). They place themselves at the center of everything their company does. Act courageously. Put yourself at the center of your brand wheel.

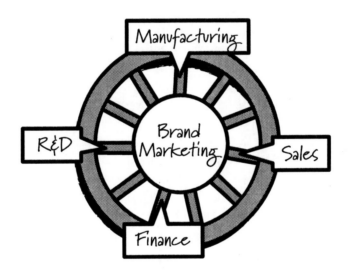

As Alan Mitchell states in his article "Out of the Shadows," which appeared in the *Journal of Marketing Management*, "An organization can only 'walk the talk' when its managers deliberately shape its internal reality to align with its brand promise . . . [the brand's] values must be internalized by the organization, shaping its instinctive attitudes, behaviors, priorities, etc." It's the job of brand marketing management to direct the focus of the organization in building the brand to the specifications of the Brand Positioning Strategy Statement.

But it is unlikely, unless you are the Chief Marketing Officer, that you will be able to re-engineer your company to institute brand management, no less position it as the hub of the wheel. Unless you are the CMO, you probably will feel hopeless about the possibility of awakening your organization to brand management and its potential, leaving you to feel that everything you learned here is great, but not realistic. You are only fooling yourself if you succumb to this thinking.

Sweep Your Own Doorstep

Nothing will ever change unless someone takes that first step. While you may not run your organization, you are responsible for your brand. Start sweeping your own doorstep. Create small wins, and others will take notice of your success. Don't make proclamations. Go about your work quietly but resolutely to make your marketing matter. Others will follow as they look for direction that will help them be more successful. Others want to be part of something that has meaning. You can provide that meaning.

It won't happen if we bury our noses deep in our BlackBerrys fielding e-mails. We need to get beyond focusing on urgent but noncritical activities such as e-mails to dealing with critical but non-urgent activities like brand positioning. What we choose to do can make a critical difference. We need to choose to do the right things. And, "how" we think about doing those critical activities can be the way to creating brand loyalty.

Some final thoughts on how to go about sweeping your doorstep:

1.   Start with getting to better know and serve your customer. Stop with the attempt to be all things to all people. You simply do not have the resources to be able to do this. It's naïve and dangerous. Get to really know and understand your bull's-eye customer, and make a commitment to do all in your power to serve that customer better than your competitors do. Get out of your ivory tower and be with your customers. Go ethnographic or even hire an anthropologist to help bring new levels of understanding regarding what makes your Target Customer group tick. Learn to think as your target customers think, and anticipate their needs, wants, and desires. Become a champion for them.

2.   See your brand as something bigger than it is. Imagine the possibilities, as brands such as Gatorade and McDonald's imagined and became. Create a

Perceptual Competitive Framework, and use it as your North Star to guide the development of the brand. Make that star your compass, and use it to filter all ideas and activities, not just from marketing but from all the functional areas of the company that support your brand.

3.   Don't be content to sell a product. Strive to market a brand in everything you do. Get beyond the product's features and attributes to explore ways in which the product can serve and benefit your customers. Use the Benefit Laddering tool to assist you in exploring what the brand can become in the minds of your customers. But keep it real. Compare and contrast your Benefit Ladder with one for your competitors. Create differentiation and you create space to win your target customers.

4.   Create your own Reason-Why support. Product research and development provides you with intrinsic reason-why support for the brand's positioning Benefit. But that's not marketing. Chances are those reasons-why are the same as your competitors'. Instead, emulate John Smale, the former chairman of Procter & Gamble, who as the brand manager for Crest Toothpaste secured the American Dental Association's endorsement for the brand. Find, secure, or create an extrinsic reason-why that will differentiate your brand from the competition and form a bond with customers. Don't be afraid to think big. As the advertising legend Leo Burnett, founder of the agency that bears his name, said, "When you reach for the stars you might not get one, but then you won't come-up with a handful of mud either."

5.   Give your brand a winning personality. It has a personality. But, more than likely, it is not one to help it get noticed. And, if it does get noticed, it is probably not one to encourage customer affiliation.

6.   Check out your brand positioning and that of your competitors in the marketplace. Enlist the help of your marketing research manager to learn how customers currently perceive you in the absolute and relative to competition. Compare and contrast. Identify indicated actions, and share your learning with your management.

7.   Market internally as well as externally. As Tom Steward astutely puts it, "Internal marketing is probably much more important than external marketing. That's even more true today than it's ever been." Pull your managers on board with you step by step to build an enduring brand.

8. Establish a quality process to iterate your way to success. Author and entrepreneur Jay Conrad Levinson states, "Marketing is not an event, but a process . . . it has a beginning, a middle, but never an end, for it is a process. You improve it, perfect it, change it, even pause it. But you never stop it completely."

9. You don't have to go it alone. We at BDNI are here to assist you. Use the tools from our productivity toolbox to assist you. They will help leverage "what" you think to help you get better results. Subscribe to and read DISPATCHESᴛᴍ, the weekly e-articles we publish that provide insights from the marketing front to keep you learning and to stimulate your thinking. Weigh in on our blog. Attend one of our seminars, or, if appropriate, engage us to facilitate a collaborative strategic brand planning session that will tap into the collective wisdom of the functional groups within your organization.

10. Remember to think brands. Think different. Think differently. Think *big*. And don't forget to act decisively.

Thank you for allowing us to share our learning with you. Best wishes to you in developing competitive positioning leading to creating brand loyalty and in making marketing matter.

APPENDIX A

The Top 10 Most Commonly Asked Questions about Brand Positioning

Appendix A

The Top 10 Most Commonly Asked Questions about Brand Positioning

Over the course of our rather long and multi-category careers working with marketers in a wide variety of sectors throughout the world we have been asked many questions about brand positioning. Invariably, our questioners are seeking our input based upon the many experiences we have had as brand builders, consultants, and teachers of the art and science of brand positioning. Here are the 10 most commonly asked questions:

Q10. *For marketing teams that are relatively inexperienced in classical marketing, isn't it best to defer to your communications/advertising agency to lead the brand positioning work?*

    A. Regardless of "classical marketing" experience level, we believe the client marketing team needs to take the leadership role in the development of the brand positioning strategy. No one knows the customer, "whole" product, competition, and company capabilities better, or has a clearer idea of the direction that the company should take the brand, than the "brand team." Additionally, brand positioning is about more than what you say in your marketing communications, such as advertising. It is about everything you **do**, from product development to packaging to medical congresses to website to merchandising and so forth. The communication/

advertising agency typically works with just a few marketing mix elements and, therefore, cannot be expected to have as broad a perspective, or accountability for transforming a product into a brand, as the client marketing team.

Ideally, this should be a multifunctional team, led by the marketing team, which includes a wide range of expertise, and comprising both internal and external experts. By all means, the communication or advertising agency (both their account service *and* creative service members) should be a key part of this team. Not only do agency account personnel and their creative teams work with a broad range of clients (and therefore see a wide range of strategic approaches in the marketplace), but they usually provide a much-needed external perspective, as well. Having said this, though, we reiterate that brand positioning decisions must ultimately be undertaken and made by the company, under the leadership of its brand marketers.

Q9. ***I'm not involved in actual brand positioning development (which is done at headquarters or by Franchise Management); why do I need to learn how to develop a competitive brand positioning?***

A. Everyone who is involved in taking the brand to market should be familiar with the brand's positioning strategy—to ensure they spend the brand's resources consistently against the desired "brand blueprint." Often, marketers who work in the field or who receive Brand Positioning Strategy Statements from a central or global HQ team insist that they are charged only with "downloading" the positioning and implementing it in their markets. Voila! What better reason to understand the essential elements of the Brand Positioning Strategy Statement, to speak the brand positioning "common language," than this? How can anyone implement a brand positioning strategy if he really doesn't (a) understand it, and (b) comprehend why it is built the way it is? There's yet an even better reason for even field marketers to have the same understanding of a brand positioning as their HQ teammates: so they can, when called for, add value to the strategic thinking, "push back" on their HQ counterparts when appropriate, and convincingly argue for some positioning flexibility related to their truly different market situation. How can you negotiate effectively or influence strategic thinking when you can't even speak the language?

Q8.   *My brand (a prescription drug) has a relatively short patent life. Do I really need a Brand Character statement in my Brand Positioning Strategy Statement?*

A. Every brand, regardless of its lifespan, can benefit from a distinguishing Brand Character in its Brand Positioning Strategy Statement. The truth is that any given brand has a brand character or personality, even if the marketing team decides *not* to consciously develop one. In that case, the dilemma is always this: Is the brand character that's "out there" the one you want? Is it the one that can help further differentiate your brand—in a meaningful way—from competition?

Marketers of prescription drug brands typically face a tougher challenge in developing a differentiated Brand Character than do most fast-moving consumer brands, and not just because of a relatively shorter life. Drug brands usually lack those everyday brand character drivers—like clever nomenclature and packaging—that most consumer brands use day in and out to reinforce their brand's character. Still, there are examples of prescription drug brands with differentiated characters. The Zithromax brand of antibiotic successfully positioned its brand personality as being the more "approachable, consumer-friendly" brand (to both patients and doctors) via its innovative packaging nomenclature, the "Z-Pak," and its "Five Days and You're Done" direct-to-consumer advertising.

The same goes for marketing medical devices. It is important that these marketers develop a Brand Character too. We have spoken with many surgeons over the years and it is clear that they see distinct differences in brand character. A character may be present for the brand, the company, or both. It is influenced by both perceptions of the brand, their experience with the company, sales and customer support personnel and, even, how the company conducts its business with them (e.g., terms they offer, etc.). It is essential that this strategic element of a brand positioning be thoughtfully developed in order to enhance the competitiveness of your overall strategy and, ultimately, your brand.

Q7.   *My brand (a prescription drug) has a relatively short patent life. What's wrong with going for as many new indications (that is, benefit claims) as possible during that life — even if the benefits do not relate to or link with one another?*

A. There is no denying that drug brands face enormous pressure from their companies and their companies' shareholders to maximize the high-profit volume while still on patent. So you have to admire those forward-thinking marketers who are constructing their early-phase clinical trials (that ultimately provide the data required by the FDA to support new indication Benefit claims) in a way that logically builds indication upon indication. For example, while it took the brand awhile to get there, Lipitor eventually had the clinical data to support its marketing as a preventer of coronary heart disease—and this was a logical indication built upon Lipitor's rock-solid cholesterol-lowering indication.

On the other hand, there are a good many other drug brands that have attempted to add an indication later in their patent life that "came from left field," simply because the manufacturer opportunistically discovered that the drug had other applications. But, because these other applications had nothing to do with what the brand already stood for, they often failed to gain any marketplace traction (particularly with consumer patients). One example of this is the Botox brand. Very few brands in recent memory have established so clearly and so well what they stand for as has the Botox brand— wrinkle removal, yielding a noticeably younger appearance. About four years into the brand's life, however, Botox added a new indication: reduced sweating for people with excessively sweaty armpits. Excuse me? Net, adding new indications for drug brands is akin to adding line extensions to consumer brands; to best protect and build upon the positioning investment companies have made, it's always better to plan ahead and make it easy for consumers/customers to see how everything fits under the brand name.

Q6.   *My company has the capability to call on every customer in the market. So why not also position the brand against every customer (that is, everyone) in the market?*

A.   There is a simple, financially based answer to this question: Your brand may be able to afford sales calls on all customers, but it cannot afford to invest equally well against everyone in the market. And, when the company's salespeople spend the extra time required to try to win over a customer who is not really a positioning "prime prospect" (i.e., has the psychographic profile, driving attitudes, and needs that are an ideal fit with what the brand offers), they are depleting the brand's precious—and not unlimited—resources against a long shot, instead of concentrating them against the prospects with the likeliest, biggest return. Even brand Coke, with all its resources and marketplace muscle, cannot afford to divert precious positioning resources against lifetime-loyal Pepsi drinkers or against lemon-lime-only soda drinkers. They are much more likely to earn an attractive return on their positioning dollars—advertising, merchandising, sponsorships, line extensions, promotions, and so on—by concentrating them against Coke loyalists, cola switchers, and occasional cola drinkers.

This same question is often posed another way: "My product is so far superior to competition that everyone would want it, so why shouldn't I go after everyone?" Well, anyone who has experience in marketing should have learned that you cannot be all things to all people. It is a sure way to waste resources and, more often than not, fail. Borrowing from the military theorist and strategist, Carl Von Clausewitz, we need to concentrate our efforts if we are to defeat our competitors. This requires that we practice the art of discipline and thoughtfully select our Target Customer group and marketing mix elements that provide us with the most significant return-on-investment (ROI).

Q5. *When we are trying to articulate a brand positioning (for my brand or for a key competitor), how do we express it: as it **currently** is or as we expect it to be in the future?*

A. The answer is both. You cannot know where you want to take an existing brand's positioning without first knowing where it is today. And we've found that the best way to confirm where a brand's positioning is today is by getting input from a group of the brand's loyal users (or, for drug brands its heavy prescribers and for medical devices its high volume surgeons). They should be the ones who know it best. It is also a good idea to see how users of competitive brands perceive your offering. Once you have a good read on the current brand positioning, the next step is to display it, right next to it, the brand positioning you intend to evolve to. The Brand Positioning Matrix is an ideal tool for enabling you to display your thinking and visualize the differences for you and others, for the management team to appreciate. Then it's a matter of identifying those specific initiatives the brand will take to actually implement that evolutionary positioning.

Q4. *I already have a communication (or advertising) strategy. Why do I need a Brand Positioning Strategy Statement too?*

A. Since any sub-strategy—like a product development strategy, a pricing strategy, or, yes, an ad strategy—follows from the brand's positioning, you have to wonder where the communication/ad strategy mentioned in this question came from in the first place! Nevertheless, there are marketing teams out there that start by developing a communication strategy. Perhaps, with luck, this communication strategy will be a good one for the brand; even so, it is still geared to guide only what the brand *says* in its communication materials, not everything it *does*. Every brand needs a direction-setting, overarching strategy in the form of a Brand Positioning Strategy Statement to guide product/new indication development, pricing, promotion, merchandising, PR, and on and on, in order to transform a mere product into a brand that commands the loyalty of its customers.

Q3.   *When should a brand reposition itself?*

A. Maybe a better first question might be, "When *shouldn't* a brand reposition itself?" It's a better question because, in fact, most brand repositioning efforts do not work—because they come too late. The brand is already declining at accelerating rates (and likely has been for some time); what's worse, the brand is often losing money. Not many general managers have the appetite for investment spending behind a brand in these straits. So, a brand typically has a much better likelihood of achieving some success with a repositioning when it occurs, say, before the brand's volume has been declining for a period of time at an increasing rate.

As we explained in chapter 10, on Power Positioning, however, we are not big believers in repositioning (having seen too high a percentage of repositioning efforts fail). Rather, we prefer to proactively position, or *Pro*sition, the brand by sustaining a steady flow of innovation. And the best *Pro*sitioning efforts happen when the brand team launches the innovation (in whatever form it takes—line extension, packaging, merchandising, advertising) just as the rate of growth begins to slow at an increasing rate. With the right innovation, the growth rate picks right back up again, leading to a higher, extended growth S-curve for the brand. This S-curve takes the brand lifecycle higher and to the right, yielding more sales for a longer duration. Marketers and their organizations who can do this need never worry about repositioning.

Q2.   ***How many Brand Positioning Statements should a brand have? Or, asked another way, if I market to both consumers and doctors, should I have two Brand Positioning Strategy Statements?***

A.   While there are some general managers and chief marketing officers who advocate (sometimes insist upon!) having only *one* brand positioning for their brands, the best answer to this question we've found is this one: *A brand needs only as many Brand Positioning Strategy Statements as it takes for the brand to win in the marketplace.*   Practically speaking, that means that if a brand competes in both a "consumer marketplace" and in a "professional marketplace" (e.g., among surgeons, nurses, pharmacists, and the like), it may very well require two Brand Positioning Strategy Statements, one for each marketplace—to help it win versus its competition. Think about it. A Brand Positioning Strategy comprises five essential elements, among which are Needs and Benefits. But how often are the Needs and Benefits in the consumer market the same as those in the professional market? More often than not, consumer patients are looking for a kind of relief from their affliction or condition; physicians who treat those consumer patients may be looking for something quite different—like improved patient compliance so that the patients can get the relief they want. If Needs and Benefits are different, by definition you have two different Brand Positioning Strategies.

There is no reason why these two different Brand Positioning Strategies cannot be linked in some important ways, such as by having similar Reasons-Why and Brand Character. And it always makes good sense to display these different positioning statements side by side in the Brand Positioning Matrix and to look for opportunities over time to bring them even closer together. But, to ensure the optimal day-to-day management of the brand against quite different "constituency markets," having separate Brand Positioning Strategy Statements for each is, quite simply, a best practice. It will ensure that you are thinking competitively as opposed to glazing over critically important strategic issues and diluting the meaning of the brand in the marketplace.

By the way, just as different targets, such as consumer patients and physicians, can make for different markets in which a brand competes, so obviously can different *geographic* markets make for different markets—and different brand positionings across those markets.

Which leads nicely to our Number 1 most often asked question about brand positioning:

Q1. *What do you think of global brand positionings?*

A. The first thing we think is that a productive global brand positioning is relatively rare. When you put your mind to identifying brands that truly have the identical positioning and meaning to its customers across the globe, well, it's hard to come up with a number of brands that's more than you can count on two hands. The usual suspects come to mind—McDonald's, Coca-Cola, Marlboro, Heineken, BMW, and Mercedes—but the list quickly dwindles. We infer from this either that creating a successful global positioning is very hard to do or that it's not necessarily the best thing to do. Actually, both of these inferences are probably true. Once again, we refer to part of our answer in Question 2: A brand should have only as many Brand Positioning Strategies as it needs to win in the marketplace.

In many product categories and in some drug classes, the market development varies greatly from continent to continent, and country to country. Probably more than any other single fact, this explains why so many brands have multiple Brand Positioning Strategy Statements—or, at the very least, brand positioning variations—in different regions. Here's one way we like to think about this. Imagine your analgesic brand is the market leader in North America and has been for years. Its positioning as an effective family pain reliever that is also safer than most others is very well established. And no wonder, because its product compound is perhaps the gentlest known; no other leading brand in North America has the exact same 100% gentle compound. This brand desires to replicate its dominance around the globe. There is just one problem: Many other markets in Europe and in Asia already have a brand composed of the exact same, gentle-on-the-body compound that already owns the same brand positioning. How, honestly, can the North American brand "win" in these European and Asian markets by entering with a global approach that's me-too?

Net, our take is that having a global Brand Positioning Strategy may be the envy of marketers everywhere—but it may not always be the best way for a brand to win everywhere. You decide! We leave it in your hands.

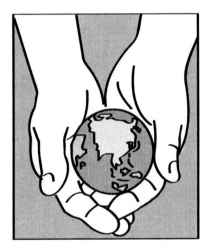

DISPATCHES™

Insights On Brand Development From The Marketing Front

TOTAL QUALITY POSITIONING

"TQM is a management approach for an organization, centered on quality, based on the participation of all its members and aiming at long-term success through customer satisfaction, and benefits to all members of the organization and to society." (Wikipedia definition of Total Quality Management, taken from the International Organization for Standardization)

You remember Total Quality Management, or TQM, as it is more commonly known, right? Whether you learned about it in school, worked for a company pursuing TQM via specialized training, or simply heard about it around the water cooler, most people in business have at least a passing familiarity with the concept. Actually, it is more than a mere concept: As originally conceived in Japan back in the 1950s, it was intended and articulated as a business management *strategy*. Note the following, also from Wikipedia: "TQM is a business management strategy aimed at embedding awareness of quality in all organizational processes. TQM has been widely used in manufacturing, education, call centers, government, and service industries, as well as NASA space and science programs." That's pretty widespread adoption. But—did we miss something—where was TQM ever used for *brand positioning*?

As far as we know, TQM has never been seriously adapted for and then pursued in the development of brand positioning. And this strikes us as pretty strange. After all, TQM is inherently a business management strategy, and brand positioning is certainly a business management strategy. TQM is customer-centric, and brand positioning—to be competitive and effective—*must* be customer/consumer-centric. In practice, TQM has typically been perceived as an *operational* methodology, and what is the implementation of a brand positioning if not operational in nature? So, even though TQM may have had its heyday in the 1980s and 90s, we think it's high time to apply it to the development and implementation of brand positioning, a strategy we're calling

Total Quality Positioning. Over the next several weeks, we'll delve into this strategy more in an effort to help marketers and their general management teams to improve the quality (especially the *competitive* quality) of their brand positionings.

But, for starters, let's go back to some of the language in the Wikipedia definitions. Our aim in doing this is to examine more critically some of the inherent traits of real TQM and adapt them to TQP. This initial examination will serve as our Boats & Helicopters this week.

BOATS & HELICOPTERS

"TQP is a management approach for an organization . . . based on the participation of all its members": The linchpin of the original TQM strategy was precisely this very simple trait. The intention of TQM could not be clearer: It is intended to be understood and practiced by the *entire* organization. And one of the most basic causes for a lack of Total Quality Positioning is that brand positioning is typically neither understood nor known by an entire organization and obviously, therefore, cannot be implemented by an entire organization. Think about it. Do the vice presidents of R&D, manufacturing, and logistics understand the brand positionings of your company's core brands? Do they retain copies of the current Brand Positioning Statements for those core brands—and refer to them when considering, say, cost reduction initiatives? (At one point, a client of ours was in the process of improving cube utilization by redesigning the case pack of the market-leading, premium-price brand, moving from laying down the individual packages within the case to standing them up. But there was trade-off in the form of more product breakage with the "stand-up" approach—a trade-off Manufacturing regarded as minimal, but about which no testing had been done with the consumer to see how she felt about more breakage in her preferred, higher-priced brand. In this case, management by TQP would definitely have insisted upon consumer research and most likely would have precluded a move to a stand-up case.) Building a brand according to its "positioning specification" absolutely demands that everyone in the organization know and follow the approved Brand Positioning Statement—that's TQP!

"TQP (is) centered on quality": Well, sure, TQM was and is all about delivering a quality product. No. It is really about much more than that, because one of its bedrock tenets is that *continuous improvement*, the kind of quality sought in TQM and therefore in TQP, is *better* quality. That means, first of all, that a brand positioning stands for better quality versus other, competitor brand positionings only when it embodies meaningful differentiation, either real or perceived. And, second, continuous improvement means that a brand positioning must keep getting better over time, must keep ahead of competitive moves that might diminish or neutralize its differentiation. Simply said, TQP requires evolution over time—albeit smart (not reckless or knee-jerk) evolution that reflects a continual search by the organization to position and market preferred brands.

"Aiming at long-term success": Companies create brands in lieu of mere products because they believe in the selling advantage of building a long-term relationship with customers and consumers. A strong brand becomes like a person—someone a customer can know and trust over the long haul. When companies merge or are sold, much attention is paid by investors to the equity value of the company's brands. If these things were not true, there would be no reason to build brands in the first place. And while it may be true that every brand has a "life cycle" curve, every brand builder seeks a brand life that will last a long time. No wonder, then, that the brand positioning must be designed with a longer-term perspective. As noted earlier, there will surely be some evolutions along the way, but a fundamental premise of TQP is that a brand positioning must exhibit a long-term perspective.

"Through customer satisfaction": Ahhh. We finally get to the heart of the TQM/TQP matter. Just as TQM in, say, manufacturing aims at consistently producing a better product for the customer/consumer than competition, so in Total Quality Positioning must marketing aim at a *promise* and *relationship* with the customer/consumer that delivers, that delights, that satisfies—completely! More specifically, you can immediately recognize a Brand Positioning Statement that is built on customer/consumer satisfaction in two ways: (1) meaningful differentiation "leaps off the page," and (2) back-up preference data from market research are noted in the document (most likely in the Reason-Why section). In short, TQP is ultimately all about building a brand positioning that is derived from the customer/consumer in every aspect (rather than one that is derived from the chief marketing officer or the managing director).

APPENDIX B

Glossary of Key Terms

Appendix B

Glossary of Key Terms

Absence of Negatives   Within the Brand Positioning, a class or type of Reason-Why that refers mainly to what negative or perceived harmful features are *not* part of the product. As a Reason-Why, it must support a positioning Benefit. For example, a sweet snack made without sugar might be said to support a positioning Benefit of preventing weight gain (thanks to the absence of the negative, sugar).

Benefit   One of the essential elements of a Brand Positioning Statement: the one that answers the target group's question "What's in it for me?" It is sometimes also referred to as the brand's promise. It provides a pay-off to the customer's needs. May occur in any one (or combination) of three ways:

- *Product Benefit*—literally, what the product *does*
- *Customer Benefit*—what that gives or provides the Target Customer
- *Emotional Benefit*—how that makes the Target Customer feel

The Product and Customer Benefits are both "functional" or "rational" benefit types.

Benefit Ladder   A simple tool that enables marketers to assess the potential of the three types of Benefits a brand might include in its Brand Positioning. As the name implies, it is laid out in ladder-like format, starting at the bottom "rung" with the important product features and attributes (each of which could be considered as a potential Reason-Why). Subsequent rungs deal with Product, Consumer/Customer, and Emotional Benefits. The best use of the ladder occurs when marketing teams check it for differentiation on each rung and there is strong linkage from rung to rung. Often a brand will explore several Benefit Ladders to determine which one has the most competitive potential.

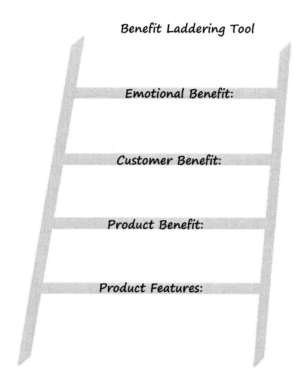

Benefit Laddering Tool

Emotional Benefit:

Customer Benefit:

Product Benefit:

Product Features:

Brand   A brand is more than a product or trademark. It's a meaningful entity that: 1) Goes beyond mere physical product attributes to incorporate meaningful intangibles; 2) Encompasses a constellation of values -- both rational and emotional; and 3)Provides the totality of the experience enjoyed by customers … leading to a perception of added value to, and a special relationship with, the Target Customer.

Brand Character   One of the essential elements of the Brand Positioning Strategy Statement: the one that identifies *who* your brand is and what personality your brand embodies (it is therefore sometimes also called brand personality). Unlike tone or tonality, which is an executional consideration during the creation of certain marketing initiatives, Brand Character is a strategic element that guides the brand's direction. As with all other elements of the brand positioning, the Brand's Character should be differentiated *and* should be highly appealing to the brand's target. In the words of a longtime creative head at a major ad agency, the Brand Character should represent, for the target, *"someone like me, someone I like, someone I want to be like."*

Brand Positioning   How we want customers to perceive think and feel about our "brand" versus competition.

Brand Positioning Add-Valuator   A checklist designed to objectify our subjective judgment in assessing the technical and strategic correctness of the Brand Positioning Strategy Statement. The Brand Positioning Add-Valuator provides a basis for assessing each element (i.e., Target Customer, Benefit, etc.), as it relates to the "Five Cs" (see below), of the Brand Positioning Strategy Statement. This should be used less as a report card and more as a guide in the preparation of the Brand Positioning Strategy Statement.

Brand Positioning Strategy Statement   A written, strategic statement that clearly articulates the way marketers want their consumers/customers to perceive, think, and feel about their brand relative to competition. The statement should include these six essential elements: Target, Needs, Competitive Framework, Benefit, Reason-Why (or Reason-to-Believe), and Brand Character.

Competitive Framework   One of the essential elements of a Brand Positioning Strategy Statement. There are two dimensions to the framework: the Literal and the Perceptual. The former answers the target's question "What should I use this brand instead of?" The latter answers the target's question "How should I perceive this brand relative to others in its same class or category?"

Consumer/Customer Needs One of the essential elements of a Brand Positioning Strategy Statement: the one that identifies the specific rational *and* emotional wants and desires that your brand can *win* with in the mind of the Target Customer. Identifying these winning needs requires not only market research but also an ongoing series of "discovery mechanisms" put in place by the marketing team to keep up with changing trends and emerging demands.

The Five Cs A memory tool to aid marketers in assessing the *technical competence* of any strategic thinking/document. For example, a Brand Positioning Strategy Statement that is technically sound must satisfy each of the following:

The 5-Cs

Clear—language is incapable of being misunderstood

Complete—contains all essential elements and parts

Competitive—expresses differentiation; creates preference

Cohesive—all the parts are well linked

Choice-Full—it's single-minded; not all things to all people

Literal Competitive Framework (LCF) One of the two dimensions of the framework: the one that identifies the competitive set a brand competes with, interacts with, and sources volume from. (See *Competitive Framework*)

Marketect A marketer who: 1) develops the blueprint for transforming a product into a brand (the Brand Positioning Strategy Statement); and 2) undertakes the stewardship to ensure the brand is built to the specification of the blueprint. On a qualitative basis, the Marketect is also a state-of-the-art marketer, someone who transforms his brand and his brand's category by getting consumers/customers to see the category in an entirely new way—a way that benefits his brand and not the competition. When running a hard third in market share to Motorola and Ericson back in the 1990s, Nokia implemented Marketect thinking by getting mobile consumers to see their cell phones in an entirely new way: as a personal fashion accessory.

Marketing Objective   A customer "behavior" objective essential to achieving the brand's Business Objectives of sales, market share and profits. Marketing Objective behaviors include penetration, switching, trade-up to new product, etc. A brand will typically have more than one Marketing Objective. However, a given marketing mix element, for example communications, will typically have only one behavior objective per tactic. Specific marketing mix elements have their own behavior objectives and are labeled according to the element. For example the communications objective is referred to as the Communication Behavior Objective; promotions the Promotion Behavior Objective. Marketing and marketing mix element behavior objectives provide concrete goals and a basis for assessing Return on Investment (ROI). All behavior objectives are interlinked and guide the achievement of the brand's Business Objectives.

Mode-of-Action   A class or type of Reason-Why that is intrinsic to a given product. It articulates the way a particular set of ingredients, a compound, or a mechanism works. As an example, a given prescription drug may claim to relieve indigestion because of its unique mode-of-action—it "turns off acid producing pumps in the stomach."

Official Brand Positioning Strategy Statement   A format that aligns the six essential elements of a Brand Positioning Strategy Statement with the marketplace research, data, and intelligence that support each element. It is "official" because it is backed up with facts and because it is signed by the company president.

Perceptual Competitive Framework (PCF)   One of the two dimensions of the framework: the one that identifies how the marketer wants the brand to be perceived relative to other brand choices in the same category or class. (See *Competitive Framework*)

Positioning Matrix   A "displayed thinking" tool that literally lays out a number of brand positioning strategies—typically including those of the key competitive brands within a given category or class—in a side-by-side format. This allows for analytical cross-checking among them to determine which brand positioning strategy is the most competitive. The format has many other creative uses, such as to assess regional or geographic differences in positioning strategies for a brand or to identify alternate brand positioning options for a new brand to check out with customers. Another important use of the format is to articulate a "family portrait" of a mega or parent brand (one that has many line extensions and sub-brands); this is commonly referred to as a Portfolio Brand Positioning Matrix.

Power Positioning   Everything that a brand *does* to implement its positioning as articulated in the Brand Positioning Strategy Statement (not merely what it says in its communications).

Prositioning (or Proactive Positioning)   A preferred alternative to *repositioning*, that often "last-gasp" act a brand takes to save itself as its volume and market share decline at accelerating rates. *Pro*sitioning is responsive and proactive as opposed to reactive. It is the conscious building and evolution of a brand's positioning via innovations that are consistent with that positioning. It is undertaken when the brand's rate of growth begins to decline and well before the brand's volume begins to decline. When done artfully it can move the brand's lifecycle up (as in higher sales growth) and to the right (as in extending the lifecycle of the brand).

Psychographics   One of the seven elements within a Strategic Target Customer Statement (that is within a Brand Positioning Strategy

Statement).   It is typically captured in a short, three- to four-word "label" that derives from a segmentation study (e.g., "Light Green Environmentalist" to describe someone interested in improving the environment, but not to an intense or radical degree).

Reason-Why   One of the essential elements of a Brand Positioning Strategy Statement: the one that supports and provides credibility (evidence!) for the brand's benefit(s). Reasons-Why are tangibles, usually comprising features and attributes inside a product; they may also comprise tangibles outside a product, such as studies and endorsements. There are two general types:

- *Intrinsic*—features, attributes, processing methods, modes-of-action, sources of materials, and the absence of negatives

- *Extrinsic*—professional endorsements, clinical studies, preference tests, self-created seals and institutes, and borrowed interest from a trademark "equity bank"

Repositioning   The act of (radically) changing a brand's positioning strategy. Repositioning most always occurs following declines in sales, when the brand is on the downward slope of its lifecycle. As such, it is reactive and is usually unsuccessful. The likelihood of success declines the more radical the departure (i.e., revolutionary) from the original positioning strategy. Repositioning also occurs inadvertently when a marketer takes over the management of a brand and sets off in a new strategic direction. This most frequently occurs in the absence of an Official Brand Positioning Strategy Statement.

Segmentation   Segments are **groupings** of (potential) customers that share attitudes, needs, values, etc., to provide a focus for selecting the Strategic Target Customer Group, allocating resources, etc.

Target Customer (the Strategic Target)   One of the essential elements of a Brand Positioning Strategy Statement; it should comprise the following seven components:

Strategic Target Customer

1. Demographics
2. Psychographics
3. Patient-Condition/Lifestage/Targeted Occasion
4. Attitudes
5. Current Usage and Dissatisfactions
6. Telling Behaviors
7. Needs—Rational & Emotional

Telling Behaviors   One of the seven components within a Strategic Customer Target Statement; these consist of a few key habits or acts that are "very telling" in that they give further insight into the way a particular target thinks. Again, for example, you would expect that a target labeled psychographically as being "Light Green" would have these kinds of telling behaviors: she recycles if it is not too inconvenient; she has considered or test-driven a hybrid vehicle; she reads labels and avoids some products with harmful chemicals.

Trademark Equity Bank   A term that refers to a certain type of extrinsic Reason-Why—more specifically, a type that typically involves one brand "borrowing" interest or credibility from another, big-equity brand. For example, if Volvo were to launch a new kind of motorbike, it might borrow from the big-brand Volvo's equity bank by supporting the new bike's safety advantages by citing a "Volvo Safety Rating."

Acknowledgments

This book did not just spring out of the earth. It is the result of a lot of planning, cultivation and just plain hard work. Not just our work but the work contributions of many, many others too numerous to list here. (If we tried to list everyone the hook would undoubtedly come out to yank us off center stage by our scrawny necks and you'd probably demand your money back.)

So forgive us these broad strokes of acknowledgement:

This work would not have been possible without our many wonderful clients who in entrusting us to help develop their managers and brands enabled our development. Doing and teaching provide us with rich and varied experiences, and push us to learn and grow. Our students, with their inquiring minds and fresh perspectives inspire us to consider and address the very real marketplace issues they face, in real time, which we have reflected throughout this book.

Our colleagues at Brand Development Network International, Dave Roche, Brenda Bence and Bill Atchinson, enrich us with their experiences, keen observations and insights. Our operations support team of Lori Vandervoort, Sherry Greve, Donna Budreau and Cindy Finley worked tirelessly on the manuscript to help us look our very best. Jeri Farmaghetti made every effort to edit our manuscript to ensure our writing would be grammatically correct. But lo and behold we continued to write, and self edit, negating her best efforts. (Therefore, any errors are ours to bear.) Brent Fagerburg plied his creative talent to design the striking book jacket, including the heart made of brand logos.

Of course our families had a part in this too. They have been more than patient with our incessant travel, obsession with all things marketing, writing the weekly DISPATCHES articles (which they have likened to "writing a term paper every week" and usually takes place on weekends), and frequent, sometimes bothersome inquiries about their ethnographic observations, purchasing habits and attitudes which have provided us with a depth of understanding of how things work that we could not achieve on our own. Their selflessness provided us with the wings to take flight and doggedly pursue our work. They are, always, a source of inspiration and encouragement.

Our past teachers (managers, colleagues and partners) also deserve recognition. They truly paved the way and built the foundation from which our work has sprung forth. You all have given us broad shoulders on which to stand.

Each and every one of you deserve to be acknowledged. You have our heartfelt appreciation. Thank you one and all.

Richard Czerniawski   **Mike Maloney**

Index

About the Authors

Richard D. Czerniawski and Michael W. Maloney are managing partners of **Brand Development Network *International*, Inc.** They are both successful former client marketing managers with Fortune Top 100 companies. Richard and Mike are co-authors of the book **Creating Brand Loyalty: The Management of Power Positioning and Really Great Advertising**. They also co-author and publish DISPATCHES^{TM}, weekly email articles to the marketing community regarding marketing excellence, brand building, brand positioning and marketing communications (most notably advertising) development towards the common objective of creating brand loyalty.

Richard and Mike have assisted, and continue to assist, many leadership brands, and their companies, in furthering the development of brand loyalty. Additionally, they have trained thousands of marketing managers worldwide, in locations around the world. With vast experience managing the most admired brands for the most admired companies, they bring more than 70-years of successful practices and experience to their work.

Richard Czerniawski

Richard Czerniawski is the founder of Brand Development Network *International*. His client experiences include key marketing positions with Procter & Gamble, Johnson & Johnson, Richardson-Vicks, and the Coca-Cola Company (where he served as Director of Marketing for all soft drink brands in the United States). He has held every position in marketing from Brand Assistant to Chief Marketing Officer to General Manager to Board Director of a start-up company in the natural healthcare category. Richard has contributed to the successes of well-known brands such as Folger's Coffee, REACH Toothbrush, Band-Aid Brand Adhesive Bandages, and Coca-Cola Classic.

In his role as a consultant Richard has lead scores of critically important assignments in a wide variety of industries. In addition to Fast Moving Consumer Goods (FMCG) in the food, beverage and a wide variety of other categories, Richard has lead client teams in pharmaceuticals (e.g., Oncology, HIV, all areas of Metabolic Syndrome, Opioid Analgesia, etc.), Over the Counter (OTC) products, Medical Devices, B2B, Financial Services and many other industries.

Richard holds a BS in Education and an MBA. He is a former Naval Aviator and Officer who served as an Instructor Pilot. Additionally, he is the author of numerous articles on marketing management (e.g., *Journal of Consumer Marketing, MWorld*). He has served as a guest lecturer for the MBA programs at DePaul University, Lake Forest College and Thunderbird International School of Management. Richard is a certified fourth-degree black belt in TaeKwonDo and fourth-degree black belt in HapMooDo. He is also a senior instructor in both arts and co-founder of the Moodo Martial Arts Club.

Michael Maloney

Michael Maloney (Mike) is a Managing Partner with Brand Development Network *International*. Mike has held key marketing positions with Procter & Gamble, the Coca-Cola Company, Tropicana Products, and PepsiCo. During his 7-year tenure with PepsiCo he worked in both the domestic and international snack businesses. At Frito-Lay, he served as Vice President of their "Salty Snack" portfolio; he also served as the General Manager of their overall snack operations in the Northeast and Midwest territories of the U.S. And, with PepsiCo Foods International (now known as Frito-Lay International), he led their worldwide marketing team. Mike has contributed to the successes of such well-known brands as Puffs

Facial Tissue, Sprite, Coca-Cola, Tropicana Pure Premium, Doritos Tortilla Chips and Ruffles Potato Chips.

Mike joined BDNI, as Richard's business partner, in 1992. He, too, has led a score of critically important strategic consulting assignments for leadership companies in a wide variety of industries throughout the world. He relishes his role as one of the lead teachers for the BDN Institute in which he, along with Richard, co-developed the Brand Positioning & Marketing Communications College and High Impact Communication College programs.

Mike holds an MA in English from the University of Texas, and an MS in Personnel Counseling. He is a former Air Force Instructor Pilot, and he has taught English at the U.S. Air Force Academy. As a Managing Partner in BDNI, Mike co-authors the weekly e-articles, *DISPATCHES*[TM], which provides marketing insights and tips to a worldwide distribution of over 7,000 brand-builders. Mike is a life-long reader and avid race-walker; he lives in Austin, Texas, and part-time in Bangkok, Thailand.